ALL WE'RE MEANT TO BE

ALL WE'RE MEANT TO BE

Biblical Feminism for Today

Letha Dawson Scanzoni
and
Nancy A. Hardesty

ABINGDON PRESS

Nashville

All We're Meant to Be

Copyright © 1986 by Abingdon Press

This book is printed on acid-free paper.

Library of Congress Cataloging in Publication Data
SCANZONI, LETHA.
All we're meant to be.
Bibliography: p.
1. Women (Christian theology)—Biblical teaching. 2.
Women—Social conditions. I. Hardesty, Nancy.
II. Title.
[BS680.W7S28 1986]   261.8'344   85-21437
ISBN 0-687-01021-7

Unless otherwise indicated Scripture quotations are from the Revised Standard Version of
the Holy Bible, copyright, 1946, 1952, and 1971, 1973 by the Division of Christian
Education, National Council of the Churches of Christ in the U.S.A. and used by
permission.

Scripture quotations noted NEB are from the New English Bible. © the Delegates of the
Oxford University Press and the Syndics of the Cambridge University Press 1961, 1970.
Reprinted by permission.

Scripture quotations noted JB are from the Jerusalem Bible, copyright © 1966 by Darton,
Longman & Todd, Ltd. and Doubleday & Company, Inc. Used by permission of the
publisher.

Scripture quotations noted NIV are from the Holy Bible: New International Version.
Copyright © 1973, 1978 by the International Bible Society. Used by permission of
Zondervan Bible Publishers.

Scripture quotations noted TEV are from the Good News Bible—Old Testament:
Copyright © American Bible Society 1976; New Testament: Copyright © American Bible
Society, 1966, 1971, 1976.

Verses marked TLB are taken from *The Living Bible,* copyright © 1971 by Tyndale House
Publishers, Wheaton, IL. Used by permission.

MANUFACTURED BY THE PARTHENON PRESS AT
NASHVILLE, TENNESSEE, UNITED STATES OF AMERICA

CONTENTS

A Personal Word from Nancy

"*Your* book changed my life!"

During the past ten years hundreds of women and men across the country from Seattle to Augusta, Los Angeles to Boston, have walked up to me and uttered those words. Each time I have felt a bit overwhelmed and humbly grateful to God for the impact this book has had on so many people's lives.

This book has also changed my life.

Its publication opened doors for me across the country. I have talked with all kinds of people in colleges, seminaries, universities, churches, on radio and TV, in the press. I have dialogued and sometimes fiercely debated. I have been challenged and chastised, defended and denounced. One woman who had been my role model from the time I was twelve years old informed me, after a lecture I gave at a theological seminary, that I was teaching "pure blasphemy." Some in the student body there were so abusive in their responses that the faculty voted to extend me an apology. Yet there and throughout the country I have also found supportive sisters and dear friends.

From the beginning I had to rethink continually what I had written, reexamine the issues, reread the Scriptures, and rethink the theology. My appreciation for Scripture has deepened and widened. I have delighted in the wealth of scholarship that has blossomed—the biblical work of Phyllis Trible and Elisabeth Schüssler Fiorenza, the theology of Mary Daly and Rosemary Radford Ruether. They have stretched my mind, moved my heart, and sent me back to the Bible.

And so have the people I have met. The book had been off the presses less than a week when I found myself doing a radio interview. Suddenly the young interviewer was reading what I had said about homosexuality in my chapter "The Single Woman." I heard it with new ears. I realized that this woman, and perhaps others in her audience, were lesbian. Before, homosexuality had been merely a matter of abstract ethics and theological propositions;

now it became a matter of people, of real life. I realized that the words I had written were not only mean-spirited but wrong.

While we wrote the book originally, I was teaching writing at Trinity College, Deerfield, Illinois. I enjoyed my students very much, but I decided that I wanted to work on my Ph.D. By the time this book was published I was deep into a doctoral program at the University of Chicago Divinity School in the history of Christianity. In 1976 I received my degree and moved to Atlanta to begin four years of teaching church history at Emory University's Candler School of Theology. *Women Called to Witness: Evangelical Feminism in the Nineteenth Century* is a revision of my dissertation, and some hints of that work will be found here.

The nearly ten years I have spent in Atlanta have been very difficult ones. During our first faculty retreat I learned that the Episcopal church had at last voted to allow women to become priests. During the writing of this book, I had sensed a growing call to ordained ministry, a renewal of the call I had felt as a teenager to be a missionary. And so I went through a program with the Diocese of Atlanta, testing that call. At the end of a very turbulent year, both I and the church decided that I was not to be ordained. I felt as if God had led me into a cul-de-sac. I still do not know why, and that is painful.

Since 1982 I have been a free-lance writer, editor, and lecturer. I have learned to live by faith; I have tested and found that God is faithful. The risks still sometimes give me cold sweats in the night (or are those the onset of hot flashes?), but the rewards are exhilarating.

I am still single as of this writing, but I have learned to love and to risk relationship. I have enjoyed the delights and survived the depressions of relationships. I have learned to fight and to forgive, and I plan to love again. Most of all, I have learned to love myself and to know that God loves me. For my "life verse" I have taken the words of Virginia Mollenkott: "Nothing you can do will make God love you more, and nothing you can do will make God love you less." Or as God told Jeremiah: "I have loved you with an everlasting love; therefore I have continued my faithfulness to you" (31:3).

God has been good, very good during the past decade. My prayer is that God will continue to use this book and my ministry to free us all to live more fully for God's glory.

Nancy A. Hardesty
Atlanta, Georgia
Epiphany 1985

A Personal Word from Letha

*S*everal years ago, I saw a cartoon in which a woman announced that she had finally found herself. Her problem, she said, was that she hadn't been looking high enough. With all too few exceptions, we as women have not been encouraged to look high enough, to discover our full potential, to be all we could possibly be.

Nancy and I hoped, in writing the first edition of this book, to challenge prevalent teachings that have used the name of Christianity to restrict women's service, limit the vision and aspirations of women, and crush women's sense of self-worth in countless ways. We wanted to show that such teachings stemmed from a misinterpretation of Scripture and a misrepresentation of God's purpose in creating both sexes in the divine image. We wanted to show that by failing to help women "look high enough," the church not only kept women from being all we were meant to be, but the *church itself* could not be all that God intended it to be. Why? Because wherever there is discrimination based upon ethnic origin, social class, or gender, there cannot be the oneness Galatians 3:28 sets forth as God's plan for the church: "There is neither Jew nor Greek, there is neither slave nor free, there is neither male nor female; for you are all one in Christ Jesus."

As we send out this new edition of *All We're Meant to Be,* we want to issue the same challenge to the church and the same hope to women who have felt blocked and undervalued. More than fifteen years have passed since Nancy and I first met and began work on the book; and they have been fifteen years of enormous changes in society, in the church, and in each of our personal lives. Growing older in itself brings changes. (My two sons, who were twelve and nine years old when we began this project and who watched it with such interest, are both now married and living in another state. And I have just learned I will soon be a grandmother.)

But one thing hasn't changed: my firm belief in the principles and goals emphasized in this book—equality, justice, love, compassion, responsible stewardship of talents and abilities, and freedom from bondage and oppression of any kind. Knowing that such principles are rooted in God's very nature and that God cares about all the concerns and struggles of women, offering both the *empowerment* and the *comfort* of the Spirit, gives me strength to go on—even amidst weariness, signs of burnout, great difficulties, and the slowly healing pain of much personal trauma that I had never expected to experience at this stage of my life.

Yet the call of God remains with us at any time of life and in and through any circumstance—the call to press on, to run toward the goal, to "take hold of that for which Christ Jesus took hold of [each of us]" (Phil. 3:12 NIV). In other words, to be all we're meant to be.

Nothing less.

Letha Dawson Scanzoni
Greensboro, North Carolina
May 1985

PREFACE
to the Original 1974 Edition

---

*S*everal years ago, after observing reactions of fellow Christians to some of my views on woman's role in the home, church, and society, it occurred to me that all too little creative Christian thought had been given the subject. The phrase "women's liberation" was not yet in use, but stirrings indicating a new surge of feminism were apparent. Betty Friedan's *Feminine Mystique* was on the best-seller list, and articles on "trapped housewives" were beginning to appear in the popular press. Yet, for the most part, it seemed that Christians were sitting on the sidelines saying nothing about the "woman question"—except once in awhile to voice dismay at the way things were going and to warn of dire consequences for society if women were to forget that their place is in the home.

The idea of writing a book on the subject began to grow in my mind, and I wrote a few articles on woman's role in a Christian perspective for *Eternity* magazine. Reader reaction varied, but I was especially encouraged by the interest shown by an assistant editor, Nancy Hardesty. We corresponded only briefly and infrequently; but from the clippings she sometimes sent for my files, I perceived that we had similar viewpoints. The thought of inviting her to join me as coauthor of a book about women flashed through my mind. But I dismissed it, thinking she was too busy with her editorial responsibilities even to consider it. I laid the project aside to accept other writing assignments.

In 1969, a visit from an unmarried missionary friend rekindled my interest in the projected book. She freely confided her heartaches, struggles, and questionings and urged me to write on the woman issue and especially to include some help for single women. Again I thought of Nancy. She had once recommended a book dealing with this topic, and I knew she must have thought a great deal about singleness on the personal level.

However, I debated about writing her. For one thing, I hesitated to invite someone I didn't even know to join me in such a major project. Also there was the matter of timing. In spite of my writing activities, something of the "restless housewife problem" was creeping up in my own life. I felt this might be the time to return to school to complete my interrupted college education and wondered about the wisdom of getting involved in writing another book. On the other hand, perhaps the book would be just the outlet I needed.

I asked the small group of Christian friends who met weekly in our home for prayer and sharing to pray with me for God's guidance. I then planned to write to Nancy Hardesty and ask if she would like to join me in writing such a book. At the same time, I would investigate the possibilities of applying college credits from years before to a degree in religion at Indiana University. Whichever of the two paths opened up I would accept as God's leading. I never expected *both* to be his answer—but that is what happened.

God's timing was perfect. Unknown to me, Nancy had just moved to the Chicago area, only a five-hour drive from my home, making it possible for us to meet soon after I wrote her and to have many delightful visits together since. I expected to find in her a writing partner, and I did. But more than that, I found a friend. And sister. During my year of completing my university studies, she stood by me with constant encouragement and faithful prayers. She also tried to help me work through the many practical problems of combining family responsibilities with the time and energy demands of a writing career, just as I've tried to help her work through the challenges of living as a single woman in a couple-oriented society. Both of us have come to understand the "woman issue" in a broader and deeper sense then ever before, in relation to both married and unmarried women, because we have learned to understand, love, and appreciate each other.

Special thanks are due to my husband, John, who encouraged us all the way. We are grateful for his willingness to serve as a sounding board for our ideas and for the many research suggestions he gave us. (It helps to be married to a sociology professor who is also doing research and writing in the area of women's roles!) And we want to thank him for those times when, during Nancy's visits, he somehow managed to put up with *two* "liberated women," whose long talkathons sometimes lasted until two or three in the morning and whose engrossment in putting together the book sometimes seemed to take precedence over putting together his dinner! But he bore up well, as did sons Steve and Dave. Our thanks to all three.

Letha Scanzoni
Bloomington, Indiana
1973

Preface

The year 1969 marked a turning point in my life. Bitter about the way my life was going and homesick for the Midwest, I agreed to take a teaching position at Trinity College in Deerfield, Illinois. This involved two things I had vowed never to do: teach, and work for another Christian organization.

During my first frustrating month I received a letter from a woman I had never met and knew only by name from her writing, Letha Scanzoni. She asked if I were interested in joining her as coauthor of a book on women. She warned me that the project was a lonely and controversial one, but suggested that we seemed to have the same views and so might stimulate each other's thinking. In my reply I warned her that I was no longer a professional writer but an "old maid schoolteacher" and had no answers to the problems of singleness. But I accepted the offer to share the search for some answers to the whole "woman question."

As Robert Frost says in his poem "The Road Not Taken," "that has made all the difference." In the past few years I have been traveling an entirely different road, one which God set me on despite my own logical calculations to the contrary. I have found that I enjoy teaching immensely—enough to motivate me to go back to graduate school for the necessary Ph.D. My writing career has blossomed in several directions. And my relationship with Letha, nurtured by sometimes almost daily letters and frequent visits, has radically changed many areas of my life.

We have written a book together. It could have been merely an intellectual and business collaboration. Instead it has been a union of two souls. I came to her a bitter, lonely, insecure, frustrated, and troubled person. And I found in Letha someone who was interested not only in my intellectual ideas, but also in the wounds of my heart. I found acceptance, empathy, and love. It revolutionized my life. She has shown me God's love until I can now truly believe that he loves me. She has understood and supported me until now I can accept myself and step out onto new pathways. She has probed and challenged my thinking as I have probed and challenged hers. Together we have struggled with all aspects of what it means to be a woman, married or single, in today's society.

You have in your hands our answers. We hope that our thoughts will stretch your mind, inspire your spirit, and deepen the love in your heart for all of your sisters.

Nancy Hardesty
Chicago, Illinois
1973

INTRODUCTION

Jesus Christ came to set us free, to make us whole. The world is in slavery to sin, suffering, selfishness, and the fear of death. Jesus spoke of making us "free indeed" (John 8:36). He described his own mission in Isaiah's words: "to proclaim release to the captives and recovering of sight to the blind, to set at liberty those who are oppressed" (Luke 4:18).

Women were certainly oppressed in the days that Jesus walked the earth, as they have been at all points of recorded history. Nearly all cultures have been patriarchal, ruled by the patriarchs, the fathers. They have insisted that women be kept in a clearly delineated, subordinate place. Opportunities for self-fulfillment, for personal development, and for achievement and leadership in public life or organized religion have been greatly restricted. Women have been expected to be seen and not heard, to bear and rear children, to remain in the home away from the busy, important world of men.

Yet Jesus' attitude toward women gave promise of liberation from the chains of custom. Women who followed him, supported him, spoke with him, and listened to his teaching could not help contrasting his treatment of them with the way they were ordinarily treated. Christ's message of God's love and offer of redemption contained seeds from which could sprout possibilities for human dignity and authentic personhood for all people—regardless of race, class, or gender.

In speaking of "women's liberation" for the Christian woman a decade ago, we were thinking not of an organization or a movement but rather of a *state of mind* in which a woman comes to view herself as Jesus Christ sees her—a person created in God's image, one whom Christ came to set free so she could be whole, grow, learn, utilize fully the talents and gifts God has given her as a unique individual. Men and women alike can be freed from gender-role stereotypes and traditions which hinder development into the true humanness intended when God created male and female in the divine image to delight in fellowship with God and with each other.

The first two chapters of Genesis show us that God did not plan for man and woman to be in conflict or competition. Rather they are to be equal partners—both in sustaining family life (the two are to "become one flesh," are to be "fruitful and multiply") and in carrying out God's will on earth (the two are to "subdue it; and have dominion"). The redeeming power of Christ makes it possible to be again fully human and to reclaim our original destiny. Christ has restored our relationship with God and wants to restore our distorted relationships with other people.

As liberated Christian women, we learn to appreciate our worth as persons created by and for God, possessing unique gifts bestowed upon us for use in glorifying God and benefiting humanity. We are not content to settle without thought into the constricting patterns society expects of its members who happen to have been born female. Instead, we are free to know ourselves, be ourselves, and develop ourselves in our own special ways, creatively using to the fullest all our intellect and talents. It is in the hope of waking more Christian women and men to the possibility of such a life that this book has been written—and rewritten.

This ideal is what some people call "feminism." Because we believe in the Bible's authority and begin with what Scripture has to say about us and about God, we call ourselves "biblical feminists." A decade ago we could only talk about a state of mind, but we and this book became part of a movement among Christians for women's full participation in the life of the church.

While we were writing this book originally, a group of evangelical men were becoming increasingly concerned about the social and political conservatism that many fundamental and evangelical Christians have wedded to their faith. In 1972 Robert G. Clouse, Robert D. Linder, and Richard P. Pierard asked Nancy to contribute a chapter called "Women and Evangelical Christianity" to their volume *The Cross and the Flag.* Contributers to that book and others interested in the issues were invited to a meeting at the YMCA Hotel in Chicago over Thanksgiving weekend in 1973. The group, calling itself Evangelicals for Social Action, drafted the "Chicago Declaration."[1]

After lengthy debates in which the handful of women present convinced the group that discrimination against women was a major issue to be dealt with alongside racism, militarism, and greed, the group included a paragraph that declared, "We acknowledge that we have encouraged men to prideful domination and women to irresponsible passivity. So we call both men and women to mutual submission and active discipleship."

The group agreed to meet again the next year, this time including a group of minority representatives and women. Nancy was asked to serve on the steering committee, and she volunteered to coordinate the list of those invited since minorities and women were given quotas. At the 1974 meeting, participants divided into various task forces, one of which became the Evangelical Women's Caucus. They passed resolutions supporting passage of the Equal Rights Amendment, the ordination of women, inclusive language in Bible translations and Christian education materials, and an end to discrimination against women in Christian institutions. A group of women from Washington, D.C., volunteered to plan and host a national conference the next year.

Thus the first national conference of the Evangelical Women's Caucus was held Thanksgiving weekend 1975 at the 4-H camp in Washington. The group has since held conferences in Pasadena (1977), Grand Rapids (1978), Saratoga Springs (1980), Seattle (1982), Boston (1984), and Fresno (1986).[2]

Looking back since the first publication of this book, we can see that we have come a long way. And yet it still seems to us that women and men have far to go toward mutual submission and active discipleship. We wait, as Paul said all creation does, "with eager longing" for the time when all of us will be set free from our bondage and will obtain the glorious liberty that is our promised heritage as children of God (Rom. 8:19-21).

1.
BIBLICAL FEMINISM

THE ORIGINAL PUBLICATION OF THIS BOOK MORE THAN TEN YEARS AGO launched a movement which has been called "biblical feminism." Although many have argued that the Bible opposes equal rights for women and that *Christian* and *feminist* are antithetical terms, many women and men have come to believe that a truly biblical Christian faith opposes all oppression whatsoever.

Perhaps some definitions are in order. We define *feminism* as a belief in and commitment to the full equality of men and women in home, church, and society. We believe that *sexism,* the systematic oppression of women, is one of the oldest expressions of original sin. Some call sexism "patriarchy," or "patriarchalism," the rule of the fathers or patriarchs.

We call ourselves "biblical" feminists because we believe that the Bible, correctly interpreted, does have good news for women. Although the Bible has been used by the patriarchal power structure to oppress and perpetuate injustice against many groups, throughout the Bible God appears on the side of the oppressed and the downtrodden. As Mary declared, God has consistently

scattered the proud in the imagination of their hearts,
. . . put down the mighty from their thrones, and exalted those of low degree;
. . . filled the hungry with good things,
and the rich . . . sent empty away (Luke 1:51-53).

Thus we take the Bible as our authority too; it is not simply the book of the patriarchal elite.

We do not call ourselves "biblical" feminists in the sense of excluding other religious feminists. Certainly many other religious women and men strive for human equality on the basis of various biblical and theological stances. We do for the most part, however, represent the evangelical wing of the church for which the Bible has particular authority.

"Evangelical"

For us, the word *evangelical* means a commitment to the authority of Scripture and a belief in the importance of a personal relationship with Jesus Christ as Savior and Lord. The word has a variety of historical meanings. The Greek word *euangelion* means "the gospel, the good news." In many parts of the world *evangelicals* are synonymous with Protestants or Lutherans because of Martin Luther's emphasis on justification by faith. John and Charles Wesley nurtured the "evangelical revival" in eighteenth-century England. The word came to be associated with the revivalist tradition in the United States as well. Although fundamentalism captured much of the movement in the early twentieth century, its ecumenical breadth was renewed in the Billy Graham crusades and in growing segments of the academic community which realized that simplistic answers could not meet complex questions.

Individuals unfamiliar with history have suggested that biblical feminism, and indeed all evangelical social action, are simply belated attempts to jump on a secular bandwagon. Certainly secular feminists are aware that the contemporary women's movement—usually dated from the publication of Betty Friedan's *Feminine Mystique* in 1963—has affinities with the black civil rights struggles and the anti-Vietnam peace movement of the 1960s. However, some conservative Christians were already being stirred by the publication of Carl F. H. Henry's *Uneasy Conscience of Modern Fundamentalism* (1947) and Sherwood Wirt's *Social Conscience of the Evangelical* (1968). Nazarene historian Timothy L. Smith had suggested in his *Revivalism and Social Reform: American Protestantism on the Eve of the Civil War* (1957) that evangelical Christians had not always been political conservatives but were indeed the force behind the abolition of slavery. Since then Donald W. Dayton in *Discovering an Evangelical Heritage* (1976) and Nancy A. Hardesty in *Women Called to Witness* (1984) have also shown that our evangelical "mothers and fathers in Israel" considered social reform an integral part of their Christian faith. Said revivalist Charles G. Finney, "Revivals are hindered when ministers and churches take wrong ground in regard to any question involving human rights."[1]

The first woman's rights movement in this country essentially grew out of an evangelical Christian context. The motivation of its leaders was to create a more Christian society, free of oppression of blacks and women, with greater opportunity for the poor, un-threatened by alcoholism, drug addiction, and war.

Biblical feminists today share this perspective. It is not simply a movement of white, educated, middle-class women who want more economic and ecclesiastical opportunity, but it is also a movement of men and women committed to eliminating all forms of oppression and to building a more just and peaceful society with greater economic and social opportunity for everyone and better stewardship of our natural resources.

Why Bother with the Bible?

Despite the valiant attempts by Antoinette Brown, the first woman ordained in the United States, to articulate a biblical feminism in the early woman's rights conventions of the 1850s,[2] the group eventually gave up on that effort. When Elizabeth Cady Stanton published her two-volume *Woman's Bible* in the 1890s critiquing various biblical passages, it proved an embarrassment to the movement because Stanton stated bluntly, "Whatever the Bible can be made to do in Greek or Hebrew, in plain English it does not exalt and dignify woman."[3] Many today would agree with her. When compared with writings of other religious feminists, our book has always been placed toward the conservative end of the spectrum because of our defense of the Bible. Although a great deal more biblical scholarship has appeared since the original publication of this book, and although our interpretations of some Scriptures have changed, we are still convinced that the Bible, rightly interpreted, does support, indeed does demand, full equality for women.

We believe that all who would call themselves Christians must grapple with the Bible. We must take seriously the Scriptures as we find them, primarily because they represent the central locus of authority in the Christian tradition. To depart too far afield from Scripture and church tradition is to create one's own religion. Thus while we understand some feminists' attempts to resurrect goddess worship, we choose to stay within the Judeo-Christian tradition.

Interpreting the Bible

However, Scripture must be carefully interpreted. That is known as he*rmeneutics,* "the principles for interpreting Scripture." Except for some of the Wisdom Literature (such as Proverbs), most of the

Bible is written not in pithy aphorisms but in logically developed paragraphs, sections, and books. Not primarily logical propositions, cogent arguments, or crafted essays, the Bible is a collection of historical narratives and prophetic utterances, an ancient Hebrew legal code, four short biographical studies, and a handful of first-century letters. Jesus taught by example and in parables. What Jesus, the apostles, and the prophets *did* was as important as what they said. In many cases someone else wrote it all down much later.

Thus, in studying Scripture, we must continually ask: What really happened originally? What was the author trying to say about it? What is the context of this particular passage? Under what circumstances was it written? What do we know from history, archaeology, language study, or other disciplines that might shed light on the culture of the people from which this portion sprang and to whom it was addressed? How can this knowledge help us better understand the meaning of this passage? How is what I think it means influenced by two thousand years or more of interpretation? What is its application in today's culture and for my life?

Thoughtful Christians recognize that such questions are attempts not to destroy or disaffirm the Bible but to comprehend what it has to say to us. The Bible seems to have always been subject to interpretation and reinterpretation. When King Josiah found a scroll containing the Law in the Temple, he sent the priests to inquire of the prophet Huldah whether or not it was authentic. She declared that it was and told the king what to do about it (II Kings 22). When the people of Israel returned from the Babylonian captivity, Ezra and other priests "opened the book in the sight of all the people . . . [and] helped the people to understand the law" (Neh. 8:5, 7). After the Resurrection, Jesus appeared to a couple on the road to Emmaus, "and beginning with Moses and all the prophets, he interpreted to them in all the scriptures the things concerning himself" (Luke 24:27). We too, in the light of the New Testament events, interpret the Old Testament differently from its original readers and from Jews today. We view certain passages as allegorical or figurative and others as literal. We understand certain instructions to be addressed to a particular person or group (e.g., II Tim. 4:21; I Tim. 5:23). To interpret other instructions, we must know the customs of the time in which they were given. The teachings on meats offered to idols (I Cor. 8 and 10), for example, require some understanding of the situation in Corinth when Paul was writing. From this understanding we go on to find principles of Christian liberty for today.

Most Christians do not feel that they are breaking a divine

command by not following the "letter of the law" in regard to some matter seen as culturally conditioned. While some Christians are adamant about one or two Levitical injunctions (usually concerning sexuality), they feel perfectly free to wear shirts of cotton and polyester and to eat shellfish despite clear prohibitions against both (Lev. 19:19; 11:9-12). Few Christian women today feel they are sinning if they wear gold jewelry, attractive clothing, or braided hair, even though I Timothy 2:9 and I Peter 3:3 are on the pages of Scripture. Most churches do not require men to lift their hands while praying (I Tim. 2:8). Modern paraphrases have not hesitated to change the "holy kiss" of I Corinthians 16:20 into a handshake. This is interpretation and application. One might even call it "picking and choosing."

Christians who claim to follow exactly what the Bible says nevertheless *interpret* its meaning. If that were not the case, there would be complete uniformity among us. Matters of church polity would be settled once and for all; there would be no episcopal, presbyterian, and congregational forms of government, each citing the Bible's support for its position. The Lord's Supper and baptism would be understood and practiced in the same ways throughout Christendom. Questions about prophecy would be resolved in total agreement. Discussions about proper Christian dress, conduct, and forms of entertainment would have definitive answers. Yet we know that these are all areas of disagreement among Christians. As Willard Swartley has clearly demonstrated in his book *Slavery, Sabbath, War, and Women,* interpretations of Scripture on major issues such as slavery and war have changed drastically over the years—as they have concerning a host of other issues.[4]

This brings us to *theology*—the stepping-stone between revelation and application. The theologian—and consciously or unconsciously all of us are theologians—tries to understand the nature of God and the whole of God's revelation in Scripture in order to make generalizations about the nature and destiny of human beings and God's will for life. Based on the Bible, theology is also open to other ways of understanding God's world. If all truth is God's truth, then insights from philosophy, history, the physical and social sciences help us understand the biblical message better.

Some Christians, of course, feel that they do not need to use a theological interpretation. They claim to be able to read the Bible "literally" and to apply it in a literalistic manner to their lives. "The Bible means exactly what it says," they assert. First, however, they usually betray inconsistencies when it comes to the literal application of such commands as "if any one would sue you and take your coat, let him have your cloak as well" (Matt. 5:40) and "if your eye causes you to sin, pluck it out" (Mark 9:47). Second, on issues of prophecy they often have all kinds of fanciful, allegorical interpretations which change with the headlines from the daily newspaper. Third, they betray sexist theological assumptions, for example, by interpreting the word *head* (Eph. 5:23), which literally refers to the appendage atop one's body, to mean "authority" (cf. Today's English Version, which incorporates that error into its translation).

What Does the Bible Say?

In order to formulate a position on any issue, a Christian must take into account a number of factors. First is the Bible. In order to understand what the Bible has to say about any subject, one must consider the whole Bible. Several years ago Georgia state legislators debated a so-called head of household bill, seeking to change a law which stated, "The husband is the head of the family and the wife is subject to him; her legal and civil existence is merged in the husband." A representative defending the older law read from a photocopy of Ephesians 5, while another legislator arguing for equality of husband and wife under the new law read from a complete Bible. That scene graphically illustrates the issue. Proof texting is not enough; one must bring all aspects of God's Word to bear.

In terms of biblical feminism, this point is most important. In this book we will deal primarily with passages that speak explicitly about women's roles, but we must always remember that women as well as men are recipients of the entirety of God's revelation. God's word to women is more than the few passages usually referred to as "the problem passages." When God says, "All have sinned and fall short of the glory of God" (Rom. 3:23), that means the sons of Adam as well as the daughters of Eve. When Paul writes, "You are no longer strangers and sojourners, but you are fellow citizens with the saints and members of the household of God" (Eph. 2:19), he includes Gentiles as well as Jews, women as well as men. As the old hymn says, "Every promise in the book is mine!"

However, even in considering the whole Bible, we must remember that the book was primarily written by men in patriarchal cultures; that the canon was defined by men, who left out many books now known to us to be more favorable to women; that Scripture has been interpreted for two thousand years by male exegetes and theologians in support of male supremacy. Even reference books betray male bias. Thus as feminist Bible scholar Elisabeth Schüssler Fiorenza suggests, a "hermeneutics of suspicion" is always in order.[5]

In looking at specific passages, we must understand the message of the entire book, the entire section, the entire paragraph, in which the verse or verses are located. For example, does this passage use themes and images the author has already used and defined earlier in the book? We must investigate the author, the time of writing, and the recipients of the message. Does this author or this type of biblical literature have certain perspectives that influence this section? What are the cultural customs of writer and recipients reflected in this passage? That is what it means to take Scripture seriously.

Finally, in dealing with a specific passage, we must know what it actually says, what the words literally mean. Sometimes, particularly on issues concerning women or prophecy or sexuality or other emotional issues, we let our theology tell us what the words mean rather than let the words tell us what the writer meant! With the wealth of reference materials available in bookstores, church libraries, and public libraries, even we amateurs can research the meaning of Hebrew and Greek words and phrases. Commentaries are helpful here if they and we distinguish between exegesis of what a text says and theological commentary on what a text may mean.

Male and Female

Our hermeneutic tends to be two-dimensional; too often we look at Scripture as a simple interaction of "us" and "it," forgetting that we are inhabitants of the twentieth-century Western world and that the Bible is a collection of writings from more than a dozen centuries and several cultures two millennia ago! We are at least worlds apart! And the Scriptures themselves reflect a variety of viewpoints.

The English word *sex,* derived from the Latin word *secare,* which means "to cut or divide," suggests the idea of separateness or distinctness. Many are asking today, What *is* maleness and femaleness in relation to humanness? As Christians we ask, What does it mean to be male and female when both are created in the image of God? Just how distinct are the sexes?

Throughout recorded history there has been a tendency to see the sexes as a polarity, the most basic duality. As Simone de Beauvoir noted in *The Second Sex,* "he is the Subject, he is the Absolute—she is the Other."[6] The relationship between the self and others becomes distorted into a dualism of male superiority and female inferiority.

Psychoanalyst Karen Horney, who has explored the attitudes of men toward women in various cultures and historical periods and has described the role of religion and philosophy in the conflicts between the sexes, points out that the very fact of *differences* inevitably results in *comparisons.*[7] Generally one of the sexes comes to be thought of as superior to the other, and an ideology is then set up to justify the roles assigned to each. When this ideology is said to be divinely ordained and labeled as "God's will," its potency is great indeed. Discrimination becomes not only condoned or excused but actually encouraged—on the basis of principle. In our day one still sees such ideology used to legitimate the physical abuse of women.

The noted historian of religions Mircea Eliade has written of the primitive world's fascination with polarities—both cosmic polarities (heaven/earth, right/left, day/night, life/death) and the polarities of human existence (male/female, we/they, and so on.). He notes that where dichotomies are perceived to exist, there is "opposition, clash, and combat," which raises the question of how such conflicts may be mediated or resolved.[8] Having projected dualism and dichotomy onto the human race, men have then woven it into culture in various ways. As Rosemary Radford Ruether has outlined over and over, "This is fundamentally a male ideology and has served two purposes: the support for male identity as normative humanity and the justification of servile roles for women."[9]

Four approaches to the male/female distinction are evident in a study of the myths, customs, and rites of a variety of cultures. All four are also evident in Judeo-Christian Scripture.

First is *debarment,* the exclusion of women from full participation in the major rituals of a faith, from any positions of leadership in the religion, and from any input or place of importance in its theology. Emphasis is placed on a supposed radical distinction between the sexes, usually with corollaries concerning women's responsibility for sin. Menstruating women were barred from the Hebrew temple and synagogue as well as from some early and medieval churches. Antithesis is stressed through patterned exclusiveness or segregation. Apartheid in South Africa and "Jim Crow" laws in the United States are forms of the same ideology. The exclusion of women from the Hebrew, Mormon, Eastern Orthodox, Roman Catholic, and Southern Baptist ministries illustrates the same tendency.

A second approach is *complementarity.* The sexes are viewed as different but complementary. In theory each sex is considered equal in ultimate worth, but each has its own sphere to fill. Implicit in the complementary approach is the notion that a person is incomplete without a spouse. In nineteenth-century America the spheres of men and women became rigidly defined. "Man's world" included all public functions such as business, work outside the home, and political and social leadership. "Woman's sphere" was restricted to keeping the suburban home or farmhouse, tending the children, and supporting the church. Contrary to what many people believe, this arrangement is not found in Scripture, nor was it the medieval pattern. It is a by-product of the Industrial Revolution, and it is concurrent with the development of the modern nuclear family.

Where the complementarity approach is followed, any overlapping of the spheres is precluded or at least strongly discouraged. Gender-role stereotypes function to keep everyone in the "proper" place. Both ancient Chinese Taoism with its yin and yang and Jungian psychology with its *anima* and *animus* define the female principle as passive and receptive while the male principle is active and initiating. The male and female elements supposedly create an equilibrium, alternating, rotating, and balancing each other, but in practice they tend to perpetuate male supremacy. One sees Paul struggling with this balance in I Corinthians 11:8-9, 11-12.

A third approach to the male/female distinction is *synthesis,* in which the two antithetical elements (still defined as antithetical) are united. Male and female blend or merge to form a new entity. In practice again it does not work so smoothly. In recent times men and women have said that they want to share the roles traditionally assigned to the other; yet women who work outside the home still do most or all of the housework and men still hold most of the power positions in business and politics. When women became bank tellers, men fled to upper management, and the banking industry became noted for its low wages for women. The same is true of teaching, secretarial work, and many other professions.

The example of synthesis most likely to come to Christian minds is marriage because Jesus says that "the two shall become one. So they are no longer two but one" (Matt. 19:5-6).) But as Blackstone defined it legally in his eighteenth-century *Commentaries on the Laws of England:* "By marriage the husband and wife are one person in law; that is, the very being or legal existence of the woman is suspended during the marriage, or at least is incorporated and consolidated into that of the husband: under whose wing, protection, and cover she performs everything." The early church fathers assured pious women that in heaven we would all be male.

In feminism the term *androgyny* has been discussed at length. Some Christians have referred to Jesus as the perfect androgyne.

Again in practice the traditional ideal androgyne has all too often been defined in male terms or from a male perspective, and female elements, however those may be defined, have been subsumed. Or else the term has been defined in such a way as to imply that individual men and women are incomplete half-persons.

A fourth approach is *transcendence*. In religion this is the attempt to overlook or deny any sexual distinctiveness insofar as the realm of the sacred is concerned. It suggests that there exists an altogether new dimension where the polarity is somehow dissolved or rendered meaningless. Some Christians have assumed that this is the state in heaven. However, such a theological stance denies the reality and value of the body. It usually concentrates on sexless, disembodied souls, contrary to Scripture's teaching of a bodily resurrection (John 20:19-29; I Cor. 15:35-50). Some Christian feminists have gravitated to the transcendent approach by taking as the *locus classicus* of their theology Galatians 3:28: "There is neither Jew nor Greek, there is neither slave nor free, there is neither male nor female; for you are all one in Christ Jesus."

However, theologian Rosemary Radford Ruether has constantly reminded us that all duality, all polarity, is evil. Psychotherapist Anne Wilson Schaef calls dualism one of the primary characteristics of the "white male" or addictive system.[10] We make such distinctions to put ourselves up and others down. We stigmatize and stereotype the "other" in order to oppress. All distinctions between people—male and female, rich and poor, black and white, gay and straight, Western world and Third World, Christian and non-Christian—are attempts to deny our common humanity. Divisions between human and animal, animate and inanimate, allow us to rape the earth and dominate it for our own greedy ends. A truly Christian, truly feminist theology continually seeks to root out all dualism, which at bottom is an outgrowth of original sin, the desire to separate and dominate.

Doing Theology

That brings us back again to theology. All of us approach Scripture with certain theological presuppositions. Too often they are simply a loose collection of ideas we have gleaned from preachers and Sunday school teachers through the years. It is helpful to sort out those ideas in some fashion and check them.

Formal and informal theology is usually drawn from four sources. Since we are evangelicals and biblical feminists, our first source is Scripture. To interpret and apply Scripture we draw on other sources: our various church traditions and the whole of church history; our own personal religious experiences and those of people we know; and reason. Methodists speak of these four sources as a "quadrilateral." Tradition was one of the first sources of authority in the church; they taught what the apostles believed and taught. Feminist theologians stress the importance of women's experience—women speaking out of the authority of their own experience, and all people considering the religious experiences of women as well as those of men. Reason includes the consideration of the findings of modern science—the physical sciences, medicine, psychology, sociology, and so on—in our theological thinking. It also includes using our reason to correlate the findings from the other sources or to make choices between them when their evidence conflicts. We often do this automatically without analyzing it. In the past such decisions have often been made on the basis of sexist assumptions. We are challenging those assumptions.

Jesus himself reinterpreted Old Testament materials from a theological perspective that sometimes conflicted with the theological leaders of his day, the Pharisees and the Sadducees. For example, in regard to the commandment against committing adultery, he went beyond the letter of the law to disclose its *spirit*—a spirit that can be violated in thought and attitude completely apart from a sexual act (Matt. 5:27-28). Similarly, his theological interpretation of "Thou shalt not kill" included violating our sisters and brothers through hatred, insult, contempt, and neglect as well as actual murder. Never was Jesus satisfied merely to repeat traditional interpretations of Scripture; he constantly sought to uncover fresh meanings and new insights that had escaped others. He revealed the heart of God's message to his hearers. When asked to define his central theological principle, he quoted from the Old Testament: "You shall love the Lord your God with all your heart, and with all your soul, and with all your mind. This is the great and first commandment. And a second is like it, You shall love your neighbor as yourself. On these two commandments depend all the law and the prophets" (Matt. 22:34-40; Luke 10:25-28; Mark 12:28-34).

Our Theological Presuppositions

All of us come at Scripture, tradition, reason, and even our own religious experiences with certain assumptions and biases. These are often rooted in, or at least reflected in, our view of God. To be explicit about our own theology, we believe that "God is love" (I John

4:8) and that God loves us, loves every human being equally and unconditionally. As our friend Virginia Ramey Mollenkott is fond of quoting from Rosalind Rinker, "Nothing you can do will make God love you more, and nothing you can do will make God love you less."

God created humankind in God's image, both male and female equally in the image of God. When we had sinned, Christ came to die for our sins and to restore us to that image as full and equal members of the body of Christ, the church. The essence of sin is not pride but dualistic division and domination, the desire to lord it over one another that we see so graphically displayed in sexism, racism, homophobia, classism, nationalism, and militarism.

God is also a God of justice. Throughout Scripture God is on the side of the oppressed. God promises to make of Abraham and Sarah, through Isaac, a great nation (Gen. 12:1-3), and God also makes the same promise to Hagar and her son Ishmael (Gen. 21:18). God delivers the Hebrew slaves from Egypt and from Babylon. God is a "father of the fatherless and protector of widows" (Ps. 68:5). God scatters "the proud in the imagination of their hearts," puts down "the mighty from their thrones" and exalts "those of low degree," fills "the hungry with good things," and sends the rich away empty (Luke 1:51-53). Jesus defined his own ministry with the words of Isaiah: "The Spirit of the Lord is upon me, because he has anointed me to preach good news to the poor. He has sent me to proclaim release to the captives and recovering of sight to the blind, to set at liberty those who are oppressed, to proclaim the acceptable year of the Lord" (Luke 4:18-19). Therefore, those who attempt to legitimate the power of a political ruler, a church authority, a husband, or any man on the basis of a descending hierarchy (God, man, woman, children, dogs, lizards, blueberries, thorns, rocks) are ignoring the thrust of Scripture. God is on the side not of the powerful and the dominant but of the powerless and the dominated. God does not coerce us with force; God loves us, forgives us, and shows mercy toward us.

The Language Issue

The major reason that we chose to revise this book rather than simply reissue it was because of our naïveté concerning the language issue in the first edition. We raised the issue in an early chapter yet we continued to use male pronouns not only for God but also for singular indefinite human persons, including all children. We find that no longer acceptable usage.

Many people think that the language issue is trivial; we did at one time. But the passion which the issue generates belies that conclusion (witness the furor raised by the *Inclusive Language Lectionary,* on which Virginia Mollenkott worked with a committee of the National Council of Churches). Indeed, since our thoughts and our theology are expressed in language, changing our language affects every bit of our thinking to the core. Changing our theological language to include the female is a most radical proposal since all "official" theology to this point has not been "objective" as men would like to have us believe, but *masculine* in authorship, content, and premise. The female has been excluded not just by grammatical conventions but by the authors' intentions. And most of us have gotten the message, at least subconsciously. In *Children's Letters to God,* one little girl wrote, "Dear God, are boys better than girls? I know you are one but try to be fair."[11] Yet women have just as much right as men to think of themselves in God's image and of God as similar to them. Men have no more right than women to think of themselves as God's image bearers, God's representatives.

Some argue that the Bible uses masculine language exclusively. Conservatives argue that this means that God is indeed masculine, if not male. *Christianity Today* editors revised an article to read "the male gender of God,"[12] a statement most careful theologians would find ludicrous if not blasphemous. Yet C. S. Lewis argued that "God Himself has taught us how to speak to Him. To say that it does not matter is to say either that all the masculine imagery is not inspired, is merely human in origin, or else that, though inspired, it is quite arbitrary and unessential. And this is surely intolerable."[13] To Lewis at least. Many radical feminists, taking such rhetoric at face value, conclude that Christianity is sexist to the core, the Bible a male fabrication to prop up patriarchy, and decide to have nothing to do with any of it. If the conservatives are accurate in saying that God is male and the language of the Bible is exclusively masculine, then radical feminists are right and we should all join them in the exodus.

The conservatives are not right, however. They simply have not read their Bibles thoroughly or perceptively. They also do not make a crucial distinction between God-language and human language. Assuming that the Bible is God's self-revelation, does God use exclusively masculine langue about *himself*? No, *she* does not. Jesus does speak at times of the Father in order to point to his intimate relationship to God and to the relationship that God offers to us as heirs in Christ. But that is not the only image of God in Scripture. In Isaiah 42:14 God says, "I will cry out like a woman in travail, I will gasp and pant." Isaiah 46:3 continues the image:

"Hearken to me, O house of Jacob, all the remnant of the house of Israel, who have been borne by me from your birth, carried from the womb." Again God asks Israel, "Can a woman forget her sucking child, that she should have no compassion on the son of her womb? Even these may forget, yet I will not forget you" (Isa. 49:15). God promises, "As one whom his mother comforts, so I will comfort you" (Isa. 66:13). The psalmist also has no difficulty picturing God as a mother: "I have calmed and quieted my soul, like a child quieted at its mother's breast" (Ps. 131:2). Virginia Mollenkott, in her book *The Divine Feminine,* discusses the biblical images of God as bakerwoman, mother hen, homemaker, Dame Wisdom, midwife, female pelican, and she-bear.[14]

In Scripture, particularly the Old Testament, God is spoken of in a myriad of images both personal and impersonal—judge, shepherd, friend, lion, bread, rock, and fire, among others. All of us know when we think carefully about it that all our language about God is metaphorical and analogical. God is beyond our limited, finite categories. God is not someone we make in our likeness. The mystery of God's essence is beyond all human language.

Nor is the maleness of Jesus emphasized anywhere in the New Testament. A more careful translation of the word *anthropos* usually used to refer to him would make that clearer; the use of "person" or "human" would be better than "man" (e.g, Rom. 5:12-21). The same translation for other people in the New Testament would indicate that it was addressed to both women and men, sisters as well as brothers. The Bible in the original language is less sexist than male translators have made it appear in English.

Concerning people language in our writing and speaking, basic justice as well as accuracy make it imperative that we speak of both men and women, of people instead of just "man" and "men" unless we specifically mean to exclude women. The masculine is no longer "generic," if it ever was. It is possible to use inclusive language—textbook publishers found that out years ago—so it is rather ironic for Christians to lag so far behind. A number of books are available to help those who are still struggling with how to break old habits.[15] One can speak of God without using male pronouns, as this book will demonstrate. One can include women in one's language without being ungrammatical or convoluted. It is simply a matter of being aware and trying. It is a matter of practicing what we say we believe—that women and men are both made in the image of God, redeemed by the blood of Jesus Christ, restored to wholeness by God's ever-healing love and grace.

2.
IT ALL STARTED WITH EVE

We are borne ruinous
For that first marriage was our funerall:
One woman at one blow, then kill'd us all.
—John Donne, "First Anniversary"

THE BIBLE BEGINS WITH TWO ACCOUNTS OF CREATION. THAT SAY quite different things about the creation of woman and man and have been appropriated quite differently by theologians seeking to explain sex roles. The second, and older, account has been used to label woman as secondary and the source of all sin. The first account does not speak of sin at all and suggests that male and female were created simultaneously in God's image.

In the beginning, male and female were created by God, created in God's image, created to be fruitful and to care for the earth: "So God created man ['adam] in his own image, in the image of God he created him; male and female he created them. And God blessed them, and God said to them, 'Be fruitful and multiply, and fill the earth and subdue it' " (Gen. 1:27-28). What does it mean to say that male and female are created in the image and likeness of God? Those who stress the differences between the sexes sometimes talk as if God's attributes of justice and love, righteousness and mercy, wisdom and goodness were divided between the sexes, with each containing only half God's image. A corollary is that human wholeness, or completeness, can only be realized within marriage. Other writers stress the intellectual nature of the image. We are rational creatures capable of communicating with and comprehending God. God is Spirit. Thus our bodies are not part of the image and are indeed irrelevant to it. This dualism in which reason and spirit are identified with the divine while the body is denigrated has a long history. Procreation is the only purpose of sexual differentiation and sexuality, according to this view.

We believe that the image of God is not only rationality but also "relationality." All persons, male and female, are created fully and equally in the image of God. All have rational self-awareness and the capacity for self-transcendence, the ability to know themselves, to know God, and to relate to others. The fellowship of lovers and of families and even the fellowship within the church reflect the dynamic mutuality and reciprocity of the Trinity, which agreed, "Let us make [humanity] in our image" (Gen. 1:26). God wanted persons who could not only understand and communicate with God but also respond to God and each other in love. God created us mind and body; Jesus was God in human form. Thus our relating and loving, both emotional and physical, are in the image of God.

After the Fall, the fact that humanity is made in God's image is reaffirmed (Gen. 5:1). Although the Fall marred the image, cracked our mirror, the New Testament promises Christians that we "have put on the new nature, which is being renewed in knowledge after the image of its creator" (Col. 3:10). Although our human nature has been corrupted, we can "be renewed in the spirit of [our] minds, and put on the new nature, created after the likeness of God in true righteousness and holiness" (Eph. 4:23-24).

What part does sexual differentiation play in this image? It does not appear to reflect a sexual differentiation in the Godhead. Yet it is important because God created it and pronounced it good. Those who see sexuality as evil and part only of our fallen nature are more Platonic and Gnostic than Judeo-Christian. Sexuality is necessary so that we might propagate the race, though that is not the only way to fulfill God's command to be fruitful and multiply nor is propagation the only purpose of sexuality. After all, God could have devised some other method of reproduction, perhaps on the parthenogenetic model of some other animals. Instead God chose to make men and women dependent on each other to carry out this task and to have two people responsible for each child. The necessity for relationship is thus "built in" to human nature.

Although marriage is one expression of such communion, it is not the only way in which human beings reflect the relational dimension of God's image. God's statement in Genesis 2, "It is not good that [*ha-'adam*] should be alone," has implications beyond marital union. It shows us that no human being is self-sufficient, but all experience humanness only in relation to others and to God. We need one another—old and young, women and men—both within and across gender lines. Jesus desired that his followers experience the oneness he shared within the Trinity (John 17:22-23). Such interdependence and unity is surely a manifestation of God's image.

Sexual differentiation does not dictate social roles. Genesis

1:26-28 does *not* say, as Billy Graham once told readers of the *Ladies' Home Journal,* "The biological assignment was basic and simple: Eve was to be the child-bearer, and Adam was to be the breadwinner . . . wife, mother, homemaker—this the appointed destiny of real womanhood."[1] Scripture speaks of no separate spheres or different functions. Both sexes were created with the biological and psychological capability for parenthood, and both were also given what theologians call the "cultural mandate." Agriculture, animal management, ecology, education, industry, government, commerce, the arts—every human being is equally responsible under God for all aspects of life on this planet.

"And God saw everything that [God] had made, and behold, it was very good" (Gen. 1:31).

Was Adam a Rough Draft?

Theologians through the centuries, however, have concentrated on Genesis 2 and ignored Genesis 1. Genesis 1 deals with the ordered progression of creation from earth, light, waters, vegetation, the heavenly bodies, birds, fish, animals, and then humankind, but the writer of Genesis 2 focuses the spotlight on humanity created before the animals and then divided from each other and, in the Fall, from God. Because the two accounts are so different, even contradictory, the temptation has been to build theology on one account and ignore the other. Paul, for example, seldom refers to the first story at all. According to biblical scholarship, Genesis 2–3 is the older account, imbedded in Jewish folklore from more primitive times.[2] Genesis 1 is a more recent account, perhaps an editorial attempt to counter some of the more antifemale and anthropomorphic interpretations which the other account had occasioned. Read as a unit, however, the first three chapters of Genesis seem to answer different questions that people have always pondered: How did the world begin? What is the relationship of the sexes? How did the world get in such a mess?

Genesis 2 tells us that God created a human being from the dust of the ground—an earthling from the earth, to echo the Hebrew pun—and breathed into that being the breath of life (2:7) *Adam* has been considered the earthling's proper name and therefore its gender male, but in Hebrew the word *'adam* is generic for "person" or "human being" (cf. Pss. 36:6; 104:14; 135:8; Prov. 3:4; all use *'adam*). That meaning is reinforced in this passage by a prefacing article, *ha-'adam,* "the person." It is related to *ha-'adama,* "the earth" or "the dust." As Phyllis Trible argues in her outstanding work *God and the Rhetoric of Sexuality,* there is no indication of this first person's gender or indeed if it had any.[3]

Living in a perfect garden and talking to God face-to-face were not sufficient for this creature. God said, "It is not good that [the person] should be alone" (Gen. 2:18), and so the animals were created. The earthling rationally understood the essence of each and so named them; yet among them the first person could not find one with whom intimate relationship was possible.

The next step was also part of God's creative activity. God placed the person in a deep sleep, and in another mysterious creative act, created from the one, two human beings, male and female. Those who see here an old man fashioning a clay doll beside a riverbed or a white-gowned plastic surgeon building a human body around one rib miss the point of the narrative. So do bumper stickers saying, "Adam was a rough draft" and "When God made man, she was only joking." Details of the actual creation of the first and second human beings are shrouded in mystery. We do know, however, that in each case creation was a direct act of God. God did not simply saw an original androgyne in half, as Plato and Jewish speculation suggest.[4] God's use of a rib has provoked preachers to note that woman was "taken from man's side to be his equal, taken from under his heart to be his beloved," and so on. But perhaps more instructive is linguistic evidence that "rib" is related to the word for "life."[5] Adam and Eve shared the same life; they were not two species but "one flesh." Woman is not simply an object within the created world, as sinful men have been prone to view her, but a complete human person.

God created a second human creature, Eve, to be "an help meet" for the first person, *ha-'adam* (Gen. 2:18, 20 KJV). From this rendering stem many of the warped ideas that surround woman's role. Subsequent translations have corrupted the phrase into "helpmate" which has engendered visions of an assistant, if not a servant.

The key Hebrew words here are *ezer,* "help," and *neged,* "meet." *Neged* is a preposition meaning "before," "in the presence of," or "in the sight of." Psalm 16:8 says, "I keep the Lord always *before* me." Psalm 23:5 promises, "Thou preparest a table before me *in the presence of* my enemies." "Suitable," "corresponding to," or "adequate" to meet all another's needs for physical, intellectual, and social communion might be better translations for the Elizabethan *meet.*

Ezer, used as a noun meaning "help" or "helper," appears twenty-one times in the Old Testament. Sixteen refer to a *super*ordinate helper, not a *sub*ordinate one. "From whence does my *help* come? My *help* comes from the Lord," says Psalm 121:1-2.

Psalm 146:3, 5 tells us, "Put not your trust in princes, in a son of man, in whom there is no *help*. . . . Happy is he whose *help* is the God of Jacob." At no time is *ezer* used to indicate a subordinate helper.[6]

What then does "an help meet for him" mean? Scholars offer such phrases as "a mirror of himself, in which he recognizes himself," "a vis-à-vis which has the character of a Thou."[7] *Ha-'adam's* response upon awakening reveals an instant recognition of an identity, a oneness, with this new creation. The grammar at this point is chaotic—Adam's response was much like ours when we are surprised and delighted. The repetition of the word *this* indicates a loss for words to describe the joy. Adam could only point:

> *This* at last is bone from my bones,
> and flesh from my flesh!
> *This* is to be called woman,
> for *this* was taken from man (Gen. 2:23 jb, italics ours).[8]

In these final two lines the words for male and female (*ish* and *ishshah*) are used. Thus, Trible argues that gender appears in this second act of God's creation during Adam's deep sleep.

The story is followed by an editorial comment, "Therefore a man leaves his father and his mother and cleaves to his wife, and they become one flesh" (Gen. 2:24). It is the *man,* not the woman, who leaves and cleaves, suggesting a matriarchal family model rather than the patriarchal one which prevailed in the Old Testament. The term *leave* means "to abandon" or "to forsake" and is generally used of forsaking strange gods. *To cleave* means "to establish a deep personal attachment." The word is used of Ruth and Naomi (Ruth 1:14), of the people and King David (II Sam. 20:2), and eight times of Israel and God.[9]

Many people use this story to suggest that heterosexuality is mandated by creation. This seems to be a theological extrapolation rather unwarranted by the story itself. Certainly unwarranted is the use of this story to buttress arguments that all licit sexual acts must be procreational. The story itself says nothing about sexual relations at all; it is a rather simple account of the creation of humanity and the creation of two genders. Even the editorial comment does not mention begetting children.

Its explicit application to marriage comes from the words of Jesus spoken in regard to divorce: "Have you not read that he who made them from the beginning made them male and female, and said, 'For this reason a man shall leave his father and mother and be joined to his wife, and the two shall become one flesh'? " (Matt. 19:4-5). Joining Genesis 1 and 2, his point here says nothing about sexual or marital roles or about the desirability of marriage at all, but simply that sexual union, becoming one flesh, is under God's law; it is not at the whim of men.

Yet Christian theologians have taught with Augustine that God created us male and female in "a kind of friendly and genuine union of the one ruling and the other obeying."[10] Usually referred to as "the order of creation," this assertion is sometimes said to be based on the order in which human beings were created (males first, females second) or more broadly on a general belief in the subordination of women to men due to woman's weaker nature (sometimes more bluntly referred to as her "inferiority"—though it does seem strange that even Christian men would think it fitting to take advantage of and oppress those who are weak and inferior).

Is One First? Is First Better?

Is there an order of creation, and is it of any cosmic significance? Those who believe in such an order look not to Genesis but to I Timothy 2:13, which prohibits women from teaching because "Adam was formed first, then Eve." Genesis 1 and 2 actually differ concerning the order of creation. In Genesis 1 male and female are said to be created simultaneously by God as the culmination of creation. If beings created first are to have precedence, then the animals are clearly our betters. In Genesis 2 *ha-'adam* is created prior to the animals, but the culmination of God's creative activity is Eve. (What difference any of this makes in regard to women teaching in the church is not made clear by the writer of Timothy.)

The issue is approached from a different angle in I Corinthians 11:8-9: "Man was not made from woman, but woman from man. Neither was man created for woman, but woman for man." The second creation narrative has been construed to say that the female was made from and for the male, but the theological leap from this to woman's subordination is a traditional rabbinic (and one might add "Christian") understanding that is not supported by the Genesis text.[11] After all, humanity was made from dust, but this does not make us subordinate to the earth. Rather, both Genesis 1 and 2 indicate that we are to care for the earth and tend it so that it will sustain us with food—a mutual submission.

In the Corinthians passage, Paul is aware of the incompatibility of such statements with the tone of Genesis and with his own statement in Galatians 3:28. He says, "Nevertheless, in the Lord woman is not independent of man nor man of woman; for as woman was made from man, so man is now born of woman. And all things are from God" (I Cor. 11:11-12). Verses 11-12 so directly contradict verses 8-9 that we agree with those scholars who suggest that the first passage is not Pauline at all but the words of another party in the factious Corinthian church. Paul Jewett considers both passages Pauline, but he suggests that "here we have what may be the first expression of an uneasy conscience on the part of a Christian theologian who argues for the subordination of the female to the male."[12] Unfortunately, few theologians since then have had such tender consciences!

First Corinthians 11 raises at least two other questions relating to our understanding of Genesis and the order of creation. Verse 7 contains the curious statement that "a man ought not to cover his head, since he is the image and glory of God; but woman is the glory of man." Some have tried to avoid apparent problems by suggesting that "image" refers to the "order established for marriage" (since the words translated "man" and "woman" could also be translated "husband" and "wife") rather than to the *imago Dei,* but the verse stands in seemingly direct contradiction to Genesis 1:27, which says that both male and female were created in the image of God. The author does not say explicitly that woman is *not* in the image of God.

The emphasis seems to be on *doxa,* "glory." To be the glory of someone is "to manifest, reveal, or represent that person" (see Ezek. 1:26-28; Exod. 33:18; Isa. 40:5; John 1:14-18). A wife's behavior reflects on her husband (as indeed his does on her); a wife represents her husband. Paul may be using what seems to us a rather curious rabbinic interpretation to underscore his instruction that in order to glorify God alone in worship, men should have uncovered heads while women should cover their heads (to obscure the "glory of man").[13] Helmut Thielicke points out that this passage sounds almost like the Gnostic doctrine of emanation by which man, being created first, was the higher emanation and contained a more clear and distinct representation of God, while woman, created later, was a dimmer, more indirect reflection.[14] Similar thinking has portrayed woman as earthy, sensual, less spiritually capable, and more concerned with inferior, corporeal, and temporal things.[15] This suggests that verse 7 may be attached to the following two verses as the assertions of Paul's opponents. (One way to deal with the apparent contradictions in this passage as well as I Cor. 14:34-35 in relation to vv. 36-40 is to see it as part of a pattern throughout the book of Paul's quoting from his opponents and then rebutting their arguments, cf. 3:4; 6:12, 13; 8:1, 4; 10:23.)

Whatever the case, it seems a rather convoluted rabbinic argument to suggest that men should not cover their heads during worship but women should. The practice of wearing the yarmulke or skullcap or of placing a prayer shawl over their heads had not yet become standard practice among Jewish men. Both orthodox Jewish men and women now cover their heads in worship. We deal with this larger question of what the entire passage is saying or not saying about head coverings in chapter 5 on women in the church.

The basic theological argument for male supremacy begins, however, with this assumption that man is made in God's image. This statement is a classic example of how sexist language waffles. Women usually assume that the statement is generic, that it means "humanity is made in God's image," as the Bible indeed teaches. However, it readily becomes apparent that most theologians have meant that males (i.e, they, themselves) are made in God's image and thus reflect the glory of God, image and glory being translated as representing God's authority, power, dominion, and supremacy.[16] God rules the whole created universe but has delegated some of that authority to "man." Genesis 1:28 clearly states that such authority has been given to both women and men, but theologians have insisted that it has been delegated to males only. They have done so largely based on a misunderstanding of the Greek word for "head," *kephalē*. Some writers use the phrase "*kephalē*-structure" as a synonym for the "order of creation."[17]

Head

The most blatant example of this perversion of God's word is Today's English Version's rendering of I Corinthians 11:3: "But I want you to understand that Christ is supreme over every man, the husband is supreme over his wife, and God is supreme over Christ." The fact that the Council of Ephesus in 431 declared the idea contained in the last phrase heretical might have alerted TEV editor Robert Bratcher that he was on the wrong track, but he was evidently too busy buttressing male authority with the second phrase to notice! In a 1971 edition of *The Living Bible,* Ken Taylor does similar gymnastics with this passage, putting the shoe on the other foot, so to speak: "But there is one matter I want to remind you about: that a wife is responsible to her husband, her husband is responsible to Christ, and Christ is responsible to God." Notice that Taylor has also neatened up Paul's "haphazard" writing by rearranging the order of the phrases to place them in an ascending hierarchy. Apparently the male egos of both men got in the way of their commitment to scriptural accuracy. They are not alone in this character fault; they are simply obvious examples of the androcentrism of all biblical translations, commentaries, and theologies of the past.

First Corinthians 11:3 says very simply (and accurately in the RSV): "But I want you to understand that the head of every man is Christ, the head of a woman is her husband, and the head of Christ is God." It says absolutely nothing about supremacy or authority or power. This is a perfect example of how we too often read our own cultural assumptions back into the words of Scripture while we ignore what the writer is actually saying. Many people read twentieth-century scientific and business models into the New Testament "head." Some argue that husbands should make all decisions in marriage and men all decisions in society because the head is the home of the brain, which makes all decisions for our bodies. One is free to subscribe to that scenario, but it is wrong to call it biblical. In biblical times people simply did not know that the brain directed the body. Indeed they believed that they thought with their hearts. Thus Jesus said, "For out of the abundance of the *heart* the mouth speaks" (Matt. 12:34), and he declared that "out of the *heart* come evil thoughts" (Matt. 15:19). He "perceived the thought of [the disciples'] *hearts*" (Luke 9:47) and spoke of understanding with the *heart* (Matt. 13:15). Mary "kept all these things, pondering them in her *heart*" (Luke 2:19; italics ours here and above).[18]

Even more farfetched biblically is the idea that "head" means the chief executive officer, the "head" of a company, and thus since a business is supposedly more efficient and profitable if one person makes all the decisions, business becomes the biblical model of marriage. Since the business corporation was only invented a couple of centuries ago, this is another anachronistic image. A more honest and less anachronistic image is that of a monarch as "head" of a realm. Hence God is supreme; Jesus is Lord; and the man can lord it over the woman, the husband over the wife (that is ambiguous because *gunē* can mean either "woman" or "wife," *anēr* either "man" or "husband"). This obviously contains more than a grain of truth. God is indeed all in all (cf. I Cor. 15:28). Jesus is Lord. However, the question is: Is that what Paul was trying to say in using the concept of "head"? We think not.

Paul uses the image of head and body repeatedly, not just for marriage. Indeed in Ephesians 5 he tells us, "This mystery is a profound one, and I am saying that it refers to Christ and the church"

(v. 32). He uses it primarily as an image of Christ and the church (see Rom. 12:3-21; I Cor. 12:12-27; Eph. 1:22-23; 2:1-22; 3:6; 4:1-6, 12, 15-16; 5:29-30; Col. 1:18-24; 2:9-14, 18-19; 3:12-15).

Paul uses the image as a "tied," or literal, metaphor. That is, he likens Christ and the church, the husband and the wife, to a literal head and body. In I Corinthians 12 he speaks at length about various organs and parts of head and body, obviously the human body. To say that the image is a "free" metaphor for some abstract idea or concept, such as hierarchy, the order of creation, or chain of command, is absurd. Paul is talking about an ordinary, literal human being. His point is a simple one: united head and body we live; severed head from body we die. It is a variation of an image Christ used, that of the vine and the branches (John 15:1-17). As Christians united to Christ we who were once dead now live (Eph. 2:1-6; Col. 2:9-14). As husband and wife become "one flesh" and live in unity, the marital relationship lives and flourishes.

Several recurrent themes show clearly how Christians—including partners in intimate relationships—are to relate to one another. A primary theme is mutual submission. We are not to think of ourselves more highly than we ought to think but are to love one another with deepest affection and "outdo one another in showing honor" (Rom. 12:3, 10)."Live in harmony with one another; do not be haughty, but associate with the lowly; never be conceited" (Rom. 12:16). "The eye cannot say to the hand, 'I have no need of you,' nor again the head to the feet, 'I have no need of you' " (I Cor. 12:21). "If one member suffers, all suffer together; if one member is honored, all rejoice together" (I Cor. 12:26). "Forbearing one another in love. . . . Be subject to one another out of reverence for Christ" (Eph. 4:2; 5:21). "If one has a complaint against another, forgive each other; as the Lord has forgiven you, so you also must forgive. And above all these put on love, which binds everything together in perfect harmony" (Col. 3:13-14).

Some people have trouble seeing the relationship between Christ and the church as mutual. They identify the husband with Christ as Lord rather than with Christ as Savior and Suffering Servant, as he is portrayed by Paul in most of these passages. The emphasis is on Christ's completed work on the cross, on his continuing intercession for us in heaven, and on his integral involvement in our growth toward *fullness* (another word used often in these passages). We love Christ because Christ first loved us and died for us (I John 4:19). Christ has already submitted unto death for our salvation; therefore, our response in submission is mutual.

Another theme is growth toward maturity. Ephesians 4 speaks of attaining maturity "to the measure of the stature of the fulness of Christ; so that we may no longer be children" (vv. 13-14). Paul says that when the whole body is joined and knit together with Christ, it "makes bodily growth and upbuilds itself in love" (v. 16). In Colossians 1 Paul urges Christians to "continue in the faith" (v. 23) and hopes to present all his converts "mature in Christ" (v. 28). In Christ we "have come to fulness of life" (Col. 2:10) and are to "put on the new nature, which is being renewed in knowledge after the image of its creator" (Col. 3:10). The incredible secret of Christian living is that we, frail and sinful human beings that we are, are becoming like Christ! Not that we are becoming divine, but we are becoming "all we're meant to be," fully human, created in the *imago Dei*. Thus this image of head and body is not intended to portray some static abstract diagram of relationships, but a dynamic living, changing, growing, and maturing process.

The other interrelated theme is giftedness. "For as in one body we have many members, and all the members do not have the same function, so we, though many, are one body in Christ, and individually members one of another. Having gifts that differ according to the grace given to us, let us use them" (Rom. 12:4-6). "All these are inspired by one and the same Spirit, who apportions to each one individually as [the Spirit] wills" (I Cor. 12:11). The gifts are given "to equip the saints for the work of ministry, for building up the body of Christ" toward maturity (Eph. 4:12). Nothing in any of these passages indicates that men and women differ in gifts. Indeed several of the passages speak of the breakdown of barriers between Jews and Gentiles, slave and free (Eph. 2:11-15; Col. 3:11)—barriers far more serious in the early church than those between men and women of the same race and class. All members of the church are gifted in some way, and those less honored by the world are to be given special honor because "God has so composed the body, giving the greater honor to the inferior part" (I Cor. 12:24).

Thus "headship" is not a unique image delineating a hierarchy of gender relationships but is one of Paul's favorite metaphors for the process of Christian living. The key is mutual submission. Christian wives submit to their husbands as the church submits to Christ (a voluntary response, not a coerced obedience). Husbands in turn do not emulate Christ in his rule of the universe (certainly a prerogative of Christ alone as God) but rather in Christ's example of self-giving oneness with his body, the church.

The point of Genesis 2 is the same as that of Genesis 1: men and women are not separate species with differing functions, capabilities, and value. Both are created by God from one substance to be "one flesh." Thus no one can say to those of another gender or another race, "You are not created in God's image; you are less than fully human." Just as the Godhead is not a hierarchy or a pantheon of gods but a loving union of three equal persons, so God has created us male and female in that image.

The Fall

That image, however, was defaced by the Fall; that unity with God and with each other was broken. The biblical story begins with the observation, "Now the serpent was more subtle than any other wild creature that the Lord God had made" (Gen. 3:1). Although diverse explanations are offered of who or what appeared to Eve, the words it spoke were those of Satan.

And Satan addressed the woman. Luther speaks for a majority of commentators when he explains that "the subtlety of Satan showed itself also when he attacked human nature where it was weakest, namely, in Eve, and not in Adam. I believe that had Satan first tempted the man, Adam would have gained the victory."[19] Others agree that Eve was singled out for temptation because she was not too smart (who goes around talking to snakes?). Woman's nature has thus been seen as naturally defective and gullible, making her less fit for intellectual pursuit, particularly theological activity. This explanation, however, seems to cast a slur on God's wisdom in saying that woman's creation was in the divine image and "very good."

Another equally valid interpretation is that both Adam and Eve were there (3:6), but Eve alone leaped to God's defense when Satan sought to discredit the Deity. Genesis 3:2 could be translated, "The woman interrupted the serpent."[20] The serpent asked if God had been so niggardly as to forbid eating from any tree. Contrary to those who say Eve did not take God's prohibition seriously because she may have received it secondhand from Adam, Eve not only sets the serpent straight—saying they could certainly eat of all the trees except one—but she also adds to God's instructions: " 'You shall not eat of the fruit of the tree . . . neither shall you touch it' " (3:3). Actually God had only forbidden eating, but perhaps Eve realized that looking and touching would lead to the temptation to eat.

Then the devil shifted ground, contradicting what God had said would happen if they ate and instead suggesting that the results would be beneficial. By denying the threat outright, Satan made it sound as though God was just withholding something good for God's own enjoyment. To this attack Eve did not know how to respond. After all, she was in dialogue with "the most subtle of all," Satan!

So she ate. "And gave also unto her husband with her; and he did eat. And the eyes of them both were opened, and they knew that they were naked" (Gen. 3:6-7 KJV). Had Adam been listening to the conversation? Did he watch her reach out to pluck the fruit without trying to dissuade her? Did he search her eyes for signs of change before accepting the fruit from her hand? Scripture offers us no further insights into details of or motives for the action. It merely records that both man and woman disobeyed God's command.

What was the original sin? From the biblical account the answer to this question may seem simple and self-evident, but theologians offer many curious speculations. A very old tradition says the sin was sexual intercourse (though how Eve would receive so much individual blame for an act that takes two is puzzling). This interpretation was offered by some early church fathers who, influenced by Gnosticism, felt that sexuality was the major source of sin in the world. But even Augustine reportedly said of this theory: "Illud est ridiculum!" The Hebrew people themselves held no Gnostic ideas concerning marriage—rather they honored marital union.

Several theories lay the blame on Eve's tendency toward liberation.[21] Early feminist Judith Murray put the case positively. She said Eve's downfall resulted from a noble motive—to adorn her mind, to quench her thirst for intellectual knowledge.[22] A contemporary writer puts it more negatively: "She unlawfully assumed the religious responsibility for the first community. . . . By the 'theological' conversation with the serpent Eve assumed a function which God had not given her." Adam was supposedly responsible for all "theological negotiations."[23] Thus by taking the lead, Eve "emasculates the man. She doesn't consult her husband. Although she was supposed to be a helper fit for him, she snatches away the meaning of his masculinity."[24] Medieval schoolmen argued that while Adam sinned against only himself and God, Eve's crime was worse because she sinned against not only herself and God but also her husband. And after her own sin, they argue—contrary to any shred of biblical evidence—that she lured, seduced, enticed her husband to sin.

Adam does, however, come in for condemnation by some theologians.He was ungentlemanly in letting her talk with a dangerous snake and eat a fruit already advertised as deadly. Out of "fond affection" and "the drawings of kindred"[25] he forsook his God and cleaved to his wife. Thus some say his sin was actually greater. Some medieval scholars (some still alive today), believers in Aristotelian biology, say that Adam's sin was worse because since he is the active principle in procreation, children would not have inherited the disease if only their mother had sinned.

None of these explanations square with the biblical teaching on original sin. All of them imply various sinful motives or actions prior to the act of eating. We know nothing, however, of the minds and hearts of Adam and Eve, except that they were created in God's image and God pronounced them "very good." Scripture says their sin was disobedience to God's command not to eat the fruit of a certain tree. They ate, and *then* sin took hold. As one scholar put it, "Adam, then, must have fallen exactly as Eve had, with as little excuse, with as great a guilt."[26] Dietrich Bonhoeffer declares, "Eve only falls totally when Adam falls, for the two are one. In their guilt too they are two and yet one. They fall together as one and each carries all the guilt alone. Male and female [God] created them—and man fell away from [God]—male and female."[27] The New Testament, speaking of the Fall, uses Adam in the generic sense and *anthropos* ("humankind") rather than *anēr* ("man") in such verses as "sin came into the world through one man and death through sin, and so death spread to all men" (Rom. 5:12; cf. 5:14-19; I Cor. 15:21, 45-49).

The immediate result of sin was a shattering of that perfect communion the two human beings had known in the garden with God and with each other. They realized their nakedness, became self-conscious, and hid. E. J. Young puts it poignantly, "Sin is secretive and breaks a pure and open fellowship . . . for sin is essentially divisive. . . . Sin renders men lonely."[28]

Immediately Adam tried to pass the buck, to blame the woman God gave him. Following her "leader," Eve blamed the serpent. God accepted neither evasion. The consequences fell on all—and equally. Estrangement is the result of the Fall—alienation from God, from others, and from nature. All participants suffer a loss of freedom, a limitation of their potential.

But first God promises redemption, release, and restoration. The broken communion, the severed cord of intimacy, would someday be healed by woman's seed (Gen. 3:15). She who was first to sin would be the first to know the Messiah.

In the meantime, humanity would suffer for their disobedience. God speaks not in wrath but in gentle reproof. God speaks of what *will* be, not what *should* be; the words are *descriptive*, not *prescriptive.* God does not institute or condone role stereotypes for the sexes but points to the sinful ways in which men and women would be limited by cultural constructions.

Genesis 3:16 outlines three ways in which woman would suffer from the Fall. First, her labor in childbearing would be multiplied.[29] Luther called this a "gracious and joyous punishment" because even in childbearing woman was sustained by the hope that her child might be the Messiah. Other theologians have seemingly derived almost sadistic pleasure from this verse, commenting that "Eve . . . had disobeyed God and sought for enjoyment contrary to God's law. She therefore will be punished in her sexual life, for not only will her pregnancy be unpleasant, but her entire life."[30] Some have used such thinking (as they have used Jesus' comment, "The poor you will have with you always") as an excuse for oppression of women in the name of God's will.

"Your desire shall be for your husband" describes the second way woman would suffer. These words have tempted scholars to speculate: "This yearning is morbid. . . . It may be normal. It often is not but takes a perverted form. . . . It is a just penalty. She who sought to strive apart from man and to act independently of him in the temptation finds a continual attraction to him to be her unavoidable lot."[31] Another describes this desire as "practically bordering on disease."[32] One whose God seems a bit sadistic suggests that desire was added to ensure the first penalty of multiplied sorrow in childbearing.[33]

Actually there is nothing morbid or pathogenic about woman's desire—it is the same as man's for restoration of the communion with his mate and with his God. Just as our communion with God is restored in Christ Jesus, so the marriage relationship in Christ can become a true "one-flesh" relationship. The Song of Solomon, which gives us an ideal picture of sexual relationship, says, "My beloved is mine and I am his. . . . I am my beloved's, and his desire is for me" (2:16; 7:10).

Katharine C. Bushnell says that a more accurate translation of this verse would be, "Thou art *turning away* to thy husband, and he will rule over thee." She notes that the word *teshuqah* is the same one found in Genesis 4:7 and Song of Solomon 7:10. The word does not connote sexual attraction or lust as so many men have interpreted it; she cites numerous ancient sources to show that it was understood to mean that Eve *turned away* from God to form an alliance with her husband. Thus God warned Eve that if she turned from God to her husband, she would find not the companionship she sought but one who would dominate her. Malicious translators have willfully ignored ancient evidence to make this verse a cornerstone of women's oppression, compounding God's prophecy.[34]

Perhaps the most famous of God's pronouncements to women is the third and last one in 3:16: "He shall rule over you." A better translation is found in The Jerusalem Bible: "He will lord it over you." Contrary to *Fascinating Womanhood,* which declares this to be "the first commandment which God gave unto the woman,"[35] even those who believe woman is subordinate in the order of creation realize that this verse represents a sinful perversion.

God is not here issuing a special commandment, "Be thou ruled by him!" or, "Thou shalt not rule!" But here in Genesis 3:16 we have a statement, a prediction, a prophecy, of how man, degenerated by sin, would take advantage of his headship as a husband to dominate, lord it over, his wife. Nowhere in the Bible is Genesis 3:16 quoted or referred to as establishing a general subordination of woman to man.[36]

Man's rule over woman "is not an imperative order of creation but rather the element of disorder that disturbs the original peace of creation."[37] Even Luther, despite all that he says elsewhere, concedes in his commentary on this verse, "Had Eve not sinned she would have raised children without any pain or sorrow. Nor would she have been subject to her husband."[38] He says this places a very heavy burden on men because it is easier to rule animals than human beings! But Adam tries. Whereas in Genesis 2:23 Eve was called "Woman," in 3:20 she is reduced to "mother of all living." Her function and sphere have been cut in half.

The consequences of sin fell not just on the serpent or on woman but also on all humanity and indeed all creation. We all toil for our food, we earn our bread by the sweat of our brows, and we return to the dust at death.

The Fall Throughout the Bible

Despite the importance attributed Genesis 3 by Christians, the Old Testament writers paid little if any attention to it. Possible exceptions are Job 31:33 ("If I covered my transgressions as Adam" KJV), in which modern versions of the Bible favor the translation "man" instead of the proper name, and Hosea 6:7 ("But at Adam they transgressed the covenant"), which some scholars believe is a reference to the place Admah, rather than to the person, Adam. The only clear reference is in the apocryphal book Ecclesiasticus:

"Woman is the origin of sin, and it is through her that we all die" (25:24 NEB; cf. Rom. 5:12).

For the Hebrew people, as we have said, the first three chapters of Genesis answer particular questions concerning the creation of the world, the institution of marriage, and the source of sin. Though the Hebrews obviously accepted these explanations as given, they did not use them to explain or excuse their own problems. When calamity befell the nation, the prophets did not say, "Our parents, Adam and Eve, sinned and thus we are being punished." Instead they declared, "All *we* like sheep have gone astray!"

Other than four references to the "one-flesh" relationship, the New Testament refers to Genesis 1–3 in five passages. Only two of these deal specifically with women, and they are an effort to settle very practical, cultural issues concerning behavior in church meetings. Eve is named or referred to twice in the New Testament: "I am afraid that as the serpent deceived Eve by his cunning, your thoughts will be led astray from a sincere and pure devotion to Christ" (II Cor. 11:3); "Adam was not deceived, but the woman was deceived and became a transgressor" (I Tim. 2:14).

These verses are surely not saying that Adam did not sin, since this would certainly contradict Genesis and the great theological teaching of Romans 5. Nor are they arguing for Eve's greater guilt or weaker mind because she was deceived. As Ambrose pointed out long ago, "In the Fall of our first parents, there is more excuse for the woman. For the man allowed himself to be tempted by his sister, his equal. Whereas Eve was tempted by an angel—a fallen angel, it is true, but nevertheless a creature superior to a human."[39] Nor would it seem logical that Eve who was deceived should be less apt as a teacher than Adam who apparently sinned with eyes wide open.

Both II Corinthians 11:3 and I Timothy 2:14 are more concerned with deception and false teaching than with women. All Christians must beware lest false teachers deceive them as the serpent did Eve. Apparently some women in Timothy's church in Ephesus had been so misled (II Tim. 3:6-7), and were barred from teaching.

Interestingly, nowhere does Jesus refer to the Fall. He does not suggest that the woman is weak and easily deceived. He does not forbid her to study theology or teach his word. He does not blame her for the first sin or remind her that men will rule over her because of it. Rather he treats all daughters of Eve as persons created and re-creatable in the divine image and likeness.

3.

WOMEN IN THE BIBLE WORLD

Look at the index of any cultural history: ancient Greece, medieval Europe, Renaissance Italy, postwar America. There, after pages of the familiar headings under which we classify the phenomena of human experience—art and architecture, games and pastimes, medicine, politics, trade, war, etc.—the reader will almost always come upon the entry "Women," in nearly every case followed by some such phrase as "position of." What won't be found is the entry, "Men, position of," for the very good reason that the history of men has been synonymous in the minds of nearly all historians with the history of civilization itself.

—Richard Gilman[1]

To UNDERSTAND THE SOCIAL POSITION OF WOMEN DURING BIBLICAL times, we must keep two things in mind. First, the Bible was written over a long period of time, and it spans thousands of years of history. In any society, time brings various changes. Second, the "Bible world" did not exist in a vacuum as some strange storybook land somehow located outside time and space. The life described in both Old and New Testaments took place surrounded by, and often influenced by, other cultures that were also working out social customs. The question, What was life like for women during Bible times? can only be answered by seeing woman's position in historical, cross-cultural perspective.

Woman's status in a given society greatly depends upon her power and position within the economic-opportunity structure of that society. As Simone de Beauvoir points out, where a woman is permitted to own nothing, she cannot experience the dignity of being a person; she herself is part of a man's property.[2] In a patriarchal society with a system of descent and inheritance through the male line (as in ancient Israel), woman's position is one of subordination (though not necessarily degradation). In societies where economic opportunities for women are greater, women hold a higher position. For example, there are African tribes in which, though the land is owned by the men, the women have ownership of the crops and control all food supplies—which obviously places tremendous power in their hands.[3]

In addition to the degree of property rights and privileges held by women in ancient cultures, another significant factor affected their position—the matter of a particular society's attitudes toward fertility cult practices and reverence for female deities. Societies which felt deep awe toward woman's maternal powers and associated her with the soil and fecundity of crops revered woman as the giver of life, incorporating this reverence into worship of mother goddesses. Various peoples also associated goddesses with overall power and wisdom.

Anthropologist Peggy Sanday sees a link between the status attained by women through their economic role in a given society and the existence of belief systems to legitimate that status. "The existence or development of female deities who have general powers can be seen as a means for recognizing and accepting female power. This can also serve to reduce sex antagonism, which seems to develop when the status of women changes in such a fashion as to threaten male power and authority."[4] If these two factors (economic power and goddess religions) are associated with woman's social status in ancient cultures, what about Israel? Israel's patriarchal family form limited woman's social-economic-legal privileges greatly; but in other respects, the Israelites gave significant honor and legal protection to women. Also, the official stand of Israel was one of opposition to fertility cults and the female deities of other nations. Would this result in a higher or lower status for Israelite women when compared to surrounding cultures? The answer requires some understanding of these other societies.

Old Testament Period

Sumerian Culture

Historian H. W. F. Saggs speaks of an initial high status for women in Sumerian culture which gradually deteriorated, and he shows a direct relationship between the society's religion and the position of women. In the early days of the city-state, women served as priestesses and temple prostitutes. Their service was valued as highly as that of the men and was rewarded with allotments from the temple. But over time this changed, and the change was related to the disappearance of goddesses in Sumerian religion.

The early myths had given the goddesses an important role in the divine decision-making assembly. In fact, the Sumerians originally believed the underworld was ruled by a goddess alone, and one myth tells how she came to take a consort.[5] Evidently, marriage ended even the autonomy of a goddess, and the male gods gradually took over the running of things. Woman's lowered position in society reflected the situation ascribed to the world of the divinities. (To state this in the reverse would, of course, be more accurate.)

Assyria

One indication of a high regard for women in early Assyrian civilization is an amazing legend about a queen named Semiramis, whose marvelous exploits and accomplishments captivated the minds of the Mesopotamian world of long ago. Abandoned by her mother (a goddess who had been involved in an amorous affair with a young mortal), the infant was found and reared by a shepherd. As a young woman, Semiramis posed as a soldier and became a war hero, whereupon she became the wife of the founder of Nineveh. Upon his death, she reigned over a vast territory that she extended in every direction, conquering kings, building great cities, and accomplishing fantastic engineering feats.

Edward Pollard makes the point that such a legend could have developed only in an atmosphere where female intellectual and leadership talents were recognized and appreciated.[6] As expressed in words attributed to Semiramis herself: "Nature gave me the body of a woman, but my deeds have equalled those of the most valiant men."

In later periods, although Assyrian girls as well as boys were taught to read and write, the amount of social freedom for women depended on their rank in society. Bare feet and bare heads characterized lower-class women as they went to the marketplace or visited the homes of friends. Higher-status women were expected to remain secluded in their homes.

The queens and women of the kings' harems were shut up as virtual prisoners in surroundings of great opulence. Occasionally the king visited his women or invited them to dine with him, but most of the time the women were idle and sought to alleviate boredom through embroidery, music and dance, conversation, and attention to dress. The average Assyrian housewife, on the other hand, filled her days with household chores. Many tasks (kneading bread, hanging the wash, and so on) were done upon the flat rooftops, making it easy for neighbor women to chat across the terraces as they worked.

Veils became important during certain periods of Assyrian history. Laws of the late second millennium B.C. required the veiling of married women and concubines. Harlots were commanded by law to keep their heads uncovered; if they dared to put on veils, they were beaten fifty stripes and pitch was poured on their heads.[7] (An awareness of the significance of veils for women in different cultures is helpful in understanding otherwise baffling Bible passages, such as I Cor. 11. Even in modern times, there remain places where veiling customs have caused problems for women desiring equality. When Princess Llalla Aiche in the late 1960s publicly removed her veil to call attention to the demands of many Moroccan women for higher rights, conservatives were shocked and whispered that the princess must surely be a prostitute! To lower one's veil in public seemed extremely risqué.[8])

All in all, we may conclude that Assyrian women had many rights during Old Testament times, but they were somewhat more restricted than another of Israel's neighbors—Babylon.

Babylon

Babylonian culture provided a fairly high status for its women.[9] Women could own property, attend to their own business, appear in public, plead in courts of justice, and even hold office. Marriage regulations, property rights for widows (including the privilege of conducting business in their own names), and other provisions of the Code of Hammurabi indicate a genuine concern for female citizens' rights. Women could be judges, elders, and secretaries. They were recognized as witnesses to documents. The Code of Hammurabi speaks of businesswomen who ran wineshops. Women were by no means mere chattels in Babylonian society.

One praiseworthy provision of the law had to do with a married woman's property rights. Her dowry (often including land or other valuable property) remained in the wife's possession and passed from her to her children. Marriage in Hammurabi's Code was more than a sale of a woman by her father to her husband (though legally there were some elements of this practice). It was also viewed as a contract between a husband and wife.

Divorce privileges, however, favored men more than women. A woman could obtain a judicial separation only by proving her husband had been cruel to her, and such proof often demanded that she undergo a strange trial by ordeal which was to serve as a sort of lie detector test. In contrast, a man could apparently divorce his wife for any cause, provided that he would return her dowry, let her keep custody of the children, and agree to pay for their upbringing. Thus, even though the husband had greater privileges in *initiating* a divorce, there was ample provision for the wife's rights and protection.

Persia

In Persia, despite the fact that fathers chose husbands for their daughters, that wives were required to be absolutely obedient to husbands (see Esther 1:10-21), and that polygamy was common, women were (according to de Beauvoir) "held in honor more than among most Oriental peoples."[10]

Marriage was the main purpose of a Persian woman's life, and posterity for the husband was considered the main purpose of marriage. Persian mothers were responsible for educating sons up to the age of seven, and daughters until marriage. If a son somehow had shown he was unworthy to receive his share of his father's estate, his mother received it. If a husband died leaving no adult son, the wife became the guardian of minor children and manager of her husband's business affairs.

Egypt

Women were highly esteemed in ancient Egypt. Even the Pharaoh recognized his queen as his equal or even superior, for as Charles Seltman points out, "to her belonged the land of Egypt itself, and the king was the man who married the daughter of his predecessor."[11] Simone de Beauvoir also calls attention to woman's high social status in the land of the Nile, including equality with men in court and the right to own property.[12]

As late as the period of the Ptolemies, marriage contracts were not unusual in which the whole of a man's property was assigned to his wife. *Either* wife or husband might own their house and fields, and husbands and wives were expected to show loving respect toward each other regardless of who was considered the owner. Ancient Egyptian writings give advice to husbands living in homes owned by their wives, warning the husbands not to be rude or demanding but to appreciate their wives and find joy in them. On the other hand, if the husband owned the home, he must likewise make his wife happy, provide well for her, and show love.[13]

However, despite the many positive aspects, woman's situation was not utopian. For all her praise of woman's lot in the Egyptian world of long ago, de Beauvoir is enough of a realist to make the following observation:

But even at the time when they had a privileged status, unique in the ancient world, women were not socially the equals of men. Sharing in religion and in government, they could act as regent, but the pharaoh was male; the priests and soldiers were men; women took only a secondary part in public life; and in private life there was demanded of them a fidelity without reciprocity.[14]

Israel

Before we look at four aspects of woman's social position in Hebrew culture (legal rights, education, occupations outside the home, and political participation), some general observations are worth noting.

First, a woman in Israel found her identity not as a separate individual but as a member of a family. She was a daughter, then a wife, and then a mother. Second, there is no denying the patriarchal nature of Israel's culture. Old Testament scholar Roland de Vaux says that the proper word to describe the Israelite family is *beth 'ab*, the "house of one's father." Genealogies recorded the father's line, and "the father had absolute authority over his children, even over his married sons if they lived with him, and over their wives" in addition to authority over his own wife.[15] De Vaux concludes that "the social and legal position of an Israelite wife was . . . inferior to the position a wife occupied in the great countries round about."[16]

We are reminded of Krister Stendahl's comment about the strongly masculine structure of traditional Jewish culture:

All the way from circumcision to burial rites it is only the male who is an Israelite in the true sense of the word. . . . The feminine ideal is in line with tradition's picture of Rabbi Akiba's wife, the student's and scholar's wife who sacrifices everything for her husband's studies, the mother who manages her own affairs subject to her husband.[17]

Legal Rights

In his book, *Hebrew Law in Biblical Times*, Ze'ev Falk warns against defining Hebrew society in terms of its laws alone. He reminds us that "the law, for instance, treated woman harshly, whereas custom operated in her favor." He also emphasizes that in discussing many aspects of the position of woman in a given society, what may be under consideration is the legal position of a *wife* rather than woman as woman.[18]

However, despite Falk's plea for caution, marital status seemed to make little difference in rights for the Israelite woman. Whether single or married, she was under the jurisdiction of some male; she was never her own person. Betrothal terms were the same as those of purchase. The word *ba'al,* which referred to a husband, meant "owner" or "master"; and a man's wife was included in lists of his possessions (e.g., Exod. 20:17). A childless widow was required to submit to the right of levirate and marry her husband's brother in order to produce offspring who would bear the name and inherit the property of her deceased husband (see Deut. 25:5ff.; Gen. 38:8). Falk concludes that although women were considered capable of commiting most offenses and incurring penalties just as in the case of men (cf. Num. 5:6ff.), the women of Israel clearly "did not enjoy equality of rights."

Yet we must not overlook the fact that legal protection was offered to persons regardless of sex. There was no sexual differentiation in the commandment that children should honor their parents (father *and* mother [Exod. 20:12; Lev. 19:3]), and a death penalty was prescribed for offspring who struck or cursed either their father or their mother (Exod. 21:15, 17). Likewise, Exodus 21 lists penalties for slave owners who hurt or killed slaves of either sex, and penalties for farmers whose oxen gored anyone, male or female.

However, from the vantage point of our own day and our own values, it is easy to see glaring inequities in the treatment of the sexes under Israelite law—particularly in regard to inheritance laws, laws covering adultery and fornication, and laws about vows.

Inheritance Laws

In ancient Israel, only sons had a right to inherit, with a double portion going to the firstborn (cf. Deut. 21:16-17). If sons survived the father, neither the widow nor daughters had any share in the inheritance. If there were no sons, the estate went to the daughters, but in their default passed to the deceased man's relatives.[19]

The origin of the custom granting inheritance privileges to daughters in the absence of sons is an interesting anecdote in the history of feminism, for it was a bona fide case of agitation for women's rights! The daughters of Zelophehad came to Moses to protest the unfairness of their father's name dying out simply because he left no sons. The five sisters asked to be given a possession among their father's brethren. "Moses brought their case before the Lord. And the Lord said to Moses, 'The daughters of Zelophehad are right. . . . "If a man dies, and has no son, then you shall cause his inheritance to pass to his daughter" ' " (Num. 27:5-8).

However, custom decreed that a woman left her old family upon marriage. Having passed into a new family, she was to assist in continuing the name of her husband's family. Thus, a proviso was added to the ruling made for Zelophehad's daughters (Num. 36:1-9). Women must marry within their father's tribe to avoid transference of the family property to another tribe. This addition to the law again ensured masculine dominance and offset whatever gains were made for women in Numbers 27.

If a man died without children, none of his inheritance went to his widow. Rather, it passed to his male kinsmen on his father's side or to his brothers. Childless Israelite widows either returned to their own fathers or remained a part of their husbands' families through the practice of levirate marriage. In cases where a widow had adult children, she depended on them for support. If a husband died while his children were small, the widow became the trustee of the money left to them and was responsible for its management. Later Jewish law recognized greater inheritance rights for widows.[20]

Laws Regarding Fornication and Adultery

In Israel, a woman was expected to be chaste before marriage and faithful afterward. This was undoubtedly related to every Israelite man's desire for sons—sons that he could be sure were his own. But judging from at least some of the legislation, this emphasis seems to have given rise to a kind of double standard.

For example, a man could accuse his bride of not being a virgin (Deut. 22:13-21). If the woman could not *prove* she was virginal at the time the marriage was consummated, the law required her to be stoned to death at the door of her father's house. However, if the bridegroom's charge could be proven untrue (because the woman's parents produced "tokens of virginity" to show to the town elders), the young man would be whipped, fined, and forced to keep the woman as his wife for life, with no divorce privileges permitted. (One wonders if the wife wasn't being unjustly punished by being required to stay married to such a man!)

The law may have seemed unfair to women on two other counts. First, it demanded virginity of the woman and provided a "test" to assure the husband that he was the first one to have sexual intercourse with her. But there was no similar provision to guarantee women that their husbands had come to the marriage bed "pure."

Second, attempts to prove virginity are unreliable. The "tokens of virginity" are usually thought to be blood-stained bedsheets or cloths smeared from the breaking of the bride's hymen during the first experience of coitus. Various cultures have had such tests over the ages, with some even requiring that items stained with hymenal blood be displayed to wedding guests.

However, the hymens of many women have been ruptured during childhood through means totally unrelated to sex relations; and there are other women whose hymens stretch rather than tear when the penis enters the vagina. The absence of bleeding during the first intercourse does not prove a woman is not virginal. Such a test could easily yield false results, and an innocent woman could be condemned to death because her parents had no tokens of virginity to show on her behalf.

Possibly the tokens of virginity were something other than this—perhaps special garments that served as "chastity belts" for unmarried girls. According to this theory, girls under their parents' supervision would have to wear such garments and submit to frequent inspection for signs of disarray.[21]

If a married woman were suspected of adultery, she might be forced to undergo a "trial by ordeal." Behind any such trial is the idea that God (or "the gods") must decide guilt or innocence and deliver the final verdict. Although such procedures were not unusual among ancient peoples, Israel rarely had anything resembling them (with the exception of casting lots to discern God's will). Thus, the "bitter water ordeal" (Num. 5:11-31) seems strange.

A man who suspected his wife of adultery but could find no witnesses to prove it could bring her to the priest for a special "experiment." After taking an oath spelling out the details of what might happen to her, the wife was forced to drink a bitter liquid concocted by the priest. (It was a mixture of holy water and dust from the tabernacle into which had been dipped the "writing pad" that contained the list of the curses.) If guilty of adultery, the wife's body was expected to swell and her "thigh fall away." If innocent, she would escape the signs of the curse and be able to bear children.

A woman could be compelled to undergo this shameful and frightening experience for no other reason than her husband's jealousy or suspicions. Yet, the law provided no means for her to check up on him if she felt he had been unfaithful to her.

Israel's requirement of a trial by ordeal for suspected adultery is by no means unique. Anthropologist Mary Douglas tells of groups having deep anxieties about "adultery pollution." A wife's unfaithfulness is thought to defile her, and this defilement would endanger her husband upon contact with her. In some cases, it is feared the couple's children (living or yet unborn) will be contaminated in some way. In one present-day tribe, if a man suffers from diarrhea after a meal, he automatically assumes that one of his wives has committed adultery. In the past, this tribe sought to determine guilt through the poison ordeal. If the woman vomited instead of suffering from the poison's deadly effects, she was considered innocent. But if she died, it supposedly proved she had committed adultery.[22]

Among Israel's neighbors, the Assyro-Babylonian river ordeal existed for the same purpose. A woman accused of adultery, who had not been caught in the act, was required to jump into the holy river. The belief was that a guilty woman would drown; an innocent one would float.

Actually, Israel's trial by ordeal was less severe than those of other cultures where women were expected to *die* if guilty (and the designated tests made death almost certain). Perhaps Israel wanted a detection system such as other societies had; yet the Israelite legal penalty for adultery (death) could only be applied if the woman were caught in the actual act. Therefore, a "more merciful" way was provided for cases where suspicious husbands accused their wives of unfaithfulness but had no real proof. The bitter waters ordeal had less severe consequences than other methods of dealing with adultery. At worst, a woman might have a miscarriage (the usual interpretation of Num. 5:27), preserving her own life at the same time it removed her husband's worst fear—that she would bear a child that was not his own.

We must keep in mind that overall there was equality of treatment in Israel's adultery laws. Not only women, but their lovers as well, were stoned to death if caught in an adulterous act (Deut. 22:22ff.). If a double standard does appear in some form, we must remember what adultery meant in ancient Israel. Since a wife was considered one of her husband's possessions, an act of adultery on her part meant disloyalty to her owner. But if a man committed adultery, his crime wasn't unfaithfulness to his own wife so much as it was an injury inflicted on the other woman's husband or betrothed (by stealing that man's exclusive sexual rights to that woman).

On the other hand, as de Vaux points out, Leviticus 18:20 ranks adultery among "sins against marriage." "Adultery was a sin against one's neighbor, but the text of Lev. 18:20 adds a religious consideration, and the stories of Gen. 20:1-13; 26:7-11 represent adultery as a sin against God."[23]

As time went on, attitudes toward adultery reflected much more consideration for the wife's rights to her husband as well as his to her. Proverbs 5:15-19 and Malachi 2:15 exhort husbands to be faithful to their wives for this is the will of God. Hosea 4:13-14 makes clear that no double standard was in effect at this stage of Israel's history; both men and women were alike condemned for their adultery (here connected with idolatry). The Apocrypha speaks of a wife's adultery as, first, sin against God; next, against her husband; and third, against herself and any illegitimate children she might bear (Ecclus. 23:22ff.).

Women and Vows

A third category of laws that seem discriminatory in regard to women concerned vows. Numbers 30 shows that a woman was considered a minor all her life. Either her father or her husband was responsible for her actions. Thus, if she made a voluntary religious promise, her father's consent or her husband's consent (depending on her marital status) was necessary in order for her vow to be valid.

If father or husband withheld consent, a woman's pledge became null and void. A widow or divorcee, however, was held responsible for her own vows, just as was a man; but all other women were under a kind of perpetual tutelage. In a patriarchal society, where a woman was under some man's authority and without independent status or means of support, the law about vows and pledges was probably given for the men's protection. Otherwise, they might be required to pay for obligations incurred by the women under their care.

Another passage on vows, Leviticus 27, evidently refers to pledges for the service of the Lord. Persons who pledged themselves or someone under their charge did not necessarily have to serve in the sanctuary. In lieu of such service, they could offer money to God, according to a specified rate scale. The amounts varied according to age and sex, with the highest valuation being placed on males from twenty to sixty years of age. The valuation assigned females in that age category was 60 percent of the valuation assigned males. Although the percentage differed according to age level, girls and women were consistently rated at a lower monetary value than boys and men.

Apparently, value was based upon assumed physical strength; and in a society that measured strength in traditional masculine terms (muscle power, ability to perform heavy manual labor, military might), women, old people, and small children would be considered of less worth in work potential.

To use this passage as a proof-text giving biblical justification for unfair pay scales based on sex is ridiculous. Occupational value today depends upon mental ability, skill, training, and talents. Christians who try to universalize this passage as God's will for all time, insisting that it "proves" women deserve lower wages than men, put themselves in an absurd position. To be consistent, they would also have to conclude from this passage that a sixty-year-old neurosurgeon should be paid less than one-third as much as a twenty-year-old grade-school dropout who washes dishes at a grill!

Education

During earliest childhood, Israelite boys and girls alike learned from their mothers—especially moral teachings. Parents were responsible to God for the religious training of both sons and daughters (Prov. 6:20-22.). The various festivals and holy days were designed to incite children's questions and educate them in the meaning of Israel's religion (cf. Deut. 6:4-25; Exod. 12:25-27).

However, as children grew, boys and girls were separated in their training. Girls remained under their mothers' control and learned to perform household tasks in preparation for marriage and housewifery. Boys were turned over to their fathers for education in crafts and trades, for instruction in their national heritage, and for specialized religious training. Prophets, priests, and elders also played a part in educating boys, because a knowledge of the Torah was considered vital in the life of every Israelite male. Boys were educated for full participation in all aspects of their society; girls were educated for the private world of the home.

Occupations Outside the Home

In Israel's agricultural economy, women shared in providing for their families in countless ways. The heavy tasks of working in the fields, looking after flocks, cooking, spinning, sewing, and caring for many offspring made Israel's women "working mothers" in a very real sense, even though they didn't have paying jobs outside the home.

However, the Israelites did not so rigidly believe that woman's place is in the home that all outside occupational endeavors were forbidden. At least by the time of the Wisdom Literature, some women did have additional careers, and they were able to combine such occupations with marriage quite successfully—as the idealization of the "virtuous woman" in Proverbs 31 shows. Apparently, it was not unusual in the later period of Israel's history for women to have income from spinning, sewing, weaving, needlecraft, and so on. The Apocrypha tells of Anna who earned money by "women's work" (weaving) and was not only paid wages by her employer but was also sometimes given a bonus, such as a goat (see Tobit 2:11-12).

Political Participation

In a patriarchal society where men were considered the authorities, women had little opportunity to participate in political affairs. Deborah's position of power during the times of the judges was the exception rather than the rule (Judg. 4:4ff.). But she and Jael (the other wartime heroine in the battle with Sisera) were highly honored by Israel, and there seems to have been no disparagement of their sex. The Book of Esther and the apocryphal Book of Judith both extol women for saving the nation. Likewise, Huldah, a prophetess during the times of the kings, played an important role in public affairs (II Kings 22:14-20). In I Chronicles 7:24, the listing of sons in the genealogies is broken to mention a daughter named Sheerah who built and fortified three cities.

During the monarchy, women were excluded from the throne. (Athaliah's rule was illegal—II Kings 11:1-16.) The line of succession went from father to son. If there were no male heirs, the rulership passed to the deceased king's brother. There is no doubt that the affairs of Israel as a nation were in the charge of the men. Women supported, encouraged, influenced, and generally served behind the scenes, if at all.

New Testament Period

In the New Testament, we see a convergence of many cultural influences, each containing inconsistencies, ambiguities, and fluctuations over time. Therefore, to understand the position of women in Christianity, we must give attention to the Jewish milieu and the heritage of the Greco-Roman world at the time Christianity began and then spread.

In comparing Greek and Roman attitudes toward women, we see strange paradoxes. For example, Rome's upper-class women had more prominence in public life than did the women of Athens. Yet opportunities for education were seldom extended to Roman girls (except for study in the home and sometimes at the primary school level, i.e., through about age eleven). For Greek girls, on the other hand, education even up through the secondary level was quite common. The Athenian Academy even had women professors.[24] Simone de Beauvoir makes the point that Greek women were, legally speaking, less enslaved than Roman women; but paradoxically, Roman women were "much more deeply integrated in society."[25]

Greek Culture

In the world of the Greeks, Macedonia stands out like the ancient Greek state of Sparta as being exemplary in granting higher status and freedom of opportunity to the female sex. Classics professor E. M. Blaiklock notes that "Macedonian inscriptions bear witness to the respected and responsible position of women in the northern Greek communities," and he suggests that the exaltation of womanhood in the Gospel of Luke and the Book of Acts fits well with the tradition that Luke was a Macedonian.[26]

Throughout the history of Greece, attitudes toward women varied—as is reflected, for example, in the great Greek plays. The philosophers disagreed about women. Plato suggested that girls be given a liberal education and that women be granted a share in the government of the republic. He wrote: "There is no occupation concerned with the management of social affairs which belongs either to woman or to man, as such. Natural gifts are to be found here and there in both creatures alike."[27] Aristotle, however, disagreed. He viewed woman's nature as being inherently defective and inferior.

Some of the Greek ambivalence no doubt stemmed from the traditional categories into which women were placed. Demosthenes summed up the three major classes in his famous remark: "We have hetairai for the pleasures of the spirit, concubines for sensual pleasure, and wives to give us sons."[28]

Among the wealthier families of classical Athens, wives were secluded and closely guarded—one reason apparently being to ensure that all offspring were those of the husband. And although ancient monuments show that many men of Athens expressed deep respect and love for their wives, honoring them as mothers of their children and managers of their homes, the fact remains that women were considered permanent minors. A woman's person and property were controlled by a guardian—father, husband, husband's heir, or even the state.

Yet, since it was considered improper to take one's wife out in public, men often found intellectual female companionship from among the *hetairai* (the word means "companion," "girlfriend," or "mistress"). Artistic, cultured, often well educated and intellectual, the *hetairai* were free to do as they pleased and were treated essentially as equals by men. Many of the great Greek scholars had mistresses from among these women; and it was common custom for a married man to invite a *hetaira* to attend a social gathering with him. Men admired the talents and highly cultivated minds of these women, but since the *hetairai* were considerd courtesans, they were not free to marry Greek citizens. They were usually foreign-born (often from other Greek city-states) and earned their living in commerce and a variety of other occupations.[29]

Elise Boulding points out that, although *any* woman entrepreneur was likely to be labeled a prostitute in that society, many of the *hetairai* "do not appear to have sold sexual services" but simply maintained an independent existence outside the system of rules and confinement for respectable married women. Thus they participated freely in Athenian public and intellectual life as poets, philosophers, mathematicians, musicians, and physicians.[30]

Demosthenes' third category, concubines, were women husbands took as temporary replacements for their wives while the wives were ill, pregnant, or recovering from childbirth. Often a man took a concubine from among his household servants.

There were other Greek women who served specifically as prostitutes. Some were slaves, and others were streetwalkers who lived a miserable existence. In a somewhat higher position on the prostitute stratification scale were the musically talented dancing flute girls. Last, there was the specialized category of prostitute-priestesses, such as those who served in the temple of Aphrodite at Corinth.

The oft-quoted remark by Demosthenes categorizes women solely from a male point of view with an emphasis on the benefits Athenian men could derive from different groups of women. Taking a sociological approach, Boulding observes that classical Athenian culture not only contained the respectable married women confined to the women's quarters of their homes and the *hetairai* but several other categories as well: slaves, poor women "who worked at the same variety of crafts and trades that poor women everywhere work at," and foreign-born women (other than the *hetairai*) who often worked as traders. High-status women past the age of sixty could participate in public ceremonies and bear messages for the younger secluded women.[31] Secluded wives also sent their slaves to do errands and shop for them. The classical scholar Sarah Pomeroy writes that the poorer women of Athens enjoyed freedom from the practice of seclusion because they did not have slaves to take care of matters outside the home. Poorer women were able to enjoy the company of other women, "for they gossiped while fetching water, washing clothes, and borrowing utensils."[32]

Roman Culture

In Rome, the condition of women was somewhat better than in Greece—not so much legally but practically. During the days of the Republic, women had been quite restricted and were under the authority of father or husband with few rights of their own. But with the establishment of the Empire, things began looking up for women. Marriage laws were changed, giving greater rights to the wife. Women were highly esteemed as wives and mothers. They shared responsibilities with their husbands with regard to children and property, were not confined to their homes, ate with their husbands and dined with invited guests, went to the public baths, and accompanied their husbands to the theater, races, and other public entertainments.

The growing emancipation of women disturbed many people, who feared a deterioration of morals and a breakdown of family life would be inevitable by-products of such female freedom. Basing their conclusions on antifeminist writings (such as the *Epigrams* of Martial and the *Satires* of Juvenal), as well as records of notorious scandals among upper-class society where wealth and leisure were often misused, some scholars paint a picture of gloom and degeneration and pin much of the blame for Rome's troubles on the changing status of women.[33]

In view of the charge that an increase in rights and privileges for women encouraged women to break up marriages, it must be kept in mind that *men* dissolved family ties just as much, if not more so, than women. The famous Cicero, after thirty years of marriage, cast off his wife in order to marry a rich young woman. The self-righteous moralist Cato also divorced his wife, but he took her back years later after learning that her second husband had died, leaving her a large estate.

It was also not unusual for a man to dissolve a marriage if the wife bore no children (infertility was always assumed to be the woman's fault). And changing mates for political advantage was very common—one sad example being the Emperor Augustus's demand that his stepson Tiberius divorce his beloved wife in order to marry Augustus's daughter Julia. The marriage was painful and disgusting

67

to Tiberius because of Julia's flagrant unfaithfulness. If one turns to the rumors of adultery, both heterosexual and homosexual promiscuity, and various scandals recorded by Suetonius showing the unsavory sides of Roman life, it is not difficult to conclude that the male sex played an even greater role than the female sex in the loosening of moral standards.[34]

The second point to be made is that wifely virtues were still praised in the days of the Empire. Morals and family stability did *not* disappear. Tombstones indicate great devotion between husbands and wives. And although divorce was not unusual, the high rates of remarriage were largely due to the death of a spouse.

Other Influences

With trade, immigration, and the movement of the Roman army, ideas from the east had spread throughout the Roman Empire. Of particular importance were the mystery cults, which stressed secret revelations for the initiate and had a triple appeal—to the *intellect* (by emphasizing knowledge), to the *senses* (by stressing terror, love, hope, ecstasy, emotional frenzy, music, dance, drama, and sometimes sexual debauchery), and to the *conscience* (through ascetic practices in efforts to gain eternal rewards).

Women played a prominent role in many of these religions, especially in the cult of the wine god Dionysius or that of Cybele, the great mother-goddess of Asia. There were temples to the goddesses Artemis (Diana) in Ephesus and Aphrodite (Venus) in Corinth. Worship of the Egyptian goddess Isis had a powerful appeal to the female sex. Called "the Glory of Women," Isis promised her women followers equality with men.[35]

Christianity spread in areas influenced not only by Greco-Roman culture but also by these various religions and their excesses. At the same time, there was its heritage from Judaism—both the strict masculine structure of the Palestinian form and the Judaism of the dispersion which Stendahl feels was different enough to seem quite attractive to women of the Hellenistic world.[36]

Thus, at first glance, there sometimes seem to be tension and inconsistency with regard to "woman's place" as seen in the New Testament writings—a subject to be explored in the following chapters.

4.

WOMAN'S BEST FRIEND: JESUS

Jesus came from God and a woman—*man* had nuthin' to do with it!
—Sojourner Truth

Jesus was a feminist to a degree far beyond that of his fellows and followers. . . . No other Western prophet, seer, or would-be redeemer of humanity was so devoted to the feminine half of mankind.
—Charles Seltman[1]

WHEN THE TIME WAS FULLY COME, GOD BECAME INCARNATE, "BORN OF woman, born under the law, to redeem those who were under the law" (Gal. 4:4-5). At last the seed of the woman was come to strike the serpent dead and break the power of the law of sin and death. No one has been more bound by that law than women.

From the moment the preparations for the Messiah's coming were set in motion, Christ's special mission to women was evident. In the light of first-century patriarchal culture, Jesus' behavior in regard to women is so extraordinary that New Testament scholar C. F. D. Moule cites it as evidence of Scripture's supernatural authenticity: "The Gospel portrait of Jesus would seem to have fairly forced its way through an atmosphere still . . . alien to it and still scarcely comprehending."[2]

As Dorothy Sayers has said so eloquently, many women then and now find Jesus a compelling figure because he never made jokes about them, never treated them as either "The women, God help us!" or "The ladies, God bless them!" Jesus always took women seriously and never "urged them to be feminine or jeered at them for being female." He did not have a patriarchal ax to grind or a "male ego" to defend. He simply treated women as human beings.[3]

Women responded gratefully and wholeheartedly from the very beginning. Men were somewhat more dubious. When Elizabeth realized that she was bearing the forerunner of the Messiah, she acknowledged immediately, "Thus the Lord has done to me" (Luke 1:25). When the angel Gabriel told her husband Zechariah that his aged wife would conceive, he realized at once the scientific improbability and questioned the angel's veracity—which left Zechariah speechless (Luke 1:20).

When the angel told Mary she would bear the Messiah, she responded, "I am the handmaid of the Lord; let it be to me according to your word" (Luke 1:38). Joseph, on the other hand, found Mary's story of a virgin birth a bit difficult to believe and so sought "to divorce her quietly" until an angel told him not to (Matt. 1:18-25). Some radical feminists have charged that Mary was a pawn in this affair, "used" by God. Yet in an extremely patriarchal society, God did not send an angel to ask permission of Mary's father or of Joseph. God came directly to the young woman and presented her with the plan. She, with admirable courage, accepted.

Some scholars have presented Mary as having a "retiring nature, unobtrusive, reticent, perhaps even shrinking from observation so that the impress of her personality was confined to the sweet sanctities of the home circle."[4] We would not cast aspersions on Mary's behavior, but an unwed pregnant girl who sets off on a journey to visit relatives (Luke 1:39-40) does not seem like a reticent homebody! The joyous poetry of the Magnificat (Luke 1:46-55) does not sound like the response of one retiring and shy.

She bore her baby among strangers (Luke 2:7). She, not Joseph, called her young son to account for staying behind in Jerusalem (Luke 2:48). She initiated Christ's miracle working (John 2:1-11). She once came to fetch him home (Mark 3:21-35). She went to Calvary to witness his death (John 19:25-27). And she was in the Upper Room at Pentecost (Acts 1:14). All of which does not exactly add up to the image of one who shrank from the public eye. Luke 2:19 summarizes her response to the events of her life: "Mary kept all these things, pondering them in her heart." A proper, quiet, "feminine" attitude? The verse is modeled on similar responses by Jacob and Daniel (Gen. 37:11; Dan. 7:28). Mary reacted not as a woman but as a person to the mystery of God's incarnation.

Part of the mystery is that Mary brought forth a *son*. Why did God choose to become flesh in male form? Philippians 2:7-8 says that in Christ, God "emptied [God]self, taking the form of a servant, being born in [human] likeness. . . . And being found in human form [God in Christ] humbled [God]self and became obedient unto death." Men usually do not think of themselves as the "form of a servant," but as Virginia Ramey Mollenkott has so aptly noted, only as a free man could God demonstrate a radically new way of relating in terms of mutual respect and service.[5] Women and slaves were servants by law and custom. Respect was demanded from them.

On the practical level, Jewish women were kept in subjection and sometimes even seclusion. A female Messiah might have had little scriptural knowledge because according to Rabbi Eliezer ben Hyrcanus in the Talmud, the Torah should rather be burned than transmitted to a woman.[6] Barbara Streisand's movie *Yentl* illustrates the difficulties Jewish women have had in studying Torah, even into the twentieth century.[7] A female Messiah would not have been allowed to teach publicly in the synagogue, nor would she have been believed if she had, since the testimony of women was not accepted as veracious. And with her monthly "uncleanness" making her ritually impure at least one-fourth of the time, a female Messiah would have taken at least an extra year to complete God's mission!

However, if one truly believes in the virgin birth and not in some pagan myth of a male god in the sky who copulates with comely human virgins, then Jesus was undoubtedly genetically female even though phenotypically male, as one evangelical scientist has argued.[8] If Jesus had only one human parent, Mary, then his genes must have been XX rather than XY, even though scientists now understand cases in which female fetuses grow into babies that appear to be male. Thus Jesus may well have been biologically both male and female.

Certainly, whatever his biological makeup, Jesus was human and not simply male in an exclusive sense. His maleness was and is a part of the "scandal of particularity" in the fact that God physically entered human time and space. Jesus was a man, a first-century Jew, probably with dark hair, dark eyes, and swarthy skin. If the Shroud of Turin is to be believed, he was probably about five feet eleven inches tall and weighed about 178 pounds. He spoke Aramaic, knew something about carpentry, and maybe learned a bit about fishing from his friends. He hiked around a lot but never traveled far. He never visited Athens, Rome, or Alexandria, never saw the Seven Wonders of the ancient world. The theologians of the New Testament and the first four centuries who debated his nature were aware of that. In Greek one can make a distinction between *anēr* ("male") and *anthropos* ("human"). When speaking of the Incarnation, the New Testament writers almost without exception choose *anthropos* (see Phil. 2:7; Rom. 5:12, 15). The Nicene Creed originally asserted that Jesus became human (*anthropos*), not man.

Jesus came to earth primarily not as a male but as a person. He treated women primarily not as females but as human beings. Without sentimentality, condescension, or undemanding indulgence, he accepted them as persons in a way that moved them to repentance and love. Jesus associated with all sorts of women—wealthy and politically prominent ones as well as poor and morally disreputable ones (Luke 8:2-3). Some, like the Samaritan and the Syrophoenician women (John 4:7-42; Mark 7:24-30), were outsiders altogether.

Despite Billy Graham's assertion that "with all the new freedom that Christ brought women, He did not free them from the home,"[9] Jesus seems to have encouraged women just as much as men to become disciples. He commended Mary for listening to his teachings and reprimanded Martha for being overly concerned with household chores (Luke 10:38-42). As Dorothy Sayers comments of that story:

God, of course, may have His own opinion but the Church is reluctant to endorse it. . . . Mary's, of course, was the better part—the Lord said so, and we must not precisely contradict Him. But we will be careful not to despise Martha. . . . We could not get on without her, and indeed (having paid lip-service to God's opinion) we must admit that we greatly prefer her. For Martha was doing a really feminine job, whereas Mary was just behaving like any other disciple, male or female; and that is a hard pill to swallow.[10]

Jesus instructed all disciples, "If you love me, you will keep my commandments" (John 14:15). He never implied that male might be better or even different. Nothing recorded in the Gospels as the acts or words of Jesus supports patriarchy.

Women responded by following Jesus, traveling in the band of disciples, and supporting him financially (Matt. 27:55, Luke 8:2-3). Interestingly, the Bible mentions no other monetary contributions to his ministry.

In a day when most rabbis refused to teach women because they were "lightminded," supposedly incapable of grasping God's truth, Jesus taught women openly, even in the Temple's Court of Women (Luke 21:1-4). He did not confine himself to "feminine" subjects either. Some of his greatest truths were revealed to women. Jesus first declared himself the Messiah to the Samaritan woman (John 4:25-26). He also reminded her that God is Spirit and that true faith can be found and practiced without regard to national or religious boundaries (John 4:19-24). Christ's assertion, "I am the resurrection and the life," brought comfort to Martha, grieving over her dead brother Lazarus, and provoked from her an affirmation identical to Peter's: "Yes, Lord; I believe that you are the Christ, the Son of God" (John 11:25, 27).

Jesus also incorporated in his teaching objects and incidents with which women were familiar: wedding feasts, lost coins, grinding corn, putting yeast in bread. Never is a woman or something feminine ridiculed or rebuked (nor is anything particularly male or masculine lauded, though he certainly rebuked male religious and political leaders in Luke 11:37-54). C. I. Scofield, whose annotations of Scripture are widely revered among conservative Christians, had no basis for his footnote, "A woman, in the bad ethical sense, is always a symbol of that which, religiously, is out of its place. The 'woman' in Matt. 13:33 is dealing with doctrine, a sphere forbidden to her (I Tim. 2:12)." Jesus used various familiar household images to teach the disciples that the kingdom of heaven will spread throughout the earth if they will be like yeast, salt, or a lamp set on a stand.[11]

Jesus not only talked with women, but he went so far as to touch them publicly—something unheard of in Jewish society where some men would not allow a woman to count change into their hands. Luke 13:10-17 records how Jesus' healing touch brought relief to a woman crippled for eighteen years. He even called her a "daughter of Abraham," a distinction rarely used, though men are often called "sons of Abraham." Rather than rejoicing in her wholeness, the men standing nearby condemned Christ's "working" on the Sabbath.

In return women felt free to touch Jesus. A most poignant illustration is the healing of the woman with a hemorrhage. For twelve years she had spent all her money on doctors who could not relieve her constant menstrual flow (Mark 5:25-34). Her condition meant that she was ritually unclean and beyond all human contact (see Lev. 15:19-30). Realizing this, she dared not address the teacher, but with courageous faith she reached out secretly to touch the hem of his robe. Christ immediately stopped and demanded, "Who touched me?" The poor woman must have been frozen in terror: she had been discovered. Surely the Rabbi would rebuke her sternly for imparting her uncleanness to him. Trembling, she came forward and, falling at his feet, confessed. Instead of a tirade of instructions for cleansing rituals, she heard those beautiful words: "Daughter, your faith has made you well; go in peace" (Mark 5:34).

Though Jesus knew who had touched him and why, several explanations could be given for his actions. Perhaps he wanted to ensure that her relationship with him would be based not merely on "magic" but on a personal encounter. In addition to physical healing, his public recognition brought social and psychological wholeness to this outcast. This can also be cited as an instance of Jesus' encouraging women to public ministry. Undoubtedly, this woman would have praised God for her cure among family and friends; Jesus gave her opportunity for a wider ministry that continues today.

Christ publicly accepted more intimate gestures of love on several occasions from women who washed, dried, and anointed his head and feet. For an unmarried young man to allow a woman to kiss and fondle his feet was most unusual. For a respectable woman like Mary of Bethany (Matt. 26:6-13; Mark 14:3-9; John 12:1-8) to take down her hair was considered most immodest. Yet in Jesus' presence Mary felt free and pure. Christ declared that "wherever the gospel is preached in the whole world, what she has done will be told in memory of her" (Mark 14:9). In accepting the affection of the woman Luke terms a "sinner" (Luke 7:36-50), Jesus did not acquiesce to her former moral standards. He rebuked not the woman but his fellow diners who saw her either as a sex object of unsavory reputation or an irresponsible spendthrift. The woman he commended for her devotion. Indeed it was she, like the prophets of old who anointed the kings of Israel, who anointed Jesus for his mission.[12]

Although one of Jesus' male disciples betrayed him (Matt. 26:47-49), one denied him (Matt. 26:69-75), and all of them forsook him, the women followed Jesus to the end and beyond. Risking life and virtue, they dared to stand among the Roman soldiers at the foot of his cross (Matt. 27:55-56; Mark 15:40; Luke 23:27-29, 49; John 19:25) and to come at dawn to the guarded tomb, full of faith that the sealed stone would somehow move (Matt. 27:61; 28:1; Mark 15:47; 16:1-4; Luke 23:55-56; 24:1; John 20:1). Their perseverance was rewarded by the sight of the radiantly empty tomb and of the angels who announced the Resurrection and ordered them to "go, tell his disciples" (Mark 16:7).[13]

They bore first witness to the fact that Christ, their beloved, was alive. Though Jesus had repeatedly foretold his death and resurrection, the disciples "did not believe them" (Luke 24:11; Mark 16:11). Only Peter and John were moved to go and see for themselves. After a rational, analytic appraisal of an empty hole in the ground, the men went away scientifically satisfied.

John tells us that Mary Magdalene lingered, lovingly, wanting to remain close to where Jesus last lay. When she saw one whom she took to be the gardener, she emphatically, passionately, assertively demanded: "Tell me where you have laid him, and I will take him away!" Jesus did not ridicule her strength to accomplish such a task or rebuke her for such audacity. Christ rewarded her with a revelation of himself and a loving affirmation of her self: "Mary!"[14]

One could argue that the women's being first at the empty tomb was only an accident of history. But the appearances of angels and of Christ himself were deliberate acts of God. Jesus appeared first not to Peter, the "vicar" of the church, nor even to John, the "beloved." Women were the first to receive the central fact of the gospel and the first to be instructed to tell it abroad.[15]

Thus Jesus' life on earth from beginning to end outlines a paradigm for women's place. His actions upset and appalled his contemporaries, dumbfounded his critics, and flabbergasted his male disciples.[16] Since that day the church has struggled, if sometimes unenthusiastically and unsuccessfully, to cut through the barbed wire of cultural custom and taboo in order to emulate the One who promised both women and men that they could be "free indeed."

5.

YOUR DAUGHTERS SHALL PROPHESY

Bernard of Clairvaux (1090–1153), who had a great devotion to the Virgin Mary, was allegedly kneeling one day before a statue of her when the stone lips parted as if to speak. "Silence!" he cried. "It is not permitted for a woman to speak in church!"

WHEN ASKED WHAT SCRIPTURE HAS TO SAY ABOUT WOMEN'S ROLE IN THE church, many people would agree with Bernard's summary. The New Testament's direct advice to women seems encapsulated in I Corinthians 14:34 and I Timothy 2:11-12, interpreted by and within a patriarchal hierarchy. Never mind what the rest of the Bible may say or show; never mind what women have really done in the church during the past two millennia; never mind the fact that most women in the world today are now literate and most Western women are well educated whereas education was open to relatively few women in biblical times.

In comparison to the usual social roles of first-century women, Christian women were extraordinarily active. We have seen how Jesus throughout his ministry fully accepted women. They learned from him and ministered to him on a par with their brothers. Although the male apostles had great difficulty understanding, let alone imitating, Christ's attitude, women continued to play an extensive role in the early church.

Originally, Christianity was simply a Jewish sect. Judaism was, and still is to some extent, a "man's religion not only in substance and in practice, but also in its symbolic theology"[1] (of course the same can be said of Christianity!). The law commanded Israelites to "set apart to the Lord all that first opens the womb" (Exod. 13:12), but the context makes it clear that God only wanted sons. Only men were required to attend the great festivals (Deut. 16:16); a woman could and did go along, but her first duty was to serve her husband and to free him to worship God. In the Hellenistic period, Jewish women were barred not only from all religious leadership but also from worshiping alongside men. In the Jerusalem Temple and local synagogues they were walled off into a separate area. Ten men were required as a minyan, or quorum, before a service could begin; women did not count. Women were not taught the oral law; even today orthodox Jews in Israel will not let a woman, not even one with the stature of a Golda Meir, touch the Torah.

Full Participants and Witnesses

In the early Christian church, women's place was quite different. From the beginning women participated fully and equally with the men. At Pentecost three thousand *people* accepted the Christian message—not a certain number of men *plus* women and children, as would have been reckoned under Jewish custom (Acts 2:41; cf. 5:14; 8:12; with Matt. 15:38). Paul's first convert in Europe was Lydia (Acts 16:14-15), and other prominent women were among his followers in other cities (Acts 17:4, 12, 34; 18:2). In Romans 16, among the twenty-nine people greeted by Paul, ten were women.[2] Baptism, the sign of the new covenant as circumcision had been of the old, was given to both men and women believers. Both sexes worshiped together in one room, though probably men sat to one side and women to the other. Women were present in the Upper Room (Acts 1:14), and they received the filling of the Holy Spirit (2:3), which signaled the founding of the church.

From the moment of the Resurrection, women were active witnesses to the living Christ, as indeed they had been before (among the Seventy mentioned in Luke 10, some pairs were undoubtedly married couples and others pairs of women as well as pairs of men). Mary Magdalene and the others were first to tell the disciples that Jesus had risen. The two disciples on the road to Emmaus in Luke 24:13-35 were probably a married couple. As the prophet Joel had predicted (2:28-32), Peter discovered that both men and women received the gift of prophecy, the call of God to proclaim the word to others (Acts 2:17-18). Perhaps this was also spoken of in Psalm 68:11, which reads: "The Lord gave the command, and many women carried the news" (TEV).

The gospel was initially spread across the Greco-Roman world by traveling missionaries, some of them trade and business people, who preached wherever they went and visited the various groups of believers which sprang up.[3] Because Paul wrote so much of our New Testament, we think of him as the leader and of others as his followers, but actually he was only one among many equals. He names a number of people as his co-workers. Those he names as specifically serving him or as being subject to his instructions are all men (Erastus, Timothy, Titus, and Tychicus). Among the women he mentions are his "co-worker" Priscilla (Rom. 16:3), his "sister" Apphia (Philem. 2), the "deacon" Phoebe (Rom. 16:1), and the "apostle" Junia (Rom. 16:7). In I Corinthians 16:16, Paul urges the Corinthians to be subject "to every fellow worker and laborer" and to give recognition to such persons (the word translated "men" in vv. 16 and 18 is literally "such ones"; the ending is a masculine plural but that was used for all groups containing both men and women, cf. *alumni*). In I Thessalonians 5:12-13 he tells the Thessalonians to "respect those who labor among you and are over you in the Lord and admonish you, and to esteem them very highly in love because of their work."

Among the New Testament missionaries one finds the names of many women. Sometimes they are paired with the names of other women, sometimes they are paired with men's names, but there is never any indication of marital status or any classification such as virgin or widow. Some names stand alone; those of Mary and Persis, who "worked hard" in the Lord (Rom. 16:6, 12), are two examples of this. Apparently the original band of disciples took spouses along when they became missionaries (in I Cor. 9:5 Paul calls them "sister-women"). We are familiar with Priscilla and Aquila (Acts 18:2; Rom. 16:3; II Tim. 4:19) and with Euodia and Syntyche, two women who "labored side by side with [Paul] in the gospel" (Phil. 4:3). Less familiar partners are Andronicus and Junia (Rom. 16:7; despite the RSV they are not *men*, but a man and a woman "of note among the apostles"), Tryphaena and Tryphosa (Rom. 16:12; two women whom Paul calls "workers in the Lord"), Philologus and Julia, Nereus and his "sister" (Rom. 16:15; in the Greek the pairs are joined with conjunctions). A book which did not make it into the New Testament canon is the Acts of Paul and Thecla, the story of a woman converted under Paul's ministry. She joined him for a time, and then he commissioned her "to go and teach the word of God." She was a model for other women missionaries.

Apostles, Prophets, Teachers . . .

Many Jewish women had been prophets: Miriam (Exod. 15:20); Deborah (Judg. 4:4); Huldah (whom Josiah consulted about the authenticity of a book found in the Temple and whose advice he enacted into important reforms; II Kings 22:14ff.; II Chron. 34:22ff.); Noadiah (Neh. 6:14); Isaiah's wife (Isa. 8:3; she was probably the author of Second Isaiah); and Anna (Luke 2:36-38).

Christian women continued in that tradition (I Cor. 11:5), particularly Philip's daughters (Acts 21:9). Prophecy was a highly valued gift in the early church, earnestly to be sought (I Cor. 14:1), and prophets were listed right after apostles in lists of gifts (I Cor. 12:28-29; Eph. 4:11). The purpose of prophecy was primarily to convict and call sinners to account (I Cor. 14:24-25), but it was also for the "edification, and exhortation, and comfort" of the church (I Cor. 14:3-4 KJV).

Women were also teachers, and teaching is listed third after the ministries of apostle and prophet. In Acts 18:24ff. Priscilla (along with Aquila, her husband) took the learned Apollos of Alexandria aside and "expounded to him the way of God more accurately." Older women in the church were expected to "teach what is good" (Titus 2:3), as Timothy's mother Eunice and grandmother Lois evidently did (II Tim. 1:5). Nowhere is it intimated that women should teach *only* other women and small children. In fact all mature Christians (Heb. 5:12-14) should be able to "teach and admonish one another in all wisdom" (Col. 3:16). Teaching in the New Testament was not connected with any specific office but was the explication of Scripture by anyone with sufficient knowledge and piety (Rom. 15:14). Since education for women was limited, some may not have had opportunity to develop this gift. Yet some like Priscilla, who may well have been a wealthy Roman with access to private tutors, did exhibit such gifts to the extent that many have suggested her name as the author of Hebrews.[4]

Women were permitted no voice in the local synagogue or the Sanhedrin, which governed national affairs. Yet in the church, women were active in official capacities from the beginning. Women were among those who chose a successor to Judas (Acts 1:13-26). Many influential women opened their homes as meeting places for the first assemblies—John Mark's mother (Acts 12:12); Nympha (Col. 4:15); Priscilla (Rom. 16:5).

Administrators

Phoebe, of suburban Corinth and seemingly the courier for the book of Romans, is given two titles (Rom. 16:1-2): *diakonos* and *prostatis*. The latter word (translated "helper" in RSV) usually means "one who presides," the "chief of a party," a president, ruler, patron, superintendent. The noun form is used only in this passage, but the verb form appears many times. Usually translated "rule" or "manage," it refers to bishops, deacons, and elders (see I Tim. 3:4-5;

5:17; Rom. 12:8). A better translation would be "she was designated as a ruler over many by me" (Rom. 16:2).[5]

Phoebe's first title, *diakonos* ("deacon"), is a word which has the same endings for both masculine and feminine forms. Paul uses the word twenty-two times, eighteen of which the King James Version translates as "minister" and three as "deacon." Phoebe, however, is called "servant"! First Timothy 3:11 is sometimes translated to refer to deacons' wives, but it more logically refers to women deacons. Although those named in Acts 6 (whose job it was to serve the widows, already a ministering group within the church) were all men (and not specifically called "deacons"), both men and women were ordained to this office in some areas throughout the church's first millennium.[6] The duties of both sexes included the practical work of the community: serving the communal meal, taking Communion to those unable to attend services, instructing converts, assisting in baptisms, distributing food and funds to the needy, visiting the sick and imprisoned, consoling the bereaved, arranging funerals, and caring for orphans. Obviously it was a very important post in the church. Women were necessary because they could visit, instruct, and physically baptize other women, whereas society would not have permitted a man such contact. Women deacons were pushed into obsolescence with the adoption of infant baptism.

Another official group within the church was the widows. First Timothy 5:3-16 speaks of them as a definite order into which mature women of good reputation were enrolled. Early church fathers Ignatius and Polycarp as well as early church documents also indicate such a group. The widows' primary ministry seems to have been intercessory prayer, although they also went from house to house collecting gifts, helping others, and caring for orphans.[7]

Dorcas, mentioned in Acts 9:36-42, may well have been a widow, since others mourned her death. She may also have been part of a group of consecrated virgins who are spoken of in I Corinthians 7 and who emerge in the second-century Western church as a large and respected group. A third-century Syrian document speaks of two groups of virgins, divided at age fifty. They made clothes for the needy, fasted and prayed for those in distress, visited and even laid hands on the sick.[8] It is from this group that nuns evolved.

As the church developed a more structured ministry, the "elders" or "presbyters" took precedence over the deacons. Though it is often said that there is no evidence for women holding this office (which is often compared to today's "preachers" in nonhierarchical churches), I Timothy 5:1-2 refers to both *presbuterō*, "a male elder," and *presbuteras,* "female elders." These references are usually camou-flaged by translating them "an older man" and "older women." However, the chapter surely deals with established orders of ministry, because it mentions the enrolling of widows (v. 9) and of *presbuteroi* (the plural form of "elders") who rule well and labor in preaching and teaching (v. 17). Nothing in verses 17-22 indicates that the references are only to men. (The word in v. 22 sometimes translated "man" really is a more neutral "no one.") Titus 2:3 refers to *presbutidas* (feminine) who are called "reverent" (*hieroprepeis,* a word that comes the closest of any in the New Testament to describing a priestly, sacred, or liturgical function but is not applied to male presbyters or deacons); they are specifically told to teach and not necessarily just other women.

Sunergos is another word used to describe what may be another ministerial office. It is usually translated "fellow laborer," or "co-workers" in the plural, and is applied to Timothy (Rom. 16:21), Apollos and Paul (I Cor. 3:5-9), Titus (II Cor. 8:23), Clement (Phil. 4:3), Demas and Luke (Philem. 24), and others. It is also used of several women, including Priscilla (Rom. 16:3), and Euodia and Syntyche (Phil. 4:2-3). There is evidence that the word may have been interchangeable with *diakonos.*[9]

One woman apostle is even mentioned in the Bible! Junia, saluted by Paul in Romans 16:7 (KJV), is a common Roman name for a woman, but since she is identified as an "apostle," many translators have assumed the name to be a contraction for a much less common male one. Chrysostom, fourth-century bishop of Constantinople, however, had no difficulty identifying her: "Oh, how great is the devotion of this woman that she should be counted worthy of the appellation of apostle!"[10] Actually if the qualification for becoming an apostle, as Acts 1:22 suggests, is having witnessed the Resurrection, several women were highly qualified.

Into a very structured and restrictive society, the gospel of Jesus Christ came as a liberating, mighty rushing wind, overturning racial, social, and gender differences. In Christ all are a "chosen race, a royal priesthood, a holy nation, God's own people" (I Pet. 2:9). As Tertullian commented of men and women: "Together they pray; together they prostrate themselves, together they perform their fasts, mutually teaching, mutually exhorting, mutually sustaining. Equally are they both found in the church of God."[11]

But such freedom was not fully understood by those outside the church and even by some within. From outsiders the church was beset by several accusations, including allegations that Christians did away with marriage and the family (did they really hold *all* things in common?) and that they were disloyal to Rome (they did call Jesus rather than the emperor "Lord"). Inside the church some also made liberty into license—Christians considered leaving their non-Christian spouses, slaves ran away from their masters, some flaunted the fact that they ate meat offered to idols, and others courted martyrdom by openly thumbing their noses at statues of Caesar. And so early church leaders offered some strong suggestions.

Rule one was, don't rock the boat quite so hard! Christians were repeatedly admonished to respect and obey the government. Christian spouses were absolved of their marital commitments only if the unbeliever left them. Women in particular were warned to do nothing which would discredit the word of God (Titus 2:5) or "give the enemy . . . occasion to revile us" (I Tim. 5:14). Within the church "all things should be done decently and in order" because "God is not a God of confusion but of peace" (I Cor. 14:40, 33).

Head Coverings

The longest passage in the New Testament devoted solely to the issue of women in the church concerns the wearing of certain head coverings or the arrangement of the hair during worship services (I Cor. 11:2-16).[12] The exact composition and cultural background of Corinthian church members are uncertain, but Corinth was a wide-open commercial center, dominated by a famous temple of Aphrodite, whose priestesses accounted for much of the city's proverbial immorality. On the other hand, according to Acts 18:7-8, the local church met next door to the Jewish synagogue and may have had many Jews as members. Thus it is difficult to know in what context Paul is speaking.

In Jewish circles there was great aversion toward women praying with heads uncovered. (Jewish men did not begin to wear the yarmulke until the fourth century, though Old Testament priests wore elaborate headgear.) A Jewish woman seen in public without her veil was considered to be flouting her marriage vows, and the Talmud commanded her husband to divorce her. Veiling was important because Jewish teachings considered both a woman's hair and her voice sexual enticements.[13]

Greek custom is a bit more complicated. Highborn wives generally wore veils in public. Concubines and second-rank wives could wear them but not in the presence of the first wife. Single women generally did not wear veils. Prostitutes and slaves were forbidden by law to veil themselves. In cultic worship both men and women were bareheaded; temple priestesses never wore head coverings. In the home no one wore veils. Thus some Corinthian Christians may have argued that within the "household of faith," particularly if it met in a private home as many churches did, they could dispense with the veil. Perhaps eventually a compromise was worked out, because early Christian art shows a woman speaking to a mixed assembly with a head covering pulled back and fastened with a fashionable ornament.[14]

Both Jews and Greeks considered the veil and certain hairstyles symbolic of marriage. Paul did not want Christian women to act in such a manner that people would confuse them with either the pagan orgiastic cults where women loosed their hair in ecstatic frenzy or the Gnostics who degraded the body and marriage. He would not have understood modern Christians who almost unanimously disregard this injunction as cultural while clinging to silence for women, because as a Jew he considered unveiling a far more serious offense to public decency than speaking.

The exact purpose of the veil and the clear meaning of this passage have been debated by theologians for centuries. Those who interpret "head" as authority and rule see the repeated puns on the word in regard to the wife as meaning that her veil symbolizes her acceptance of her husband's authority. The key word is *exousia* (I Cor. 11:10, translated "veil" RSV), meaning "power." The question is whose? The traditional answer, "her husband's," is philologically untenable and raises two questions: If the veil is a symbol of one under authority, why does the husband not wear one to indicate that he is under God's authority? And is not the worshiping woman responsible to God alone?

Even more creative are suggestions that the word is simply a play on an Aramaic word for "veil" that is related to a Hebrew word for "rule"—a nifty word game surely, but it undoubtedly would have totally bypassed Paul's Greek readers. Another interesting theory is that the veil represented magical power which would ward off evil spirits. A bit more understandable is an interpretation based on I Corinthians 11:7. It suggests that the goal of worship is to glorify God. Since the man, according to verse 7 (though not Gen. 1:26-27), is made in the image and glory (*doxa*) of God, his uncovered head glorifies God. Since the woman reflects the glory of the man, she must be veiled before she can glorify God alone.[15]

The most textually plausible suggestion is "her own power." An insignia of respect, the marriage head covering or hairstyle would offer protection for a woman's dignity. To arrange one's head is to exercise control; to expose one's head is to court shame. Some argue that this passage is directed primarily at women exercising the gift of prophecy and that Ezekiel 13:17-23 indicates that women prophets may have worn specific veils or headbands indicating prophetic office. First Kings 20:41 indicates that male prophets also wore some insignia on the head to identify themselves. Within this context, the "angels" were considered the intermediaries who gave the prophets their message from God.[16]

On the other hand, Joseph Yoder argues that the first ten verses of I Corinthians 11 are simply a restatement of traditional Jewish teachings, but that a great change begins with the words, "Nevertheless, in the Lord." From here on, says Yoder, Paul is moving away from Jewish arguments for subordination and enunciating a doctrine of liberty for the Christian woman. She needs no veil "for her hair is given to her for a covering" (11:15). Obviously some people might be upset by such radical teaching, but to "any one . . . disposed to be contentious," Paul, according to Yoder, simply says, "We recognize no other practice, nor do the churches of God" (11:16).[17] That is, women need no covering other than their hair. Thus this passage would be similar to those arguing against Judaizers who insisted that Gentiles be circumcised.

Though it is hardly a major issue, the "angels" referred to in 11:10 have intrigued and befuddled scholars. One pastor finally conceded that it was probably a phrase Paul tossed in for effect, much like we use "for heaven's sake!" But he does seem to offer it as a justification, in addition to the "headship" argument and his rabbinic exegesis of Genesis which we have discussed earlier. Some say the angels are good ones who oversee the created order, guard individuals, and evidence God's presence in public worship. On the other hand, they might be bad angels, perhaps those who got confused at creation and worshiped human beings rather than God. Tertullian was the first to suggest that they might be evil and attracted by a woman's seductiveness unveiled. The angels may also be learning from the church and for them women should set an example of Christian modesty. Or maybe women should learn from the example of the angels in Isaiah 6:2 who modestly covered themselves in God's presence. A more down-to-earth suggestion is simply that "angels" was a euphemism for male ministers who, standing before a congregation, might be distracted by the beauty of unveiled women.[18]

The essential justification for the wearing of veils was simply social custom: "Give no offense to Jews or to Greeks or to the church" (I Cor. 10:32); "Maintain the traditions . . . as I have delivered them to you" (11:2); and "We have no such custom" (11:16 KJV). In between, Paul appeals to "nature," saying it obviously teaches that for a man to wear long hair is degrading. But this is certainly an appeal to social custom since nature unprevented would veil a man's face and head in hair much more than a woman's. Actually this is a strange comment since Jewish men often let their hair grow as a part of religious vows (something Paul and his friends had evidently done in Acts 21:24), and Greeks honored the ancient long-haired Spartans as well as their contemporaries whose long hair was a sign of asceticism or of devotion to philosophy.[19]

Silence in Services

Basically the church was concerned with what was "fitting" in its social context (I Cor. 11:13; Eph. 5:3; I Tim. 2:10; Titus 2:1). A broader view of I Corinthians illumines the issues. The New English Bible titles the section beginning in chapter 7 "The Christian in a pagan society." Chapter 11 in The Jerusalem Bible is labeled "Decorum in Public Worship" with subtitles "Women's behavior at services," "The Lord's Supper," and "Spiritual gifts." A cursory glance at the book reveals the multitude of serious problems facing this large, active congregation. The church was obviously endowed by the Spirit with an abundance of gifts (1:7), but even these required discipline if the entire group was to be edified. Women in the group were given two instructions: "Any woman who prays or prophesies with her head unveiled dishonors her head" (11:5), and "Women should keep silence in the churches" (14:34). On the face of it, these two commands are contradictory, but the context offers an explanation.

Immediately following the instructions concerning veils, Paul discusses the Lord's Supper. Indications throughout the New Testament as well as other early church writings show that meetings were divided into two parts. The first half was open to anyone who wanted to come and hear the gospel. This is sometimes called the "mass of the catechumens" because, just as in liturgical churches today, it was devoted to the reading of Scripture and discussing it, praying, and perhaps singing. Catechumens were those interested in becoming Christians but who had not finished instruction or been baptized. Thus they were barred from the second half of the service, the "mass of the faithful" who were permitted to take Communion.

Chapter 11 falls within the latter context where only bona fide
Christians were present. Women could prophesy and pray, but they
should not offend other Christians or give rise to rumors of looseness
by their behavior. In I Corinthians 14 the discussion has turned to
the first half of the service where uninitiated, unlearned unbelievers
(vv. 16, 23, 24) are present. Here Paul lays down another rule
because, as he says in 14:23, "If, therefore the whole church
assembles and all speak in tongues, and outsiders or unbelievers
enter, will they not say that you are mad?" His intent is clearly to
preserve order and decorum.

Exactly what is Paul prohibiting women to do in I Corinthians
14:34-35? Says one author, it is "a command not to take charge of the
public worship service. . . . this prohibition of women into the
pastoral office is a universal prohibition."[20]

But is Paul prohibiting women from speaking altogether? Could he
really silence women in the home church of Priscilla, Chloe, and
possibly Phoebe? No. Although there are textual questions about the
authenticity of these verses[21], they do fit perfectly with the linguistic
and thought patterns of the chapter. The word for "speak" here is
used twenty-four times in the chapter. Everybody in Corinth
seemingly wanted to speak during their services. The word does *not*
mean a formal lecture, exhortation, or teaching, but simply *talking,*
idle talk or chatter. It is used of the women in I Timothy 5:13 who are
also described as "idlers . . . gossips and busybodies."

Contemporary orthodox synagogues sometimes still have the
same problem. Women are usually confined to a screened-off
balcony or side room where they can barely hear. And since they are
not encouraged to learn as much of the liturgy, the Torah, and the
oral laws of Judaism as men do, they simply do not understand what
is going on. So they chatter and gossip to the point that it becomes
quite noisy.[22]

Paul goes on to say that "if there is anything they desire to know, let
them ask their husbands at home." Obviously these women were
interrupting the meetings with questions. Inquirers, converts from
paganism, uneducated women—they probably had many questions
more appropriate for a catechetical situation. This certainly could not
be a definitive pronouncement. Of whom would single women,
widows, or those with pagan husbands or fathers ask questions? But
one can imagine how disturbing it could be for spouses separated by
an aisle to call questions back and forth!

And so Paul forbids women so to speak; he tells them to keep
silence. Again the word for "silence" is one that has already appeared

in verses 28 and 30. If these orders of silence had been applied as rigorously as the one concerning women, our services would be silent indeed! Paul is not simply telling women to be totally silent but rather he is asking all Christians to defer to one another in order that the services might be orderly and edifying. Utterances inspired by the Spirit were permitted; other talking should cease, a suggestion still applicable today.

In support of this injunction he uses a reference to "the law." In some translations the word is capitalized as if to refer to the Law of Moses in some way, but nothing in the Old Testament prohibits women's speaking in worship contexts, nor is there any verse that specifically says they should be in subjection. Bibles with cross-references usually cite I Timothy 2:11-12 and Genesis 3:16. Since Timothy was undoubtedly written later, Paul could not have been referring to that. Genesis 3:16 says that as a result of the Fall men will dominate women. Surely Paul would not have the church perpetuate a sinful condition.

The word *law* used here rather means "what is proper, what is assigned to someone,"[23] thus their role. Again Paul appeals to social custom. If the Corinthian church were meeting in a Jewish synagogue or home, the orthodox would feel it a desecration to allow women to speak. The Talmud says a woman is subject to divorce for "conversing with all sorts of men." Another suggestion is that Chloe, mentioned in 1:11, was a highborn Greek woman who was offended by the forward outspokenness of converted lower-class women and *hetairai*. Whatever the reason, the verses do not prohibit a ministry for women in the church but simply assert that Christian meetings should be orderly.

Teaching

First Timothy 2:8-15, though usually considered synonymous with I Corinthians 14:34-35, presents many different questions, some of which we have dealt with elsewhere. Some modern biblical scholars regard the book as non-Pauline, written at a much later period when the church was more structured and institutionalized.[24] Timothy's church was in Ephesus, home of the great temple of Diana, and some of the women there seem very unstable. Although some were deacons and elders, the younger women were "burdened with sins and swayed by various impulses, who will listen to anybody and can never arrive at a knowledge of the truth" (II Tim. 3:6-7) and "idlers, gadding about from house to house" (I Tim. 5:13). Such young widows were advised to remarry, contrary to Paul's advice to Corinthian widows in I Corinthians 7:40.

The immediate context in I Timothy 2 is behavior in public worship, presumably the first part of the service with unbelievers present, since Communion is not mentioned. First, men are instructed to pray without anger or quarreling—which makes one wonder what was going on, though perhaps the reference is to Matthew 5:23-24. Then women are told to adorn themselves modestly, though they must not have been wearing veils or no one would have noticed their hair. Both I Timothy 2:9 and I Peter 3:3 inveigh against gold-braided hair, not simply braids but an especially elaborate style including false hair and jewelry interwoven—a favorite style of courtesans. If we judge by the space devoted to the subject, New Testament writers seem most concerned about how women wore their hair and jewelry! These instructions are almost totally dismissed by today's church as cultural and irrelevant, yet the verses following are proclaimed as eternal principles.

"Let a woman learn in silence with all submissiveness. . . . She is to keep silent" (I Tim. 2:11-12*b*). Though this sounds identical to I Corinthians 14:34-35, the word for "silence" is different. It means to "desist from bustle" or to "refrain from the use of language." It suggests decorum. The adjectival form of the word was used in I Timothy 2:2 to describe the type of life all Christians should lead. The word is used in other contexts to indicate the proper attitude of reverence for anyone, male or female, in the study of the Torah and Talmud.

"I permit no woman to teach" (I Tim. 2:12). In Greek the word for "teach" comes first in the sentence and is the word for formal instruction, though as we have seen, in the early church many members, including women, had this gift and exercised it. The primary concern here is not so much the role of women as the possibility of false teaching. Timothy's parishioners had already shown themselves to be confused in doctrinal matters (II Tim. 3:6-7) and "some have already strayed after Satan" (I Tim. 5:15). The prohibition is buttressed by a reference to Eve's being deceived, an occurrence cited elsewhere only in II Corinthians 11:3 where, as we have seen, Paul warns all Christians to beware lest the serpent deceive them too. Insubordinate men who were "empty talkers and deceivers" were likewise silenced in Titus 1:10-11.

The fascinating element in this instruction to Timothy (I Tim. 2:12) is the phrase "or to have authority over men." The men referred to are probably husbands. The verb is *authentein,* used just this once in the New Testament. Possible translations are "interrupt" (Dibelius), "dictate to" (Moffatt), or "domineer over" (NEB). In noun form, as used by the great Greek dramatists, it meant a "suicide" or a "family murderer." Later the noun came to mean "lord" or "autocrat." In the first century it was rather a slang word, and one can sense the writer's relish at throwing in such a juicy word. Because suicide involves deciding for oneself, taking one's life into one's own hands, to do so for others meant to become a "dictator." Thus the word came to mean "self-willed" or "arbitrary," interfering in what was not properly one's own domain, trespassing the socially proper limits.

Thus we see again a concern for maintaining the cultural status quo, for not transgressing the marital social roles. The passage seems to deal with a particular situation rather than to state a general principle. Of all the passages concerning women in the New Testament, only Galatians 3:28 is in a doctrinal setting; the remainder are all concerned with practical matters. In I Timothy the problem seems to be women who usurped authority from others, teaching when they had neither gift nor training. Perhaps one of the wealthier women thought her social position guaranteed her a leadership post. Or perhaps the church was even meeting in the home of a woman who was bossy and domineering. Maybe some women were putting down their husbands in public. Whatever the local situation, we must be careful not to consider this passage the only and final word to women. In the light of other New Testament teaching and example concerning the ministry of women, it seems feeble to rest an entire case against women's ordination on this verse, which appears to say nothing about the delegation of such authority to qualified women by the community. To receive ordination from a community of believers would not be to "usurp authority."

Although the New Testament does not repudiate the social order, neither does it make the maintenance of that order the goal of the Christian church. With "one Lord, one faith, one baptism, one God and Father of us all, who is above all and through all and in all" (Eph. 4:5-6), the church's goal is to be one building (Eph. 2:19-22) and one body (I Cor. 12:12-26). "There is neither Jew nor Greek, there is neither slave nor free, there is neither male nor female; for you are all one in Christ Jesus" (Gal. 3:28). This verse directly contradicts the prayer of every orthodox Jewish male: "Blessed are you, Lord our God . . . who has not created me a heathen . . . a slave . . . a woman." Christ prayed "that they may all be one" (John 17:21), and the church's goal has always been unity. But somehow the church has continually come unglued: Judaizers and Gentiles, East and West, clergy and laity, catholics and anabaptists, Catholics and Protestants, masters and slaves, evangelicals and liberals, men and women. Instead of being healed, the divisions have festered.

Yet Paul in Galatians is serious; he does not get carried away with rhetoric; his words are intentional. The last phrase, *arsen kai thēlu,* uses the technical terms that parallel Genesis 1:27 as quoted by Jesus in Matthew 19:4. Although the three pairs given by Paul are usually translated with identical syntax, the first two are "neither . . . nor" constructions but the last is literally "there is not male and female."[25]

Paul here is not denying certain distinctions between groups. A person could not change what he or she was born—Jew, Greek, slave, free, male, female. Paul is not following certain Gnostics who tried to deny our biological nature. None of the apostles advocated the immediate overthrow of cultural custom—Christianity was controversial enough without that! Yet they did not shy away from the radical cutting edge of the gospel which would gradually undermine society's oppressive policies and restore God's intended harmony. Both Greeks and Jews were accepted by Christianity on an equal footing. Slaves and freeborn became brothers and sisters. Men and women worked side by side in spreading the gospel. There were no second-class citizens in Christ's church.

Social distinctions are meant to be transcended—not perpetuated—within the body of Christ. Paul is certainly not talking to the Galatians in purely "spiritual" terms as some have contended "in Christ" means. He does not advise the conflicting groups to sing one chorus of "We are one in the Spirit, we are one in the Lord" and then each go off to separate meals. In fact, that is precisely what he reprimands Peter for doing (Gal. 2:11-21). In asking Philemon to receive back his slave, Paul pointedly tells him to treat Onesimus "no longer as a slave but more than a slave, as a beloved brother . . . both in the flesh and in the Lord" (Philem. 16).

All social distinctions between men and women should have been erased in the church. Yet, they have been perpetuated with a vengeance. Just how sincere has been our prayer, "Thy will be done on earth, as it is in heaven"?

6.
HE, SHE, OR WE?

Throughout history people have knocked their heads against the riddle of the nature of femininity. . . . Nor will you have escaped worrying over this problem—those of you who are men; to those of you who are women this will not apply—you are yourselves the problem.

—Sigmund Freud[1]

"VIVE LA DIFFERÉNCE!" SOMEONE IS SURE TO SHOUT WHENEVER the discussion turns to the natures of men and women. Most people assume that innate differences exist between the sexes, that they are "sexually differentiated in their entire humanness," and that this antithesis is "a part of nature," "a God-given principle," the "creation order."[2]

Strength, action, sound reason, decisiveness, aggressiveness, ambition, energy, drive, courage, and inventiveness are thought to characterize "masculine nature." The male biological symbol is that used in astronomy for Mars, god of war, and represents his shield and spear: ♂. The mirror of Venus, ♀, goddess of love and beauty, is the female symbol because "feminine nature" is thought to be narcissistic, subjective, dependent, passive, intuitive, tender, fragile, irrational, and frivolous.

Not only do the sexes inhabit differently shaped bodies, but we have been taught that God created us with "masculine" or "feminine" minds and souls as well. Thus men have been considered innately equipped to be the spokespersons, the leaders, the builders of society, while women's greatest joy and fulfillment are expected to be found in marriage, motherhood, and housewifery.

The machismo image of masculinity in our society is characterized by power. The male is expected to prove his manhood through achievements in athletics, education, occupation, and even bed. Sex becomes conquest; the object is to "score." Force, violence, and war have also been linked to the real he-man image.

"The feminine mystique," on the other hand, lies in woman's supposed innate passivity. A man chooses her as his wife and "gets her pregnant." Without her help the baby grows mysteriously inside her. All her maternal and nurturing "instincts" are devoted to her child. She finds total fulfillment in mothering her children and responding to the wishes of her husband. Her goal in life is to please other people, to sacrifice herself for them. She lives through their achievements.[3]

Are men and women as radically dissimilar as our society constantly tells and shows us that they are? Are we *innately* so different?

Biology

"Male and female [God] created them"—that is all the Bible tells us about sexual differences. The biological givens are assumed; they are never defined further or explored. Instead Scripture continually reaffirms the unity of the human race, not our distinctives but our similarities.

Each of us began life as a single cell—a fertilized ovum that contained forty-six chromosomes, twenty-three from our mother's ovum paired with twenty-three from our father's sperm. Out of these twenty-three pairs of chromosomes containing all our genetic material, only one pair determined whether we would be female or male. If that pair was an XX combination (one X chromosome provided by our mother and one by our father), we are female. If the sex-determining pair was an XY combination (an X contributed by our mother, a Y contributed by our father), we are male. The mother's contribution is always an X chromosome; the father contributes either an X or a Y sex chromosome and thus provides the determining factor for what the child's sex will be.

As the single cell divides and grows into an expanding cluster of cells, the XX or XY pattern is repeated in each cell. The cells throughout a female's body are XX, and the cells throughout a male's body are XY. The only exceptions are the germ cells (ova in females and sperm cells produced by males), each of which contain only *half* the number of chromosomes found in other cells in the body. An ovum has only one X instead of a pair, and the sperm cell has only one X or one Y instead of the XY combination of the other cells of the body.

The fact that the cells throughout our bodies designate us as either male or female (even a person who has had gender reassignment surgery and hormonal treatment—what is popularly known as a "sex change") *means only that the original cell from which we began kept dividing and growing,* repeating the original pattern of our genetic makeup. It tells us nothing about the roles of women and men. Yet, some Christian leaders have implied the existence of some cosmic, theological significance to being chromosomally male or chromoso-mally female. "Every cell of the body is coded masculine or feminine," one theologian has written, suggesting that a man is to live "in a masculine way" and a woman "in a feminine way."[4] But, of course, every cell is coded either *male* or *female*—not "masculine" or "feminine," which are cultural terms referring to the roles societies assign persons according to their gender. Our cells contain only the message of our biological sex, not biologically deterministic behavior based on our sex.

For the first couple of months of prenatal life, the embryo's genital structures are not differentiated as male or female but are exactly the same—the "buds" of what will be. If nothing is added, the body simply continues developing into a female; but if the right mix of male sex hormones is added (because the Y chromosome somehow signaled the sex glands to develop into testicles and produce the necessary hormones), a male body will result.[5] This prenatal development lays the foundation for what will be the only absolute and irreducible differences between males and females as adults. In the words of psychohormonal researcher John Money and his coauthor Patricia Tucker, "Only a man can impregnate; only a woman can menstruate, gestate, and lactate."[6] These *basic four differences* have to do with reproduction.

Certain kinds of other differences between men and women do exist, of course. Men tend to have broader shoulders, giving them greater strength in the upper body. Women tend to have wider hips, giving them a lower center of gravity and a pelvic structure suited for childbirth. Women have a higher ratio of fat tissue to muscle, and men have the opposite ratio. Recent research in sports medicine has uncovered new information on differences and similarities between the bodies of women and men. However, the differences are relative. As science writer Gary Seldon emphasizes, "It is certain that there is more variation among individuals of each sex than the average difference, if any, between the sexes" in various physiological factors related to athletic abilities. In fact, says Seldon, "Sports medicine has finally taught us what should have been obvious all along: athletic training must be geared to the individual, not the sex."[7]

John Money and Patricia Tucker make the same point:

It's not hard to find a normal man who is more like the average woman than like the average man on any count except the basic four, or to find a normal woman who is more like the average man than the average woman in this or that respect. In other words, within-group differences, even when it comes to

93

secondary sex characteristics [size of breasts, presence of facial and chest hair, pitch of voice, etc.], may be as great and are often much greater than the between-group differences.[8]

Even the muscular strength of some women exceeds that of some men. "Many female athletes today are working out with weights—dead weights of 400 pounds, for example—that many men could never hope to lift no matter how hard they might train," writes Gary Seldon. He adds that some physiologists suggest that women may have the potential of being even stronger than men "since weight-lifting records show that lighter people tend to be more powerful in proportion to weight."[9]

But doesn't the Bible say that women are the "weaker sex"? We need to keep in mind that before the advent of birth control when most women spent most of their adult lives pregnant, they certainly did appear weaker. And because muscular development has been stressed and encouraged more in males, men do generally exhibit greater bodily strength. If, however, this is still a measure of superiority, then civilization has advanced no further than our cave-dwelling, club-wielding ancestors. In our society, at least, women appear to have greater stamina and endurance under stress—witness men's earlier death due to heart attacks, their high incidence of ulcers, and suicide. There is also evidence that testosterone, one of the androgens which regulate male sexuality, may contribute to a slightly higher metabolic rate which seems to cause men to "burn out" faster. It also does not retard the aging of blood vessels and the buildup of cholesterol as the female's estrogen does.

Actually, when husbands were told to "live considerately" with their wives, "bestowing honor on the woman as the weaker sex" (I Pet. 3:7), the intention may have been an altogether different meaning from the one generally assumed. Dick and Joyce Boldrey, for example, have suggested that "weaker" as used here does not mean physical or mental deficiency but refers to one who is socially and politically *without honor*. Thus the admonition to honor the woman, since society did not. In the traditional way of thinking, honor went in only one direction: upward. But Christians were repeatedly instructed to honor those socially and politically beneath them as well.[10] As social theorist Talcott Parsons has pointed out, "There does seem to be a general tendency for the strategically placed, the powerful, to exploit the weaker or less favorably placed" in a given society.[11] This was not to be the pattern among those who loved and served Christ. To use I Peter 3:7 as a proof text to support arguments for woman's inferiority is a gross misuse of Scripture and misses the verse's main point.

But why be concerned about comparing women and men in the first place? No one denies that certain basic distinctions exist between the sexes. What *difference* do these differences make? Why should individuals be consigned to roles limited by sexual designations rather than allowed to develop fully their unique and varied capabilities?

Human beings are not predestined or controlled by instincts as are the lower animals. Even studies of the higher anthropoids (apes and chimpanzees) show that their behavior is less determined by instinct and more by learning. Biology is not destiny, and neither hormonal nor animal studies offer proof that human gender roles are innate.[12] Rather, they are assigned and reinforced through social learning.

Culture

The meaning and content of the labels "masculine" and "feminine" in terms of behavior and temperament are totally determined by culture.

Classic illustration for that statement is found in Margaret Mead's *Sex and Temperament in Three Primitive Societies* in New Guinea. Among the Arapesh both sexes are mild-mannered, gentle, cooperative people concerned primarily with nurturing the lives of their children, animals, and crops. Mundugumor men and women are ruthless, aggressive individuals devoted to fierce and sometimes violent competition in which nurturing, cherishing aspects of personality have little place. In Tchambuli society women are energetic, dominant, impersonal, unadorned managers while the men, less responsible and emotionally dependent, indulge in catty gossip, wear curls, and perfect their dancing.

As Mead concludes, if those temperamental attributes which we as Americans have traditionally regarded as "feminine" can so easily be declared "masculine" in one group and totally outlawed for the majority of both men and women in another society, then "many, if not all, of the personality traits which we have called masculine or feminine are as lightly linked to sex as are the clothing, the manners, and the form of head-dress that a society at a given period assigns to either sex."[13]

Not only temperaments but also tasks are assigned according to a person's sex. "Women's work" and "men's work" are not defined uniformly the world over. Cultural anthropologists have studied societies in which weaving or cooking or basketmaking or repairing clothing are exclusively the province of males. They also have lists of societies in which building houses or clearing land for agriculture or engaging in fishing or herding are tasks assigned only to females. In some societies, men make the pottery; in others, women do this work. In still other societies, either sex may make pottery or build the houses or cook.[14]

Human nature is unbelievably malleable, capable of taking a variety of directions. What we become is the result of cultural conditioning, enculturation, socialization. Individuals acquire a gender identity from a very early age through the process of psychosexual development. It is learned through identification with the parent of one's own sex, interaction with the other parent, and imitation of adults and peers who model societal gender-role expectations. As the child grows, she or he is constantly exposed to messages about "how girls are supposed to look and act" and about "how boys are supposed to look and act"—messages that come through books, television, advertisements, and countless other subtle and not-so-subtle ways. The child also becomes aware of the positive and negative sanctions society offers to those who do or don't conform to gender-role expectations.

In our society we have no ideal for "personhood." All aspects of life—emotional, intellectual, vocational, even spiritual—have been arbitrarily divided into two categories labeled masculine and feminine. Persons are given access to one or the other of these realms usually depending solely on whether they possess male or female external genitalia at birth.

The pervasive influence of this initial decision is incredible. At birth the baby is color-coded with a blanket. Parents accordingly choose a name which is hopefully unambiguously "boy" or "girl." Relatives bring gifts in either blue or pink. After all, it is embarrassing if we remark, "Doesn't the baby have a cute face!" when we are supposed to say, "My, he looks like a potential football star!"

The purpose of the color-coding is to apprise everyone of the category into which they are to begin to enculturate this newborn member of society. And there are radical, far-reaching differences. From birth girl babies are hugged, kissed, coddled, and controlled, while their brothers are touched less, left alone in their cribs longer, and encouraged to venture out away from their mothers.[15] Girls are taught to be affectionate with friends; boys are encouraged to shake hands, shadowbox, and wrestle.

At play girls are expected to be quiet, cooperative, cautious, and close by. Boys are allowed to be tough, rough, daring, and venturesome. Boys are given the building blocks, chemistry sets, trucks and rockets they will presumably deal with as adults. Girls are offered doll babies, miniature houses, and toy stoves. In one set of picture books[16] on the question of "What will you be when you grow up?" girls are given such choices as stewardess, model, movie star, secretary, or nurse "with white uniforms to wear." For boys the suggestions include fireman, policeman, farmer, pilot, or doctor to "help save people's lives." As a finale, the girl says, "I may even be a housewife some day when I am grown. . . . I'd love to be a mother with some children of my own." For boys, however, the book never mentions marriage or children. Instead their ultimate goal is being an astronaut or president!

The church condones and encourages society's divisions, adding to them the stamp of God's approval. A child in church notices immediately that most, if not all, of the major services are conducted by men. A study of Sunday school curricula for three-year-olds (!) found all ministers portrayed as men (in a denomination that does ordain women), all teachers as women, all men in exciting vocations, all mothers in the home, none of the girls helping their fathers, most of the girls working around the house. Little girls were portrayed as timid, fearful, unhappy, dependent victims of their emotions. The boys in the stories were adventurous, independent, self-sufficient, sociable, and happy.[17]

Formal education merely continues the process. Americans take pride in the fact that we offer equal education for all, yet this is far from true in many areas and is a relatively recent innovation for women. Girls initially do well in school because they have already been extensively socialized into behavior that teachers reward—sitting still, listening, and following orders. Because their mothers talk to them more from birth, they have the edge over boys in verbal skills. Boys have been pointed toward scientific, mechanical, and mathematical skills. Primary education concentrates on learning verbal skills and gradually boys close the gap. Girls, however, are often not given such compensatory study in the scientific areas, and they eventually fall behind.

Despite the fact that boys and girls show no significant differences on intelligence tests or college entrance exams and girls generally have higher grade point averages at all levels, women have been systematically discriminated against in education. Skills courses and vocational programs have been largely sex segregated. This means in

some cities high schools which not only offer important vocational
training but also often the best college preparation available have
been off limits to girls. In higher education women have been
discriminated against in college admission, financial aid, classroom
participation, athletic opportunities, internship programs, teaching
assistantships, and research grants.[18] The problem again is not
biological or intellectual; it is simply cultural. As one woman law
student commented, "When your advisor insists on addressing you
as 'Sweetie' you know something is wrong!"

Certain strides have been made in recent years toward eliminating
some of the gender inequities at all levels of education, and various
individual educators and institutions have worked hard to encourge
girls and women to excel in areas where the female sex has all too
often faced roadblocks. Still, many traditional attitudes about
separate educational goals for each sex persist, and some pressure
groups have begun pushing for even more rigid gender-role
differentiation in the public school curricula.

Outside the classroom, gender-role stereotypes are reinforced by
the media. Advertising portrays a woman as unable to cope with daily
living without help from men to tell her how to wax her floor, clean
her dishes, or wrap leftovers. A woman's major concerns seem to be
white teeth, clean hair, dry underarms, and an uplifting bra. Her goal
is sufficient sex appeal to attract a man.

The inordinate stress our society places on feminine beauty is
contrary to the biblical emphasis on inner grace. As William Law said
long ago:

It is therefore much to be lamented, that this sex, on whom so much
depends, who have the first forming both of our bodies and our minds, are not
only educated in pride, but in the silliest and most contemptible part of it.

They are not indeed suffered to dispute with us the proud prizes of arts and
sciences, of learning and eloquence, in which I have much suspicion they
would often prove our superiors; but we turn them over to the study of beauty
and dress, and the whole world conspires to make them think of nothing else.
Fathers and mothers, friends and relations, seem to have no other wish
towards the little girl, but that she may have fair skin, a fine shape, dress well,
and dance to admiration.[19]

The Bible, however, stresses not outward adorning but "reverent and
chaste behavior," "the hidden person of the heart with the
imperishable jewel of a gentle and quiet spirit" (I Pet. 3:2, 4). The
Christian woman's goal in life is not to be beautiful but to serve God.

In his teenage years, a boy is involved in essentially one task: deciding on a vocation and training for it. Finding a wife and establishing a family are of secondary importance and will presumably fit into and enhance his career aspirations. The teenage girl, on the other hand, is torn by conflict. In school she is expected to work hard, develop her gifts, and prepare for a career too. But from all sides she is getting the message: What do grades and degrees matter if you don't get married? Having a date for the high-school prom and getting a diamond ring for college graduation are the important accomplishments. Higher grades than one's current boyfriend must be shamefully hidden. Counselors often suggest only such traditionally "feminine" professions as teaching and nursing; if a girl prefers auto mechanics or physics, they discourage and ridicule her.[20] Parents take more pride in a girl's beauty and dates than in her grades and honors. As one girl put it, "When I turned out to be a mathematical genius, my mother said, 'Put on some lipstick and see if you can find a boyfriend.' "

By the mid-1980s, even after years of exposure to the ideals of the equality of the sexes encouraged by the women's movement, social pressures to conform to the old gender-role scripts continued. When one junior-high-school student's name was announced over the school intercom as part of a small select list of those who had achieved all A's for the semester, her boyfriend angrily rushed over to her in the school cafeteria. "Who do you think you are?" he shouted, gruffly grabbing her shoulder. "Do you think you're better than me? You're trying to show me up, aren't you! Well, don't you ever get grades like that again, or you and I are finished." He stormed away from her lunch table, as the embarrassed young teenager tried to fight back tears. Her friends rushed to comfort her and told her just to forget any guy who would treat her like that, that he wasn't "worth it." But she couldn't pay the price. She went home ill that afternoon; in the following months, her teachers noticed her grades dropping steeply. She continued dating her domineering boyfriend; and at the end of the school year, the *parents* of the two young persons joined together to throw a gala party to celebrate their first year of going steady.

Thus the bright young woman is caught on the blade of a two-edged sword. In achievement-oriented situations in school and career, she wants to succeed, to live up to her potential, to fulfill her talents. Yet society tells her that such achievement requires a loss of femininity. Men are the achievers in our world. To succeed in a man's world means that one must become masculine, or so it has been defined. A woman caught in this situation fears both failure and success—if she fails, she has not been true to herself; if she succeeds, she is going against society's expectations.[21]

Psychology

These expectations which permeate popular thinking have also been woven into all of our "official" psychologies. The "father" of modern psychology, Sigmund Freud, declared "anatomy is destiny." He was sure that all women felt themselves to be castrated males, envied the male's penis, and were incapable of cultural achievement. Their only hope was to accept their inferior role and have babies as a penis substitute. Feminist Kate Millett has effectively answered many of his assertions.[22] Freud confused biology and culture, anatomy and status. Confronted everywhere by evidence of the male's superior status, women do not envy the penis but only what persons who possess that organ have access to: prestige, power, and achievement opportunities and rewards. In many cultures men have similarly envied women's ability to bring forth human life.

Other schools of psychology also regard the cultural gender roles as innate. Erik Erikson saw in small children evidence that boys are concerned with "outer space" (exploring and interacting with the world around) while girls are only concerned with "inner space" (subjective and interpersonal experience). Thus the originator of the "identity crisis" declared that "much of a young woman's identity is already defined in her kind of attractiveness and in the selectivity of her search for the man (or men) by whom she wishes to be sought." He defined her maturity in terms of the view that a woman's "somatic design harbors an 'inner space' destined to bear the offspring of chosen men, and with it, a biological, psychological, and ethical commitment to take care of human infancy."[23] No one would dream of defining adult male identity and maturity in terms of attractiveness to women and destined fatherhood!

Cumulatively these influences add up to very well-defined and rigid personality types and behavior models. The "mentally healthy male," according to a 1968 survey of mental health professionals by Donald and Inge Broverman, is aggressive, independent, unemotional, logical, direct, adventurous, self-confident, and ambitious. The "mentally healthy female" is passive, emotional, dependent, less competitive, nonobjective, submissive, vain, easily influenced, religious, and in need of security.[24]

Basically these role definitions have been made by and for the convenience of men. Men are relatively comfortable with their identity because it is shaped by their own needs and desires. Women's identity is also shaped by men's needs and desires. If a woman is not built like Miss America, she must diet or pad. Whatever her intelligence and talent, she must make them appear less than those of her male companions. Even Christian organizations have told female workers that their ministry is to be of encouragement and service to the men staff members, that they should channel any ideas through the men. All of this encourages women in the conniving, cajoling, and coercion better known as the use of "feminine wiles."

Social and civic functions have been modeled after the masculine pattern; women participate in "feminine" functions. In order to narrow the competition, men have relegated women to an entirely different ball game. And despite all the camouflage, women's realm is clearly secondary, different, and inferior. Men hold all the important positions of leadership, creativity, and responsibility. Women's work is considered unimportant and unspecialized, and it is often unpaid or underpaid.

Male personality traits and behavior are defined as "adult" and "healthy" while those defined as "female" by society are still regarded as childish and even neurotic. The Brovermans discovered this by asking psychologists to list the traits of a "mentally healthy adult." *It conformed exactly to the list previously drawn for a male* but contrasted sharply with that for a female. A woman who exhibits "male" traits of aggressiveness and rationality is labeled "masculine," "neurotic," "lesbian." If she conforms to female stereotypes, she is not a healthy adult; if she does not conform, she is sick. It is a no-win option.

Not only are our masculine cultural stereotypes defined as adult, healthy, and superior, but also Godlike and God-ordained. Thus ours is obviously the "natural," "normal," "God-ordained" way of ordering society. Women who exhibit "masculine traits" must simply be defective in creation; those who would seek roles outside what is prescribed for them are simply rebelling against God's decrees. Although cultural expressions are entirely relative, each society seeks to absolutize its ways and to invoke divine sanction. We try to make God in our image.

What has happened is that women do conform to the stereotypes. Any group told repeatedly and forcefully that it is inferior, incapable of certain accomplishments, will soon begin to believe it and act accordingly. A woman teacher once told her all-girl class that of course their text pictured a male chef because "everybody knows" that men make the best cooks, dress designers, hairdressers, and even laundry workers. Constant repression kills ambition. Only a woman with extraordinary strength of character and an exceptional home background would have the courage and stamina it takes to fight her way into a "male" profession—thus the stereotype that women cannot succeed in certain fields and thus the fact that younger women have had few role models to follow. Drifting with the tide is much more comfortable and much less difficult than fighting it. Women take the easy way out: they conform. They either accept the image men have outlined or escape any identity crisis by becoming "Bill's wife" and "Beth's mommy."

At least they have in the past. Today women are asking more and more for the opportunity to define themselves. They are increasingly more willing to accept the challenge and responsibility of their own lives. Christian women are claiming the right to seek God's will for their individual lives and to act on God's direction rather than simply confine themselves to what society decrees as "feminine."

Fear of Change

To call gender identity and traditional gender roles into question, however, is like "picking up the ground on which we stand and shaking it," as Rosemary Ruether once commented.[25] Isolated from other cultures by our conviction that Western civilization is vastly superior, and schooled to see all other cultures through glasses tinted by our own role stereotypes, we have very few models for change. Women in particular have had no feminine heroes, no *heras,* to emulate—women have been systematically excluded from our history. Women's accomplishments have been minimized or attributed to men. Until recently, few questioned the notion that only pagan idolaters or heretics believe that there is any feminine component in the divine.

And so, many people opt for the status quo. It is comfortable (particularly if you are male, middle class, and married). It has a long historical and theological tradition to undergird it. Yet the so-called status quo is no longer an option—it has been slowly disintegrating ever since the Protestant Reformation, the American Revolution, and the Civil War. With the growing belief in the equal dignity of all persons, we have jettisoned belief in the infallibility of the papacy, the divine right of kings, and the superiority of the white race. If we really believed our myths of male dominance, we would have to take away women's rights to be educated, to vote, and to work outside the home. Few would opt for such radical retrogression. To implement rigorously the implications of our supposed gender-role concepts would clearly waste too many gifts of both men and women.

But if we are to change society, in which direction shall we go?

Some fear that the goal of women's liberation is the reversal of the traditional roles. Psychologists say that this fear of women taking over society is a fantasy based on ruling class ego and guilt. Men assume that women want to imitate them and, when given power, will inflict on men the oppression they have received. However, women do not want all the power—they simply want to have the power of choice in their own lives and to share in the decisions that shape *our* society.

A related fear sometimes expressed is that changes in gender roles will destroy the male ego. This depends on one's definition of that mystical entity. Are men so fragile that they will be shattered if they can no longer rule the roost because they wear male plumage, if they have to compete not only with other races for their jobs but also with another sex, if women no longer let them win at chess and bowling? That "ego" is based on pride and oppression. It deserves to be destroyed. Why should a person's sex organs be any more relevant to holding power than skin color, ethnic origin, or religious affiliation? On the other hand, both men's and women's egos will be supported and nourished by a society that encourages all people to achieve full potential. After all, women need self-esteem, recognition, and inspiration too.

Still other persons voice different fears. Thus, for example, professors John Money and Anke Ehrhardt, authorities on psycho-hormonal research, offer reassuring words to persons who worry that children will be confused about their gender identity if gender roles are not rigidly segregated. They do not deny that growing children need to realize that there are two distinguishable sexes but, they point out, "nature herself supplies the basic irreducible elements of sex difference which no culture can eradicate, at least not on a large scale." They refer to primary sexual characteristics (such as beards on males, voice pitch differences between the sexes, and so on). In the words of these scientists:

Provided that a child grows up to know that sex differences are primarily defined by the reproductive capacity of the sex organs, and to have a positive feeling of pride in his or her own genitalia and their ultimate reproductive use, then it does not much matter whether various child-care, domestic, and vocational activities are or are not interchangeable between mother and father. It does not even matter if mother is a bus driver and daddy a cook.[26]

Yet another fear brought up sometimes centers not so much around *gender identity* (our conception of ourselves as either male or female) but rather around *sexual orientation* (whether our romantic/erotic attraction is directed toward an opposite-sex partner or a same-sex partner). In other words, does the absence of clearly defined gender roles "cause" homosexuality to increase? The answer is unequivocally *no*. In spite of much research in recent years and a great deal of new information on homosexuality, no clear-cut, final answers have been discovered to explain why a minority of persons are homosexual while the majority are heterosexual. But we have learned that sexual orientation is primarily a matter of feelings, a way of being, whether or not those feelings are ever translated into actual sexual expression.[27] Whether or not a person conforms or doesn't conform to societally prescribed gender *roles*—the assigned scripts we are expected to follow on the basis of whether we are female or male—has nothing to do with a person's sexual *orientation*. Many males who are tender, sensitive, and interested in activities that have been more associated with females are nevertheless heterosexual. Many males who are "macho" in appearance and interests are nevertheless homosexual, including some men in professional sports. The same is true of women. Some lesbians act and dress in ways that are stereotypically "feminine," and others do not. Similarly, some heterosexual women think of themselves as "tomboy types," but this has nothing to do with sexual orientation.

If rethinking and changing rigid gender roles will not require role reversal (with women in power and men subordinate), nor efforts to "destroy male egos," nor gender-role confusion in children, nor increases in the incidence of homosexuality, won't it at the very least encourage a *unisex* society? Won't everyone be expected to be alike?

No, because a society that insisted on unisex conformity would mean limiting the full range of human potential and complexity just as surely as insistence on stereotypical male and female segregated roles has done.

A better alternative would be a society that recognizes and encourages the widest possible variety in individual behavior and temperament. Each person would be accepted as fully human and helped to develop all inner potential. This is exactly what the feminist movement is asking for: the chance for every woman to develop and test her inner capabilities without having someone say, "That isn't ladylike!" and the chance for every man to develop and test his inner capabilities without being told he isn't acting "like a real man."

Psychologist Sandra Bem, whose pioneering research on the

benefits of *psychological androgyny* has been widely acclaimed because of its encouragement of both women and men to be *"both* independent and tender, *both* assertive and yielding, *both* masculine and feminine,"[28] now sees certain problems in an uncritical insistence on such an approach. She writes:

In the early 1970s, androgyny seemed to me and to many others a liberated and more humane alternative to the traditional, sex-biased standards of mental health. And it is true that this concept can be applied equally to both women and men, and that it encourages individuals to embrace both the feminine and the masculine within themselves.

Then she points out the danger she sees: "But advocating the concept of androgyny can also be seen as replacing a prescription to be masculine or feminine with the doubly incarcerating prescription to be masculine and feminine. The individual now has not one but two potential sources of inadequacy with which to contend." She sees as even more important than this double demand for a new kind of conformity the problem of *dividing up the world in terms of gender*. She argues that "human behaviors and personality attributes should no longer be linked with gender, and society should stop projecting gender into situations irrelevant to genitalia."[29] That is the same point we are trying to emphasize in this book.

Qualities that have been linked with males (such as rationality, assertiveness, courage, initiative) and qualities that have been linked with females (such as tenderness, sensitivity, empathy, intuitiveness) are in actuality *human* qualities that should be permitted and encouraged in persons of either sex to the degree that such qualities can be a natural and uncoerced part of themselves. But no one should be required to be an exact mix of "half masculine" and "half feminine," with everyone totally alike, as some have assumed.

Women and men live out their existence in different bodies and with different experiences of the world, their differences greatly exacerbated by divergent socialization. By not paying attention to how women have experienced the world, our knowledge of the world has been distorted and one-sided. What psychotherapist Anne Wilson Schaef calls "women's reality" is different from the reality she labels the "white male system."[30] Yet, in history, psychology, and countless other disciplines, women's reality has been overlooked, and men have defined the human norm. We have already seen an example of this in our reference to the Brovermans' study on perceptions of mentally healthy *adults* and separate categories of mentally healthy women and men. A more recent effort to show how psychological theory has failed to consider women's perceptions and experiences is the work of psychologist Carol Gilligan, who has examined theories of human development and moral reasoning and the research on these topics. She writes that her goal is "to expand the understanding of human development by using the group left out in the construction of theory to call attention to what is missing in its account."[31]

Men have been socialized to emphasize autonomy, individuation, and separation. Women have been socialized to emphasize attachment, caring, and responsibility for others. Thus, not surprisingly, Gilligan has found that for women, "morality is connected to responsiblity in relationships, and they always assume a connection between self and others, whereas men tend to look at moral issues in terms of the rights of individuals to noninterference."[32] Since the male experience and mode of moral reasoning has been seen as at a "higher stage" and normative, the female approach has been viewed by moral development theorists as being less mature, less developed—in other words, deficient. Gilligan takes such notions to task.

Rather than being at odds with each other, both approaches to moral reasoning are important. "Ten years ago, I thought in terms of the work of Piaget and Kohlberg on the development of the idea of justice," Gilligan has said. "Now I see morality as reflecting two themes that are woven into the cycle of life: inequality and interdependence. These experiences are universal, and they give rise to the ethics of justice and care, the ideals of human relationships—that everyone will be treated with equal respect and that no one will be left alone or hurt."[33]

Males and females have much to teach and learn from one another. We are all created in the image of God, a God of justice and equity, a God of loving care and compassion. All of us, without regard to gender, need to reflect the totality of that image. In our rethinking of the roles and relationships of women and men, it is possible to think in terms of at least three approaches, as described by Gayle Graham Yates. We can think in terms of "women over against men," "women equal to men," or "women and men equal to each other."[34] This third approach would seem to hold the greatest promise for a world that does not need to hear more about separateness and conflict, nor about a "normative" group versus an "other" that is striving to match the more powerful group.

For the sake of *men,* as well as for the sake of women, changes need to be made. "Humanity has been held to a limited and distorted view of itself—from its interpretation of the most intimate of personal emotions to its grandest vision of human possibilities—precisely by virtue of its subordination of women," writes psychiatrist Jean Baker Miller. She goes on to point out that until recently only the understandings put forth by men were available to us. But now older ways of thinking are being greatly challenged. "As other perceptions arise—precisely those perceptions that men, because of their dominant position, could *not* perceive—the total vision of human possibilities enlarges and is transformed."[35]

Christlikeness

Christians should be the least threatened by such visions of liberation. We of all people should have a historical, transcultural perspective. We serve the Creator of all cultures who is creatively at work in every culture. We are only pilgrims here; we seek a city in which we have been told that sexual polarities will be irrelevant. Our goal in life has never been to conform to the stereotypes of this world but to be transformed into Christlikeness.

Christ came into a world dominated by ascribed roles, positions decreed by birth. Only a Jew, a son of Abraham, was one of the chosen people. Only a Levite could be a priest. Only a male could receive circumcision. Only a Roman citizen was protected by Roman law. Only privileged aristocrats were allowed in the Roman senate.

But the Good News was that *achieved* roles were what counted in the kingdom of God. "Believe in the Lord Jesus, and you will be saved" (Acts 16:31). "There is no distinction between Jew and Greek; the same Lord is Lord of all" and *all who call upon God* are recipients of God's riches (Rom. 10:12). In Christ we are no longer servants and children but friends and heirs (John 15:15; Gal. 4:7).

Jesus did not endorse the patriarchal attitudes of his culture. He never once exhorted women to be good wives and mothers. He did not shoo Mary back into the kitchen but reprimanded Martha for getting too involved in it. He commended the "gutsiness" of the Canaanite woman who would not take no for an answer (Matt. 15:21-28) and the widow who would not let a corrupt judge ignore her plea (Luke 18:1-8).

Nor did he encourage the *machismo* attitudes of his male contemporaries. He criticized their casual attitude toward divorce that considered wives as servants who could be dismissed for trivial mistakes (Mark 10:2-9). He punctured their pride in thinking that they could view women as sex objects as long as they did nothing about their fantasies (Matt. 5:27-28; Luke 7:37-50). He called their bluff when they exercised a double standard in bringing to him a woman taken in adultery while letting her male companion go (John 8:1-11). He condemned their worship motivated by ego and assertiveness (Mark 12:41-44; Luke 18:9-14). He observed that the rational and clever did not understand his teachings as well as the simple did (Matt. 11:25).

Power and dominance were foreign to Jesus' teaching and practice. When the disciples wanted to call down fire from heaven to get even with the Samaritans, Jesus rebuked them (Luke 9:51-55). He commanded Peter to put away his sword (John 18:11) and told Pilate, "If my kingship were of this world, my servants would fight . . . but my kingship is not from the world" (John 18:36). Jesus scolded the disciples for their competitive, grasping spirit and scramble for power and position (Matt. 20:25-28). Although he acknowledged that the gospel would bring division, he didn't refer to division between the sexes (Luke 12:53).

Christ himself did not conform to cultural sex roles. He never felt compelled to prove his masculinity in marriage and fatherhood. He was not afraid to be tender and loving with men, women, and children. He was gentle, meek, and generally unassertive. He wept publicly on more than one occasion. His paradoxes often confounded the logic of his critics.

But he was also strong and resolute in the face of temptation and death. His righteous anger drove the money changers from the Temple. He decisively debated and sometimes bluntly denounced the scribes and Pharisees. He declared the demands of justice and righteousness forthrightly.

Jesus Christ is our example, our paradigm. We are not told in Scripture to seek what it means to be a "man" or a "woman" in our society, but what it means to be Christlike. We are called to mature personhood in Christ's image (Eph. 4:13). And we are promised the Holy Spirit's help in that transformation.

The fruit of the Holy Spirit's work (Gal. 5:22-23) cannot be pigeonholed under "masculine" or "feminine" but only categorized as *imago Dei*. According to the New Testament, the Christlike person exhibits the best in human qualities: love, joy, peace, patience, kindness, goodness, faithfulness, gentleness, self-control, humility, integrity, meekness, sensitivity, empathy, purity, submissiveness, confidence, courage, strength, zeal, determination, compassion, common sense, generosity, and self-sacrifice.

Against such there should be no law for any person in any culture.

7.

LOVE, HONOR, AND ——— ?

If workable marriages are to exist in this latter part of the twentieth century, the artificially determined roles of male and female . . . must be discarded and replaced. . . . Modern marriage requires equality, just as world history indicates a trend toward equality among peoples regardless of sex, race, or creed.

—From *The Mirages of Marriage*[1]

SOME CHRISTIANS CONSIDER THE INCLUSION OF THE WORD *OBEY* IN the marriage vows almost as a badge of orthodoxy. They are alarmed that many modern wedding ceremonies omit this wifely pledge. Certain religious leaders voice dire predictions of the demise of the family, the emasculation of husbands, the delinquency of children, and the horrible specter of a society dominated by power-hungry women.

Articles and sermons plead with husbands to assert their leadership. Wives are told that godly submission to their husbands is their duty, that the divine order requires a woman's position in marriage to be one of subordination. Women who refuse to accept this role are told they will miss out on the joy of living in God's will. In this view, patriarchy—not partnership—is the unquestioned biblical standard for marriage.

This teaching has been so widespread in some Christian circles that few have dared to question or challenge it. Yet it bothers many young couples contemplating marriage, just as it disturbs some who are already married and who were untroubled by questions of "Who's boss?" until they heard a sermon or read a book that insisted that equal-partner marriages are contrary to God's plan.

"But why is it so wrong for persons to stand on equal footing in a relationship of love?" some are wondering. "Why must there be a hierarchy of superior/inferior, a dictatorship instead of a democracy, an insistence that one person must lead in all practical and spiritual matters—regardless of abilities—simply because of having been born a member of a certain sex?" The answer they usually hear is that God has simply designed things that way, that woman was created to meet man's needs, and that to complain that it is an unfair setup is to rebel against God.

The traditional view of marriage stressed such matters as duty, authority, obedience, and rigid role differentiation. Today another ideology emphasizes the importance of companionship, affection, self-actualization, growth, and a relationship of equals. In such marriages, the partners recognize each other as unique individuals. Each has needs, abilities, and special personal assets to contribute to the marital unit. This leaves room for creativity, flexibility, and imagination in family life-style. Each spouse has maximum freedom to explore his or her own particular talents and interests, without being cramped by traditional restraints resulting from gender-role stereotyping.

Although examples of egalitarian marriages seem to have been rare in history, the idea itself is not new. Priscilla and Aquila, two of the apostle Paul's dearest friends, provide a biblical example. Priscilla and Aquila were a husband-wife team who were united not only in their love for each other and in their devotion to Christ but also in their work. They participated in an active Christian ministry and labored side by side in a common trade (tentmaking) as business partners. Paul regards this gifted couple fondly and is grateful to God for their companionship as fellow workers in Christ's kingdom (Acts 18:1-4, 24-28; Rom. 16:3-5; I Cor. 16:19). Perhaps Paul knew of other such marriages among Christian workers; he mentions that some of the apostles had wives who traveled with them on their missionary journeys (I Cor. 9:5). There is no reason to accept the assumption made by one writer that the apostle would have been offended by the "modern idea" that a wife should be her husband's best friend.

In the nineteenth century, philosopher-economist John Stuart Mill took issue with the prevalent view of marriage in his time and provided a detailed rationale for equal partnership. Even earlier, the renowned seventeenth-century scholar and poet John Milton had challenged his contemporaries to rethink God's intention for marriage. Each of these writers envisioned the richness that could be possible in a marriage *based on true soul-companionship*. Mill spoke of a marriage between a man and a woman of similar education, opinions, and purposes "between whom there exists that best kind of equality, similarity of powers and capacities with reciprocal superiority in them—so that each can enjoy the luxury of looking up to the other, and can have alternately the pleasure of leading and of being led in the path of development."[2] Milton wrote, "It is not the joining of another body [that] will remove loneliness, but the uniting of another compliable mind."[3]

Yet many Christians are suspicious of attempts to promote equality between the sexes because they think such a notion is contrary to the Bible. "Scriptures declare unequivocally that the sexes are *not* equal," announced an editorial in an evangelical periodical.[4] With such an understanding of the Bible, it isn't surprising that a religious publisher rejected a commissioned book on Christian sex ethics because the manuscript emphasized the positive implication of equality for dating and marriage. "It is unnecessary to make woman equal to man, even at the dating level," said the publisher.

Some Christian young men quickly latch on to the notion that women were made for men. One student at a Christian college told us of her first date with a fellow student. He suggested they have a time of devotions before going out, and she gladly assented. But immediately he whipped out his pocket New Testament and read aloud Ephesians 5, beginning with verse 22, "Wives, be subject to your husbands, as to the Lord." He paused and said, "See what that says? It means you're supposed to *obey* me." "Obey you?" the young woman countered. "Why, I hardly know you, and we've never been out together before—and I'm certainly not married to you! What makes you think I have to obey you?" She said as far as she was concerned, it was "Goodby, Charlie!" She never dated him again.

Husband-Wife Authority Relations

Why are so many Christians afraid of egalitarianism in marriage? There seem to be two main reasons: (1) *a fear that the Bible will be disobeyed,* and (2) *a fear of anarchy or disorder.*

First, there is a strong unexamined conviction that the Bible upholds the patriarchal ideal as the divine pattern for marriage in all cultures and in all ages. To question this is tantamount to questioning the very plan of God. Furthermore, some argue, if one abrogates the principles of male authority and female submission, might there not be other biblical teachings that could also be questioned, argued away, or set aside? Doesn't that undermine the total authority of the Scriptures?

Again we must refer to the principles of hermeneutics discussed in chapter 1. The man-woman question must be raised in the spirit of theological interpretation. Otherwise, we are merely playing games by tossing isolated biblical proof texts at one another while all the time failing to grasp the basic principles of what it means for women and men alike to be kindred citizens of the kingdom of God, of what it means to walk anew as children of God pulsating with new life through Jesus Christ. In short, we need to learn what it means to be Christians—Christians who demonstrate that both men and women are Christ's disciples. How? By the love we have toward one another, regardless of differences of age, race, sex, or social class. And we need to learn how to exhibit the fruit of the Spirit and the signs of Christian maturity in all of life's relationships—including marriage.

But in addition to the worries over biblical authority, many people express a second fear about viewing marriage as egalitarian rather than patriarchal. Might not chaos and anarchy result in the absence of a clearly spelled-out chain of command? The egalitarian marriage ideal is thus rejected on the grounds that the Bible insists upon a *hierarchical* ordering of society.

Interestingly, the same argument was once used to keep the "common people" from having a say in government. Subjects were told that it was God's will that they submit to the higher authorities on the basis of such passages as Romans 13 and Hebrews 13:17. Kings were persuaded that they ruled by divine right, and they made no apologies for tyrannizing over their subjects.

Similarly, the issue of slavery was defended by those who twisted Paul's analogy of the church as a body (I Cor. 12). They contended that this was a picture of God's will for society, with some persons ordained to lower spheres and some to higher, yet each assigned a part to play. "The feet are as indispensable to the head as the head to the feet," wrote slavery defender James Henley Thornwell, who went on to point out that if the "feet" ever desired to be anything but feet all society would be plunged into "irretrievable confusion."[5] Slaves must be treated kindly, but kept in their place, said Thornwell. And they must be taught that their position was God's will.

Christians convinced of a God-ordained, ironclad arrangement for all society for all time understandably have difficulty thinking in egalitarian terms. They see an order or chain of command based on rank (masters-slaves, rulers-subjects, men-women, parents-children). The idea of two mature human beings relating to each other as equals within the marriage relationship strikes them as absurd. Therefore, they emphasize that the husband is to be the head of the home, and if the wife wants to be equal—well, that would mean there would be two heads. And doesn't everybody know that a two-headed monstrosity could never function well?

There are other commonly used illustrations intended to make the same point. Some argue that two riders wouldn't ride side by side on a horse, but rather one would be seated in front of the other. (However, two riders might sit side by side in a carriage with the horse pulling them—and two Christians might sit side by side in a marriage as well. Or we might ask, Even if one horseman does ride at the front of the horse and the other behind, who's to say the two wouldn't occasionally change places? The illustration doesn't stand up well.)

Then there is the illustration borrowed from government. Some say marriage requires the husband as the final authority because otherwise it would be as confusing as if a country chose two heads of state with equal powers. It is alleged that this could never work. Yet, such a plan *did* work in ancient Rome during the long period of the Republic. Keenly sensitive to the problems of unlimited powers in government, the Romans worked out a detailed system of checks and balances. Heading the government were two annually elected consuls or "presidents" of equal rank (so that power would be restricted by sharing). In case of conflict, the negative right to veto took precedence over the colleague's positive right. In practice, however, as we shall see in a later section, the consuls largely avoided conflicts in ways that might be paralleled in marriage. (No, it was *not* this dually shared leadership that caused the "fall of Rome"! The western empire crumbled centuries later under a government of one-man rule.)

However, such arguments can end in a dead-end street. We need to see that God intended marriage to be a relationship—a companionship, a covenant (see Mal. 2:13-16). Marriage is not a body needing a head (the man) and a heart (the woman) in order to function. It is not a ride on a horse nor a government in need of a king. It is a relationship between two human beings who willingly join themselves together, each investing all that he or she is and has in the new social unit being formed.

Husbands and wives are two made one. But that "one" is not the husband, with the wife's identity lost and merged into his (as so many laws and customs suggest—such as the practice of changing a woman's name to Mrs. William Jones, which means "the mistress of William Jones").[6] Rather, the two form a new unit and can think of themselves as *partners*—just as two business partners can join together to form a business in which each has an equal share and voice. We are not speaking here of a president and vice-president arrangement, or of a pilot and copilot setup, but of a fully equal partnership. John Stuart Mill argued that such an arrangement can and does work in the business world.[7] It is foolish for Christians to insist that in any voluntary association there must always be one person who has final authority in all matters. If two persons have made equal investments in a business partnership, they should have equal say about all matters concerning their mutual venture. The same thing holds for marriage.

Yet, the traditional Christian position has been opposed to the egalitarian marrage ideal. Over the ages, Christians have generally interpreted Scripture to favor male headship.

Patriarchy or Partnership—What Does the Bible Say?

In the Old Testament, there is no question about who is the head of the household. The patriarchal structure of Israelite society regarded the husband as both possessor and master. His will was the will of the house; he was the center of the family. All members of the household were expected to look up to him and obey him, no matter what the cost. Pedersen points out that a wife was supposed to be willing to sacrifice herself for her husband "because his life is always more valuable than hers."[8] A husband could arbitrarily and unilaterally divorce his wife, sending her out from his house, whereupon she was called *gerushah*, meaning "expelled."[9]

Marriage meant that a woman was *ba'al-taken* by her husband, that is, she came under his ownership. Both Genesis 20:3 and Deuteronomy 22:22 speak of a married woman as *be'ulat ba'al* which means "a wife owned by her husband." A wife called her husband *ba'al* ("master") or else *'adon* ("lord"). Thus, as Roland de Vaux points out, a woman addressed her husband "as a slave addressed his master, or a subject his king."[10]

This patriarchal arrangement was common among other peoples as well. Esther became the bride of a Persian king who had divorced his former wife for refusing to obey him. Queen Vashti's failure to bow to her husband's command upset the men of the king's court. Perhaps all the women of Persia and Media would follow the queen's "bad example"! They enjoined him not only to replace his wife with a new queen but also to send out a decree that "all women will give honor to their husbands, high and low.' . . . that every man be lord in his own house" (Esther 1:20-22).

The Apocrypha says, "Do not leave a leaky cistern to drip or allow a bad wife to say what she likes. If she does not accept your control, divorce her and send her away" (Ecclus. 25:25-26 NEB). In the Hebrew culture, even if a wife were above her husband in social status, she was supposed to consider him above her. The Midrash tells the story of a certain woman of wealth and noble birth. She married a poor beggar who never masked his delight in his masculine prerogative of lording it over her. One day he went to the sages carrying a golden candelabrum on top of which he had placed an earthen lamp. This he said was a fulfillment of Genesis 3:16, illustrating that he who was so much lower in birth and social standing than his wife nevertheless ruled over her by virtue of being a male.

Daughters of Sarah—I Peter 3

If we shift our attention to the New Testament, it again seems at first glance that husband-wife authority relations are weighted in favor of the man. However, the passage instructing wives to obey husbands in I Peter 3:1-6 deals with a special situation. These were wives with unbelieving husbands who hoped to win them to Christ. Instead of preaching or nagging, they were to follow the Old Testament pattern of modesty, submissive behavior, and a meek and gentle spirit. Such an evangelistic strategy would be the most persuasive for these men, accustomed as they were to patriarchal arrangements in the home. This instruction is counterbalanced by a message to husbands who were already Christians, appealing to them to treat their wives considerately, recognizing them as "joint heirs of the grace of life." To fail to show such consideration could result in ineffective prayers (I Pet. 3:7).

Yet many Christians see a great deal more in this passage, laying much stress on verses 5 and 6: "So once the holy women who hoped in God used to adorn themselves and were submissive to their husbands, as Sarah obeyed Abraham, calling him lord. And you are now her children if you do right and let nothing terrify you."

Some Christian writers (both men and women) find it highly significant that *Sarah* has been chosen as a model of wifely obedience here. One writer suggests that this example settles the question of how far wives must go in their submission—especially as questions arise about obedience to husbands who are cruel or heavy drinkers and the like. He writes:

Both Paul and Peter state the command to submission without qualifications. Peter's use of Sarah as an illustration of obedience is notable since Abraham *twice* in order to protect his own life, denied that Sarah was his wife and allowed her to be taken into a ruler's harem (Gen. 12:10-20; 20:1-18). The implication is not that a wife should allow her husband to sell her into prostitution if he wishes. But by stating the case absolutely, both Peter and Paul forestall capriciousness in the matter of submission.[11]

Another author calls our attention to the same passage, but from a slightly different angle. She praises Sarah's quiet submission to her husband's plan, even though it showed that Abraham regarded his own life more highly than his wife's, and draws the lesson that just as God protected Sarah because of her obedience in such a difficult situation God will also bless and protect wives who follow Sarah's example of submissiveness today.[12] (Figures on wife abuse even by Christian husbands show this faith is unwarranted.)

But what was Sarah really like? Does Genesis present her as the quiet, passive, obedient wife that some have inferred from I Peter 3? Decidedly not! Sarah was by no means a dull, colorless, subservient person; she displayed real spirit and voiced her own opinions. And Abraham did not rule with an iron hand, making decisions unilaterally, while paying no attention to his wife. In fact, perhaps he would have been better off had he *not* given in to her wishes in one instance (Gen. 16:2), for it was Sarah's idea that Abraham should have a child by her maidservant Hagar rather than wait for God's time and plan. But later, when Sarah demanded the expulsion of Ishmael (son of Abraham's union with the maidservant), and Abraham disagreed, it was *God* who told Abraham to obey his wife! "Whatever Sarah says to you, do as she tells you, for through Isaac shall your descendants be named" (Gen. 21:12).

Sarah was a woman of strong personality—a real partner to Abraham. God's plan included her by name. It wasn't enough that Abraham should have a son; it must be a son *by Sarah*. She would be blessed by God, and she would be the mother of nations (Gen. 17:15 ff.).

Genesis 18 records an incident that might be called "reverently humorous," for it includes some friendly banter between God and Sarah. In a theophany, God and two angels visited Abraham's tent. While Sarah was preparing a meal for them, she overheard the announcement that she would bear a son in her old age. She laughed to herself. The very thought seemed so utterly fantastic! God knew she had laughed in her heart and rebuked her, saying nothing is too hard for God. Then "Sarah denied, saying, 'I did not laugh'; for she was afraid. [God] said, 'No, but you did laugh' " (Gen. 18:15). Her laughter, like Abraham's (Gen. 17:17), wasn't a laughter of scorn or mockery, but was an expression of surprise and incredulity. No doubt when she and her husband named their little son *Isaac* (a word meaning "laughter") as God had instructed them, they looked back on this sharing of laughter with God—almost as though it were a private little joke between the three of them. Now it was laughter of gratitude and delight. Sarah said, "God has made laughter for me; every one who hears will laugh over me . . . Who would have said to Abraham that Sarah would suckle children? Yet I have borne him a son in his old age" (Gen. 21:6-7).

In the two incidents telling of Abraham's denial that Sarah was his wife (out of fear that powerful rulers would kill him in order to possess his beautiful wife), Abraham didn't suddenly decide to tell an untruth at Sarah's expense when danger confronted him. He had talked it over with her in advance, and she had agreed to go along with his plan (Gen. 12:11-13; 20:5, 13). Perhaps they had rationalized the whole matter and decided it was only a half-truth and not a bold, outright lie to claim they were brother and sister. They actually had been born of the same father, though of different mothers (Gen. 20:12).

Obedience to God

The marriage of Abraham and Sarah, then, doesn't really provide the kind of authority model that some Christians assume; nor is the biblical picture of Sarah one of weakness, meekness, and subservience. But there is an additional lesson here: Sarah's example certainly does *not* warrant a wife's unquestioning obedience in cases where a husband asks her to violate God's law.

Abraham and Sarah were newly emerged from paganism. Humankind was in a kind of spiritual infancy and only gradually learning the revelation of the one true God. (Even so, although the Ten Commandments had not yet been given, there was evidently common knowledge that God considered adultery sin, according to Genesis 20:3-6.) Perhaps we can excuse the conduct of Abraham and Sarah as the actions of those whose moral sensitivities were not yet fully developed. But we cannot draw the conclusion that a Christian woman today, enlightened and indwelt by the Holy Spirit, should obediently follow her husband's wishes if they are contrary to God's will. (Incidentally, it's possible that Sarah agreed to lie and risk the possibility of adultery not so much out of *obedience* to her husband as out of *love* for him and a genuine desire to preserve his life.)

To argue that a woman is responsible to submit to her husband under all circumstances—even if it violates a command of God or the wife's own conscience (and sermons have been preached to that effect)[13]—goes totally against the spirit of the New Testament. "We must obey God rather than men" (Acts 5:29). Each Christian, male or female, married or unmarried, is responsible to God.

This point comes through clearly in the story of Ananias and Sapphira (Acts 5). With his wife's knowledge and cooperation, Ananias had kept back an amount of money that had been pledged to the Christian community. The apostle Peter rebuked him for lying not to men but to God, and Ananias died suddenly in a way that convinced the church of God's judgment. Three hours later, Sapphira (not knowing what had happened to her husband) was asked about the money obtained from the property sale. She told the same falsehood that her husband had told. "How is it that you have agreed together to tempt the Spirit of the Lord?" asked Peter just before Sapphira too was overtaken by sudden death.

It is noteworthy that the apostles did not excuse Sapphira by saying, "Well, after all, wives must obey. She just dutifully did what her husband said; she had to submit. Therefore, the responsibility for sinning against God was entirely her husband's." Quite the contrary. Wives are accountable to *God*.

Susanna Wesley—A Case Study

Another question arises with regard to the I Peter passage. If Sarah is taken as an exemplary wife because of how she addressed her husband, is it the writer's intention that Christian wives should actually call their husbands "lord"? (Gen. 18:12, to which I Pet. 3:6 alludes, is obscured in modern translations which usually use the term *husband*).

Earlier we noted the custom of ancient Israel where wives *did* call husbands "master" or "lord." And some Christian women have taken I Peter 3:6 as a literal command to do likewise (although it would seem the writer was calling attention to Sarah's respect for her husband as revealed in her thoughts in Gen. 18, rather than ordering Christian women to address their husbands in a prescribed manner). However, ascribing such titles to one's husband by no means always indicates that a spiritless, passive, submissive wife is on the scene. Susanna Wesley is a case in point.

Often referred to in sermons and articles as the ideal pattern of Christian wifehood and motherhood, Susanna Wesley in truth outwardly showed submission to her proud and hot-tempered clergyman husband. All the days of their married life, she called him "my master" and "sir." But since most of the burden of rearing their large family fell to her, she and her husband often clashed over matters concerning the children, and Mrs. Wesley did not hesitate to express her opinion that her approach to discipline was best.

Disagreements were common in the Wesley household, and after thirty-five years of marriage, she confessed in a letter to her son John that their home knew much unhappiness because husband and wife so seldom thought alike.

Frequently, through what is generally called "female tact," Mrs. Wesley was able to have her own way without giving any indication that she wasn't being submissive and obedient to her husband. But one notable exception brought such a strong reaction from him that the world came close to being denied John and Charles Wesley!

After family prayers one day, Mr. Wesley noticed that his wife had not said "Amen" to his prayer for King William (whom Susanna regarded as a usurper without any right to the throne). Samuel Wesley called her into the study and asked why she hadn't said "Amen" as was her custom after his other prayers. She explained her honest feelings. Then her angry husband knelt down and called God's vengeance upon him and his posterity if he should ever come near Susanna or get into a bed with her again—unless she asked for God's and her husband's forgiveness for not praying for the king.

When the king died shortly afterward, the Reverend Mr. Wesley changed neither his mind nor his vow. He threatened to apply for a chaplaincy on a ship, and set off for London, resolving never to see his wife again. Deeply distressed about whether to obey him or stay true to her conscience, Susanna Wesley sought the advice and comfort of two close friends, a woman and a noted divine, whose encouragement sustained her during the uncertain months of separation from her husband. Eventually Samuel Wesley, moved by news of a fire in the rectory and the counsel of a fellow minister, forgot his stubborn pride and rash vow and returned to Susanna. John Wesley, called by one writer "the child of their reconciliation," was born a year later.[14]

Ephesians 5

Perhaps even more than the I Peter passage, it is the fifth chapter of Ephesians that many Christians feel ensures for all time the divine right of husbands.

Be subject to one another out of reverence for Christ. Wives, be subject to your husbands, as to the Lord. For the husband is the head of the wife as Christ is the head of the church, his body, and is himself its Savior. As the church is subject to Christ, so let wives also be subject in everything to their husbands. Husbands, love your wives, as Christ loved the church and gave himself up for her (Eph. 5:21-25).

On the basis of this passage, many religious leaders say the uniqueness of Christian marriage is clearly set forth, namely, the subjection of the wife and the headship of the husband. Couples are told that a marriage ceremony that includes the bride's vow to *obey* can be a real "testimony," instructing wedding guests in the way that Christian marriage is marked off from all other conceptions of marriage.

However, a view of marriage that considers the husband dominant and the wife submissive is *not at all unique!* In the Roman culture of that time, the *paterfamilias* ("father of a family") ruled over the entire household (wife, children, grandchildren, and slaves). He controlled the property, decided whom his children would marry, and had the final say in matters concerning everyone under him. The Romans spoke of the *patria potestas*—"the power or authority of the father."

We have seen that this view of marriage prevailed in ancient Israel and in other nations during Old Testament times. It has been the pattern in other religions throughout history. The Hindu Law of Manu demanded that "a virtuous wife must constantly revere her husband as a god"—even if he had no good qualities whatsoever and even if he were infatuated with another woman. A fifteenth-century Confucian marriage manual tells a wife to look up to her husband as her lord, never disobeying his instructions, giving him reverence and service, and looking on him as if he were heaven itself. Why? Because a wife's lifelong duty is obedience. Social customs and religious traditions the world over have long presented this outlook on marriage. There is absolutely nothing either unique or Christian about insisting that wives obey and subject themselves to their husbands.

What *is* unique in Ephesians 5 is groundwork for an altogether new ideal of marriage. The key lies in an understanding of marriage as a picture of the relationship between Christ and the church. (Similar imagery is also found in II Cor. 11:2; John 3:28-30; and Rev. 19:7 ff.) In this analogy, the New Testament writers are following the tradition of the Old Testament where the relationship between God and the people of God is frequently spoken of in terms of marriage (cf. Hos.; Ezek. 16; Isa. 54:5-8; 62:5b; also the entire Song of Sol. if it is interpreted allegorically).

Although the instructions for wives and husbands in Colossians 3:18-19 and Ephesians 5:21 ff. again appear at first glance to make the husband the unquestioned head of the house with the wife required to give unconditional obedience, we find upon closer examination that there is a real difference between these instructions and the Old Testament patriarchal tradition. There a woman was to sacrifice herself for her husband because she was of less value than he. In Ephesians 5, we read that a husband is to love his wife to the extent of Christ's sacrificial love for the church—even to the point of giving himself up for her! Husbands are told to love their wives as their very own flesh. *Both* husbands and wives are told to be submissive to one another in the realization that *all* Christians should be subject to one another (Eph. 5:21). Such attitudes, if put into practice, can't help setting up a climate in which there is no need to battle about authority rights. The teaching of Ephesians 5 provides the atmosphere in which a new and thoroughly Christian ideal of marriage can grow.

But isn't the main emphasis on the wife's subjection to her husband? No, it is not. A careful look at these verses shows that much more space is given to requirements for the husband's conduct (although articles and sermons seldom present the passage in this way). The reason for this focus is that the passage is primarily presenting the deep, spiritual truth (the "great mystery") of Christ's love for the church. Practical implications for the human marriage relationship are interwoven with this.

A New Pattern Set in Motion

Ephesians 5 allows for an "evolution" or development of the ideal of marriage as God intends it. This is often overlooked, because we get sidetracked by the words *head* and *subject* and their usual connotations. Most speakers put the emphasis on "Wives, be subject to your husbands," and "The husband is the head of the wife." Often they don't quote the remaining parts of these verses at all. But as we have seen, such a message wasn't at all new or unique. New believers certainly needed no such instructions, because the dominant-husband/submissive-wife model of marriage was the norm in the societies of that time. There would have been no reason to tell wives to submit to their husbands or to tell husbands they were the heads.

What *was* new in these instructions of Ephesians 5 was the *way* husbands and wives were now supposed to relate to each other. The headship/subjection pattern was transformed. Wives were to submit in a totally new way—as a part of the mutual submission of *all* believers to one another. It was not to be a submission rooted in fear or grudging duty but rather "as to the Lord"—a response of love, joy, and delight because of Christ's self-giving love for us which calls for our self-giving love in return.

We yearn to please and serve Christ, because Christ has given his all for us and has spared nothing on our behalf. From this, the husband takes his cue as to how he is to be the "head" of his wife—a way so startlingly different from older ideas of male headship that the first husbands who read this epistle must have been astonished. Who had ever heard of such a thing? To follow Christ's example meant that a husband must spare nothing—not even his own life if need be—in his concern and care for his wife. He must think of her as part of him, his very own flesh, and "no man ever hates his own flesh, but nourishes and cherishes it, as Christ does the church" (Eph. 5:29). As we saw earlier, Christ's headship over the church refers to his being the source of its life, making it an organic, living unity that is fed and nourished by his constant giving.

If we think of the term *head* in the sense of *archē* ("beginning," "origin," "source"), we are again reminded of the *interdependence* of the sexes, each drawing life from the other. In the creation story of Genesis 2, where the origin of marriage was described, we saw that God took from man and made the woman. But ever since, as Paul reminds us, man has come from woman. That is why he stresses that "in the Lord woman is not independent of man nor man of woman" (I Cor. 11:11). And the head or source of all things is God (I Cor. 11:12). Christ is the head of the two made one flesh.

The wife, according to the pattern of Ephesians 5, can't help responding to her husband with a fervent desire to show her love to him, just as he has expressed his love to her. The cycle goes on and on, each giving to the other and receiving in turn.

In such an ideal (and Ephesians 5 pointed toward that ideal, even though it had to begin where the people were and didn't spell out all the details and implications), marriage is not something fixed and static, with rigid roles, clearly designated duties, and places in which each spouse must stay put. Rather, Christian marriage should be something alive and exciting and on the move, as each gives and receives from the other in a continuous exchange of Christ's kind of love. The reciprocity of mutual respect, self-sacrificing concern, and deep affection serves as the dynamic that invigorates and energizes the exhilarating adventure God wants marriage to be. It is an adventure of growth together.[15]

Misusing Ephesians 5

Those who think in terms of duties, roles, and hierarchy (rather than in personalistic terms) often twist the meaning of Ephesians 5. Their stress is always on the wife's subordination. And if the husband isn't loving her after Christ's example—well, then it's the wife's fault, not the husband's! Such reasoning is an insult to the love of Christ, yet it is common in some Christian circles. The following excerpt from an article in one Christian magazine illustrates this thinking:

Do not forget that your husband spends the better part of his day with people who are not only interested in his work but who are often well-informed and stimulating. Furthermore, women he meets or works with in the business world make a consistent effort to be neat and attractive. How then is he to be excited about loving you as Christ loves the Church if he comes home to find you with your hair in curlers and so taken up with the household affairs that the most interesting part of your conversation has to do with enzyme active detergents or baby food?[16]

"How then is he to be excited about loving you as Christ loves the Church?"—as though Christ's love for us depends upon how "interesting" and "attractive" we make ourselves! Where would any of us be if such were the case? What would be the meaning of the Book of Hosea or passages such as Romans 5:8 and I John 4:10? We are not saying that wives shouldn't try to look attractive for their husbands (or husbands for their wives), but rather that Ephesians 5 is speaking of an unconditional love that accepts, overlooks, forgives, and loves—even when the other person seems unlovable.

All too many sermons and articles interpret Ephesians 5 and related passages in ways that are decidedly one-sided. They seem to support the old idea that "a man's home is his castle and his wife is his janitor," implying that this is the divine order. The wife must subordinate her interests to those of her husband; all the privileges and rights are weighted in his favor. True, such articles usually end with a reminder that a husband should imitate Christ and be willing to die for his wife—but that's a lot easier for men to take than being asked to share household tasks with her, since the former situation isn't likely to arise very often! Grudgingly, some rights are conceded wives, however, but usually in a spirit of condescension (such as the article suggesting that it might be a good idea for Christian husbands to give their wives a small allowance with no questions asked, even though the husband could assume that his wife "would probably spend it foolishly").

The picture of Christian marriage given all too often is one of an autocrat lording it over a docile child-wife who has no mind of her own, no interests but those of her husband and children, and little inclination toward personal growth. It is dangerous teaching and can only work against the Christian principles of unselfishness, love, and striving toward Christian maturity—principles that God asks of all believers, whether male or female. As Sidney Callahan points out, God desires free persons who have "grown up into Christ, not crushed automatons without freedom, without identity." She goes on to say that it is unfortunate that some women "have made too many of the wrong sacrifices; they have been guilty of a suicide of personality. For too long Christians and Christian women have confused free sacrifice, service, and obedience with passivity, servility, and self-destructive acquiescence."[17]

The usual way of teaching Ephesians 5 suggests that it is the wife who must make the self-sacrifices (just the opposite of what the text says) and unwittingly encourages the husband to be selfish, egocentric, convinced of his right to have his own way, and filled with pride and a heady sense of power. That is why the usual interpretation is so harmful. Persons or groups cannot remain unspoiled by the corrupting effect of power when they are told they hold by divine right a position of superiority in which others are duty-bound to subject themselves to them.

If the husband's example is Christ, we must remind ourselves of how Christ regards and relates to the believer. Christ never compels us against our wills, never forces or coerces. There really is no basis for insisting that wives obey husbands even if it goes against their own better judgment. One minister gave the illustration that a situation may arise in which a husband and wife disagree over which physician to call when their child suddenly becomes ill. In such a case, he said, they must call the one the husband chooses. And even if the child should die, the wife must never suggest that her choice of a doctor might have saved his life.[18]

In such sermons and articles, wives are always told to adapt and adjust to their husbands. If wives don't trim their own interests and fit into their husbands' plans, it is said the marriage will be out of balance and contrary to the divine pattern. But why shouldn't husbands do some of the adjusting? Because, such speakers and writers claim, God ordained that the wife should adjust and not vice versa. "The woman was made for the man," and she should center her entire life around her husband's plans, interests, problems, work, and needs, according to this view.

To prove this point, one Christian counselor told a troubled wife to submit to her husband's wishes because the Bible makes clear that the wife should always be interested in "how [she may] please her husband" (I Cor. 7:34). He used this verse as a proof text, but he completely ignored the preceding verse which describes the married man as one who is concerned about "how to please his wife." The verses are the same, except for the mention of husband in one and wife in the other. (And even at that, their intent wasn't to spell out marital duties so much as to show that married persons sometimes find that the energy, time, and responsibilities of family life conflict with service for God.) At any rate, an equal and mutual desire of the spouses to please each other is presented in this passage as the normal situation in marriage. That a counselor would quote only the verse about *wives* is just one more indication of the bias characterizing much Christian teaching, thereby giving the impression that wives must always be the ones to defer to their spouses' wishes.

Self-actualization for women is discouraged in much Christian teaching today. Somehow women are supposed to be different from men, being able to live through someone else (husband, children) and to find their fulfillment through self-effacement and vicarious experiences rather than through direct participation in the world. When women complain about this and ask to be able to achieve as men do, they are called "selfish" and are told they are rebelling against God. Some religious leaders still seem to think in terms of the Old Testament era when wives were considered possessions. One writer speaks of what he calls "the spiritual terms that God has laid down" for a woman in which "with delight she learns the joy of knowing it is her husband's house, his home; the children are his; she is his wife."[19]

Missing in such discussions is an effort to learn what it really *means* when husbands are told to love their wives as Christ loves the church. Christ's spirit of self-sacrifice is what is emphasized in Ephesians 5. Jesus said he came not to be ministered unto, but to minister; not to be served, but to serve. He criticized the disciples for arguing about who would be the greatest, emphasizing that the first shall be last and the last shall be first. If anyone really wants to have the privileged position and stand in first place, he said, that person must be willing to be a slave—a servant rather than a ruler. The seeking of power, prestige, privilege, and position is the world's way, not God's way (cf. Matt. 20:25-28).

In spite of such clear admonitions, Christian marriage is still considered to be modeled after the pattern Jesus condemned—lording it over, seeking privilege and power, exercising authority. If a husband doesn't have natural abilities for such a position of authority and leadership—well, then the situation calls for dissimulation.

Books, articles, and sermons tell wives to *pretend* husbands are the ones who are always right, who always know best. If a wife is more gifted and intelligent and shows better judgment than her husband, she must never let on. She must arrange things so that her ideas are subtly accepted without her husband's awareness that they were not his own ideas. And husbands must always get the real credit. Christian leaders sometimes seem totally unaware of the inconsistencies in what they are saying. One woman, for example, tried to illustrate her conviction that the husband should be the head of the family by pointing to her own childhood when everyone looked up to her father. "If Papa said it, it was just as though God had said it." But in the same breath she said, "Papa did the work, and Mama ran Papa without Papa knowing it, and it was a beautiful situation."[20]

Christian articles point out that "behind every great man is a woman," but are quick to add, "yet, she is always behind and never out in front." The "masculine ego" is said to be very fragile and can be damaged severely if a wife doesn't constantly bolster it. (Could "masculine ego" be another name for "self-serving pride"?) Training for this begins early in life when girls are told to hide their intelligence if they want boys to be interested in them. Never mind the hypocrisy; it's part of the male-female game (and isn't Christian at all).

The idea that Christian husbands fulfill the instructions of Ephesians 5 by requiring their wives to be self-effacing, nonthinking servants to be ordered about and to minister constantly to husbands' comforts misinterprets Christ's attitude toward the church. In John 15, Jesus made clear to his disciples that they had reached a point where he regarded them not as servants but as friends—those with whom he could share totally all that he had received from above (John 15:15). His ministry had been directed toward bringing them to that point. He had no desire to keep them in a subservient position so that he could lord it over them and build up his ego at their expense. The aim was toward true friendship which requires a relationship of equals.

Similarly in Ephesians 4:13-16, the emphasis is on the growth of the body of Christ, the church, toward spiritual maturity—true adulthood. The husband who follows Christ's example will likewise do all in his power to help his wife in her spiritual and mental growth. He will encourage her to be a mature, fulfilled, fully developed personality. Such a husband will not force his wife into a mold that stifles her gifts, her spirit, or her personhood. Unless he has such an attitude of deep concern for his wife's freedom and growth, he is *not* loving her as Christ loves the church.

8.

LIVING IN EQUAL PARTNERSHIP

———————

Intimacy is a two-way relationship in which the partners know each other as they really are, shortcomings and all, and yet they have no fear and do not have to play games with each other because they each are accepted genuinely by the other as a person with good times and bad, highs and lows. Intimacy is having no place to hide from your partner emotionally, yet not having any need to hide. It is a warmly personal being together characterized by self-disclosure and affection . . . the experience of close, sustained familiarity with another person's inner life. . . .

Intimacy is the product of an equal-partnership marriage. Equal marriages are not always intimate, but intimate marriages are always equal.

Intimacy demands respect and trust, and you cannot respect or trust an inferior enough to share your innermost secrets.

—From Jean Stapleton and Richard Bright, *Equal Marriage*[1]

THE BIBLICAL MODEL OF LOVE MUST DETERMINE THE CONDUCT OF BOTH husband and wife within the marriage relationship. Unfortunately, some Christians like to say that the Bible instructs only husbands to love, while it directs wives to submit. But Jesus told *all* Christians— male and female—that love is the badge of discipleship. We are to love one another as Christ has loved us, and Christ loves us as the members of the Godhead love one another! (See John 13:34-35; 15:9-13; 17:26.) This is the kind of love that a husband is asked to show his wife. And this is the kind of love that a wife is asked to show her husband.

What will such a concept of marriage mean to a couple? For one thing it will eliminate the desire to dominate, exploit, or manipulate the partner in any way. Neither spouse will consider it a right to demand his or her own way. Such a concept will mean that each one will do as much as possible to help the other develop fully as God intends. This will mean sacrifices on the part of both husband and wife. Rather than view marriage as a functional arrangement with rigid roles and fixed duties assigned on the basis of sex, the couple will look upon marriage as a living relationship between two equal partners, "each for the other and both for the Lord," as an old marriage motto puts it.

But would such an egalitarian ideal destroy the model in Ephesians 5 in which the Christ-church relationship is presented as a paradigm? After all, Christ and the believer, though united in love, are not equals. Again, we must emphasize that the marriage ideal presented was intended not to exalt husbands to the position of gods or kings but rather to draw our attention to the *way* Christ loved the church. The pattern, if allowed to work itself out over history, with mutual love and delight and self-sacrifice on the part of both husband and wife, could not help moving in the direction of egalitarianism and democracy in the home.

In other words, the New Testament writers did not call for *immediate* social change in most areas. This would have only caused societal disruption, confused the issues of the gospel, and brought Christians into further conflict with the civil government as subversives and revolutionaries. Yet certain teachings when put into practice could not help laying the groundwork for the outworking of justice and love in social institutions.

Paul, for example, sent back a runaway slave to Philemon. But as we saw in our chapter on the early church, he asked Philemon to receive this new convert as a brother in Christ and as one of value "both in the flesh and in the Lord" (Philem. 16). In other words, the fugitive was to be appreciated as a person, a fellow human being, and also as a Christian. It isn't difficult to see the implications of this teaching. Once Christian masters would begin viewing slaves as persons valuable in God's sight and as sisters and brothers in Christ's family, an atmosphere would be created for recognizing an *equality* of personhood and rights.

The same principle applies to marriage. Once Christian husbands would see that they were called to follow Christ's example of self-sacrificing love, an atmosphere would be created for raising the position of women in marriage instead of "keeping them in their place." If a wife is an equal heir of grace, she is surely not intended to be treated as a servant without any rights except to fulfill her husband's demands and wishes.

To insist that marriage must be maintained as a hierarchy because otherwise the Christ-church analogy breaks down is like saying that all nations must have a monarchy because other forms of government fail to reproduce the picture of God's sovereignty over all the earth. Or to say that slavery must be maintained in order to keep us aware of what it means to be bondservants of Jesus Christ. We are not so rigid about other models in Scripture. Why should we insist on such rigidity in the institution of marriage? It is the spirit of love—self-expending love—that is the main point of Ephesians 5.

Such love means that often the wife will give in to her husband's wishes and lay aside her own interests and desires in order to assist, encourage, and build him up in every way possible. But it also means that *just as often* the husband will put aside his rights, privileges, and personal convenience in order to aid his wife. And often they will both have to make sacrifices for the sake of the children. This will mean constant adjustments from which neither partner is exempt—and many of these adjustments will be difficult.

Decision Making in Marriage

But won't there be utter chaos (or a hung jury) if two persons haven't determined in advance to settle matters according to the wishes of one who is in a position of final authority (in traditional thought, the husband)? Not necessarily. We spoke earlier of the two equal business partners in John Stuart Mill's example. Such partners work out solutions to disagreements through discussion and compromise until they can settle on an agreeable position.

There was also the example of the Roman consuls who had the power of a negative vote so that, in the case of a disagreement, the one who said *no* prevailed. In other words, *nothing* would be done on a certain issue until both agreed. This could also work in marriage with regard to issues on which the couple is deadlocked. Or the couple might work out a compromise. Or they might decide to delegate the decision to either one—perhaps the one for whom the particular matter is most salient in a given situation.

In the Roman Republic, there were three main ways that conflicts were avoided under two-man rulership. First, there was the method of *cooperation* in which joint action was taken by the two working together in harmony. Second, there was the method of *alternation of duty periods,* with one man serving as leader one month, the other the next month, and so on. Or third, they sometimes used the method of assigning *different spheres of action*—for example, one consul might be off on the battlefields running a war, while the other consul remained at home presiding over the affairs of state.

It's easy to see how similar ways of avoiding conflicts might be used in an egalitarian marriage situation. Many couples today are trying to work out ways to divide up tasks according to abilities and interests rather than roles and traditions, or to take turns in taking leadership and responsibility in certain areas, as well as looking for ways they can grow together through cooperative ventures rather than seeing all of life rigidly marked with labels of "his" and "hers." They would prefer to see the totality of marriage labeled "ours."

Division of Labor

A marriage of equal partners requires flexibility. It will mean taking a new look at traditional patterns with a view toward change. No longer is there a clear-cut demarcation between "woman's work" and "man's work." No longer can it be asserted that "woman's place is in the home" or that "God has ordained the man to be the breadwinner." To rethink such matters demands openness and maturity. Imagining and implementing the many possibilities that may arise is not an easy matter; it may even seem quite costly in many cases.

Many persons will also find such views threatening. Aren't we tampering with God's plan? Doesn't the Bible tell women to bear children while men labor for bread by the sweat of their brows (Gen. 3:16-19)? The young women addressed in Titus 2:5 are told to be "keepers at home" or "domestic." Aren't careers, child-care centers and fulfillment outside the home contrary to God's plan for women?

If we look closely at the Scriptures, we see that what is usually thought of as a divinely ordained division of labor occurred only after sin entered the world (Gen. 3). Earlier we saw that Genesis 1 makes clear that at creation God intended both parenthood and the outside occupational realm to be the shared responsibilities of both sexes. Similarly, the Book of Proverbs and other Scriptures make it clear that mothers and fathers alike have an obligation under God for the rearing of their children. Babies, growing youngsters, and teenagers all need interaction from *both* mom and dad. All family members need to be lovingly involved with one another, enriching and strengthening one another's lives. Children need to (and long to) know and enjoy both parents as persons, as unique individuals—not as rigid role-performers operating in fixed, frozen spheres.

Both parents and children are apt to find that family life takes on a new sparkle and zest when gender-role stereotypes are broken down. Dinner conversation may include mom's anecdotes about her day on the job, just as it includes accounts of the children's school adventures and dad's latest news about his work life too. If a son feels like stirring up a batch of brownies or doing needlepoint, he won't feel that he's being a "sissy" doing "woman's work." If a daughter dislikes cooking and sewing, but enjoys building furniture or repairing cars, she needn't feel she's being "unfeminine." The children grow up accepting it as completely natural that dad does the laundry, meal-planning, or vacuuming, or that mom stays up late at night studying for the courses she's taking at the university. All in all, every family member is a distinct individual, an interesting person in his or her own right. And all feel they have a responsibility to share in the smooth-running of the household, rather than push off everything onto one person.

Passages such as Titus 2:4-5 and I Timothy 5:14 must be read in context. Women in the situations described were being told to center their interests in building Christian homes so that criticism by enemies of the faith could be avoided and "the word of God may not be discredited" (Titus 2:5). In other words, the sanctity of marriage must be upheld in the midst of charges that Christianity was a sect that would undermine the home. And new converts had to learn of their great responsibilities in Christian parenthood and in other social roles in the particular society and circumstances in which they lived. This was the reason for the *Haustafeln* (lists of household duties for persons in various positions: husbands/wives; parents/children; slaves/masters), which are provided in various epistles (e.g., Eph. 5:21–6:9; Col. 3:18–4:1; I Tim. 6:1-2; Titus 2:1-10). However, to interpret these verses to mean that God's will for all women in all times requires confinement to the home is a mistake with unfortunate consequences.

A new look at male-female roles, division of labor, and spheres of activity distresses many. They prefer to think in terms of complementarity—the old separate-but-equal idea. Many Christians thus speak of a wife's being equal to her husband in personhood, but subordinate in function. This is just playing word games. Equality and subordination are contradictions. But evidently some writers and speakers are motivated by good intentions, hoping to soften a bit of the harshness and injustice of traditional teachings on wifely subjection. Therefore, equality is elevated to the spiritual realm; and on the practical, functional level of running the home, subordination becomes the rule "for the sake of order." But regardless of terminology used, this pattern cannot indicate an egalitarian marriage. True egalitarianism must be characterized by what sociologists call "role-interchangeability." *Both* spouses can fulfill the roles of breadwinner, housekeeper, encourager, career-achiever, child-trainer, and so on. Specialization according to sex disappears.

Hard decisions may be required. If both husband and wife have career commitments and one of them is asked to make a move to another geographical location, whose career will determine the place of residence? Or should they live separately and commute on weekends? Yet, for a husband and wife who love each other and see God's guidance in finding what is best for each other and for their children, difficult decisions can be worked out creatively and satisfactorily.

New ways of family living can emerge in equal-partner marriages. New approaches to the most menial household tasks may come about, with everyone pitching in to help as much as possible. If Jesus could pick up a towel and wash the disciples' feet, why can't a Christian husband in imitation of Christ's love pick up a towel and wipe the dishes? Or cook a meal as the risen Savior did on the Galilean beach? Wives can learn to handle money matters wisely as did the woman in Proverbs 31 (an asset now and an absolute necessity should one's husband die, as so many widows have found out belatedly). The older dependency image can be cast off, as wives pursue new ways of aiding their families—without fears of "losing femininity" or "damaging husbands' egos."

In all of this, a balance must be sought. *Neither* husband nor wife must get so busy that the family as a whole is neglected—spiritually, emotionally, or physically. Traditionally, the woman has been expected to be the warm center to which all family members can retreat from the hard knocks of life. If she too is out in the hubbub of the world, who will provide the refuge that makes home a place of calm and refreshment? Who will be the binder of wounds, the healer of hurts, the ego builder, the one who always understands and has a word of comfort and encouragement? Such concerns are part of what Dr. Jessie Bernard calls "the stroking or supportive function," and a woman is expected to excel at it and specialize in it, often at a tremendous cost to herself. [2] Women, too, need emotional support, appreciation of achievement, encouragement, and so on. There is no reason why husbands and wives cannot perform the stroking function for one another, rather than expect it to be one-sided. Children, too, can develop a sensitivity to the needs of other family members and learn to minister to one another. Certainly this is consistent with Christian principles (cf. I Cor. 12:25-26; Gal. 6:2; Rom. 1:12).

The Husband and Wife As Lovers

Companionship

Many people today talk about a search for warmth, intimacy, and meaningful relationships. Yet there is a suspicion that such deep soul-comradeship cannot exist within the institution of marriage, that somehow its possibilities are destroyed once a relationship is confirmed by ceremonies and legal papers. To some young people, marriage is a societal regulation that insists on rights, duties, roles, and restrictions, forcing couples into the mold of "the establishment." They therefore conclude that relationships have more possibilities for freedom and growth in living-together-out-of-wedlock arrangements. Other young adults drift into conventional marriage patterns based on notions of "romantic love" that in time evaporate, leaving the couple with only a working relationship and little experience of deep friendship with each other. Yet, it is true companionship that is the sought-after ideal today. And sometimes it is found.

Strangely, however, some people think this ideal is contrary to the Bible! One writer has even warned husbands and wives against thinking of themselves as best friends who "hang around together" as though they share an "identical social role." He goes on to say that "when their companionship leads them to share each other's emotional reactions, the effect is to feminize the man"—something that greatly disturbs the writer, Stephen B. Clark, who describes such a "feminized male" as one who has learned to care about feelings and to be gentle and "soft" in handling situations. Clark wants to see "manly" men who don't spend so much time with women and don't therefore "identify Christian virtue with feminine characteristics."[3]

Clark's anxieties over deep husband-wife companionship are a far cry from an observation in the Apocrypha. There the writer of Ecclesiasticus speaks of three things considered beautiful, heartwarming, and delightful in the sight of both God and human beings: "concord between brothers, friendship between neighbors, and a wife and husband who live happily together" (25:1 *JB*). The New English Bible translates that last phrase, "who are inseparable."

The biblical conception of marriage is a partnership, a covenant. It is an agreement freely entered in which each gives himself or herself to the other. "My beloved is mine and I am his" (Song of Sol. 2:16). The theme that sings its way through the entirety of the Song of Solomon is the utter delight of husband and wife in each other. Mutual joy, mutual love, mutual enthusiasm and pleasure spring out of every paragraph. There is a blending of spirit with spirit and body with body within the marital union.

In a marriage where the worth and dignity of each partner is recognized, there is a possibility of the highest type of companionship. There can be a sharing of common interests, an enjoyment of common pursuits, and a desire to be informed of each other's individual interests as well. Likewise, there can be a drawing upon each other's resources, advice, and help in a reciprocal manner. A couple who enjoy each other as friends can find great delight in just being together and talking, walking, reading, or listening to music, as well as in going places together. The simple things of life take on deep meaning when they are shared with a dearly loved friend—and so it should be (and can be) in the husband-wife relationship. When both partners are devoted to Christ, they can know the joy of having all aspects of marriage permeated with spiritual awareness and the vitality that grows from the shared experience of a deep relationship with God.

The couple who want an equal-partnership marriage must steer clear of manipulation and domination, each spouse instead seeking the other's good and prayerfully striving to put into effect the principles of I Corinthians 13. They must also strive to avoid falling into the stifling trap of gender-role stereotyping, which stresses differences and separate spheres, driving men and women apart rather than drawing them together. Christian marriage should be the kind of relationship that encourages both spouses to grow in Christ and to exhibit the fruit of the Spirit (Gal. 5:22-26). That kind of partnership can't help enriching the lives of both husband and wife, their children, and the lives of others with whom they come into contact day by day.

Sex and the Christian Wife

"Do most housewives and mothers really enjoy their sex life? Or is it just something they put up with?" The question came from a listener to a radio call-in program. The guest psychiatrist replied that this depended upon the maturity of the individual, because the close intimate relationship of which sex is a part is for mature individuals (as opposed to selfish, immature, ego-centered persons). This, he said, determines enjoyment—not whether a person happens to be a housewife or mother or whatever. At this point, the program's hostess interrupted. "But doesn't it depend on whether a person is a man or a woman?" she asked. Without hesitation, the psychiatrist replied, "I don't think that has anything to do with it."

Most people seem to think that has a lot to do with it. And indeed it does in many cases. This isn't due to natural, biological differences between the sexes, however, but rather stems from cultural conditioning. Many wives have grown up with the notion that "good" women shouldn't find pleasure in sex. They accepted the idea that while husbands enjoy it, wives only endure it. During the Victorian era, even medical books emphasized that high sexual drives in a woman indicated that something was wrong with her. If a wife showed too much eagerness for coitus or much enjoyment of it, husbands often became suspicious. What kind of woman was she? The myth was that only "loose" women and prostitutes liked sex, whereas women in general considered sex to be dirty, shameful, and disgusting.

Elizabeth Blackwell, the first female physician in the United States, was one of several women who was already challenging such views in the second half of the nineteenth century. Blackwell argued that the seeming lack of sexual passion characterizing many women of her time stemmed from their hearing and reading teachings that such passion was *sinful lust,* "a sin which it would be a shame for a pure woman to feel, and which she would die rather than confess." She longed to see women view their sexuality positively as a natural part of their being, created by God for the expression of love. She also wanted them to recognize its potential for drawing them close to the Creator of life through the unique privilege of bringing new lives into the world.[4]

The research of recent decades has provided unparalleled evidence showing that women have sexual interests, desires, and capabilities for expression just as men do. In particular, the Masters and Johnson laboratory research has exploded the myth of the vaginal orgasm and has shown women's tremendous capacity for sexual pleasure through clitoral stimulation.[5] Women have been shown to be capable of multiple orgasms within a short space of time—much more so than men because of their physiological makeup.

Furthermore, although a principal disagreement among married couples continues to be disagreement over frequency of sexual intercourse, we may no longer simply assume that a husband desires intercourse more often than his wife. Increasing numbers of women have reported to marriage counselors (and in research surveys) that they would prefer to engage in coitus more often than their husbands desire. Cross-cultural studies also confirm the fact that it is not "female nature" to be passive, uninterested, and incapable of sexual enjoyment. Where women have negative attitudes toward sex, those attitudes are learned—not innate.

Some women think that their negative ideas about sex stem from the Bible, but a close look at what the Scriptures really say will correct this. The overall message of the biblical writers is that God created sex and pronounced it very good (Gen. 1:27-28, 31), and marriage in all its aspects is to be regarded as a gift from God to be received with thanksgiving and sanctified by the word of God and prayer (I Tim. 4:1-5; Heb. 13:4).

God intended sex to be pleasurable for both husband and wife. Wives can be freed from many of their fears and hang-ups about sex by meditating on all the implications of that statement. Proverbs 5:18-19 speaks of the tremendous ecstasy possible in the sexual relationship of two persons united in marriage. The idea of sex play, sex pleasure, and sexual thrill is not an idea foreign to the Bible or forbidden by it. Rather, it is encouraged.

The Song of Solomon presents a beautiful picture of a husband and wife who utterly delight in each other, and who are filled with awe and wonder at the marvelous pleasure they experience in the sexual expression of their love. There is no sense of shame as they adore and explore each other's naked bodies, but rather feelings of deep delight in this gift of beauty God has created. And they don't hesitate to verbalize those feelings. (Notice the husband's adoration in Song of Sol. 4 and 7, and the bride's praise for her beloved in 5:10 ff., for example.)[6]

A Christian wife who can look upon sex in this way will find she is no longer a passive "object" acted upon, but is rather a happy participant in a creative, dynamic, beautiful adventure with her husband. Sex doesn't have to be dull, one-sided, or unimaginative; it can be an exhilarating experience. It is a way of acting out physically the inner unity of two made one flesh. It is a way of sharing oneself with the beloved, of being fused together in union and communion. All this can take place in an atmosphere of ecstatic delight in each other and with feelings of gratitude to the Creator for providing this marvelous means of expressing love.

Even the apostle Paul (so often thought to be negative about marriage and sex) sees an equality in the sexual relationship of a husband and wife. First Corinthians 7:3-5 clearly points out that both husband and wife are expected to have sexual desire and that the body of each spouse belongs to the other. (In other words, Paul doesn't lay the stress on the woman's body as her husband's possession. He speaks of reciprocity and equality.)

What are some implications of the teachings in these verses? For one thing, we see that there is nothing indecorous or immodest about a wife's approaching her husband to initiate sex relations. Whether she does this by words or gestures, she is offering herself and her love to the man she loves and who is a part of her; and she is asking for his love to be expressed in return.

Similarly, she shouldn't be afraid to explore her own body and determine the areas that bring the most pleasure, and she should feel free to tell her husband so that he can better express his love in the ways most pleasurable to her. Likewise, she should feel perfectly free and uninhibited in caressing her husband's body and learning what is most pleasing to him.

It's important for both spouses to maintain an openness of communication and not be afraid or ashamed to tell each other what they like and don't like about their sex life. This can be handled tactfully and lovingly without tearing the other person down. Many couples participate bodily in the intimacies of sex and yet feel strangely embarrassed about discussing it together verbally. So many difficulties could be overcome, and so many new joys and thrills could be experienced, if couples could only cultivate the habit of talking things over and sharing deeply and honestly their innermost feelings.

Experimentation and imagination have their place in the marriage bed. There is no one and only "right" way or "correct" technique or "proper" position. Many couples hesitate to be innovative in sex play because of misconceptions that new techniques may indicate abnormality or may be "perversions." Most marriage counselors today tell couples that anything that is pleasurable to both partners and is not emotionally or physically harmful or offensive to either one may be engaged in without guilt or shame.

The playfulness and joy of the married couple in the Song of Solomon certainly suggest that time was allowed for full bodily pleasure; there was no hurry. All five senses came into use in savoring the experience together. There were the fragrance of spices and perfumes, the sweetness of kisses, the pleasure of caresses, the hearing of endearments, the beauty of each other's bodies—all combined to bring delight in the giving and receiving of married love.

Even where such attitudes are held, however, occasional problems arise. Difficulties in the sexual side of wedded life are not unusual and shouldn't be looked upon as indications of failure. Sometimes, for example, fatigue or worry may cause one of the partners to feel like declining the other's request for a time of loving. But this can be talked over in a mature manner and shouldn't be taken as a personal affront.

A good idea is immediately to plan together a "date" for another time—the next morning or evening, for example—and arrange schedules with that in mind. It can be made something to look forward to and planned in ways designed to create a special, romantic atmosphere. For example, they might play mood music on the stereo and the wife put on her loveliest, filmy negligee. They might dim the lamps or use candles to provide a subdued lighting effect. They might take a bath or shower together or make love in a different room or before the fireplace if possible—the possibilities can extend as far as the couple's imagination. That way the "postponed" time can take on a unique aura rather than merely be a "make-up session" to hurry through in compensation for an earlier refusal.

Another problem is often the problem of privacy—particularly as the children grow older. Again, with planning, imagination, and careful arranging of schedules, couples can work out times to be alone, uninterrupted, and totally uninhibited with each other. This may mean making love at rather unusual times on occasion, but this can add zest and excitement. Innovation and flexibility are crucial in keeping the sexual side of marriage from settling into a dull, predictable routine, in which many couples complain of boredom but aren't quite sure what to do about it.

The Christian wife shouldn't hesitate to discuss any problems about sex with her husband, or with an understanding counselor if she needs further help. Husbands and wives can pray about their sex life together, just as they feel free to pray about any other area of life in which they sense a need for God's guidance and aid. Sex isn't a set-apart area of life, unrelated to one's Christian faith. It is something God has given and about which God cares.

Occasionally, one hears a fear expressed that the sex life of a couple will deteriorate if there is an equal-partnership marriage. Such a fear has no basis in fact. In his studies of self-actualizing persons, psychology researcher Abraham H. Maslow found that freedom from gender-role expectations and restrictions greatly enhanced the sexual pleasure of both women and men.[7] Sociologists Philip Blumstein and Pepper Schwartz found in their massive study of American couples that "couples who can initiate and refuse sex on an equal basis are more satisfied with their sex life."[8] Sex, after all, was not intended by God to be an act of conquest (on the part of men) and surrender (on the part of women). There is no reason for men to feel threatened by the idea of equal sexual desires and rights for women. The marriage bed isn't a battleground, a power struggle, a place to prove oneself in some sort of performance. In fact, it's not so much an *act* (at least ideally) as it is a *relationship*—an enactment of an inner union of spirits.

If wives are self-actualizing and active with regard to sex, it doesn't mean they are being aggressive. Rather, it can mean they are *expressive*, desiring to give as well as receive love; and this can be delightfully pleasant for husbands. Such an egalitarian approach to marital sex is supported by the biblical pictures we saw earlier. There we did not see only one person bringing something to the sexual relationship (or taking something from it), but we saw two whole persons, free to be themselves, and free to share themselves completely with each other in order to experience the total joys of the one-flesh relationship.

9.
WOMB-MAN

If I am asked for what purpose it behooved man to be given this help [woman], no other occurs to me as likely than the procreation of children. . . . I do not see in what way it could be said that woman was made for a help for man, if the work of childbearing be excluded.

—Augustine[1]

The feminine situation is only established . . . if the wish for a penis is replaced by one for a baby, if, that is, a baby takes the place of a penis in accordance with an ancient symbolic equivalence.

—Sigmund Freud[2]

People say I shouldn't have so many kids—especially us being so poor and all. But they just don't understand. My babies are what I live for. I never was able to get much education, and there ain't much I feel like I can do for the world—except have babies. Every time I have a new baby I get such a good, happy feeling—like I've done something really important!

—Pregnant mother of seven to social worker

In WESTERN EUROPE, AMONG TOOLS AND ART OBJECTS DATING FROM THE Upper Paleolithic Era, archaeologists have discovered an abundance of sculptured figures of pregnant women. The bodies are rotund, with enormous breasts and greatly swollen abdomens. Each head is a mere sphere, lacking eyes, ears, nose, mouth, and hair. Sociologist Gerhard Lenski comments: "Most scholars think it is no coincidence that the artist ignored the facial features and devoted all of his attention to the symbols of fertility."[3]

For many concerned women, these fertility figurines symbolize what the "woman problem" is all about. Women have so often been viewed as "sex objects"—faceless creatures (or at least, mindless ones) whose one function in life is to mate and bear children.

Yet, the ancients didn't see this as degrading at all. They thought woman's reproductive capabilities marked her off as possessing special *mana* ("supernatural power"). A mixture of awe and fear characterized their feelings about the birth process. A tiny, living human being could come out of a woman; surely she must be linked with magic forces!

How did such veneration of woman-as-reproducer affect woman's actual status in society? Opinions vary. Some writers cite evidence indicating deep reverence for women as "priestesses of nature" equipped with special ability to affect agricultural productivity. The fertility cults worshiped female deities and had women as well as men who performed priestly functions. John Langdon-Davies suggests that mother-goddess worship is "the logical outcome of woman's chief claim to power, of her one gift which no man can share with her."[4]

Since woman's childbearing powers were thought to influence productivity of fields, woodlands, and livestock, she was given the task of cultivating the land. To ancient people "Mother Earth" was the cosmic model that human mothers mirrored. Out of the earth's fecund womb sprang life-sustaining food, but sometimes that womb was closed and the people suffered. Women understood such things. They seemed to be at one with the earth; surely they would be able to coax fruitfulness from its stubborn, barren soil. Therefore, for magico-religious reasons (not because men were forcing them to become drudges), women took over horticultural tasks. In societies that stress this close connection between women and agriculture, matriarchal systems of social organization are not uncommon.[5]

Some authors argue that although woman's procreative functions call forth male awe and worship, these same powers may make men resentful and envious. Langdon-Davies refers to the theory that men seek to compensate for their inability to bear children by being creative in other ways—by becoming "pregnant in soul" and bearing "children of the mind," giving birth to ideas, as stated for example in Plato's *Symposium*.[6]

A comparable view is presented by psychoanalyst Karen Horney who suggests that "our entire culture bears the masculine imprint" because man, filled with admiration for woman's reproductive capabilities, has set about to create in other ways to make up for the childbearing powers denied him. She credits the male sex for "essentially" producing government, religion, art, and science.[7]

Reasoning along similar lines, Ashley Montagu goes so far as to suggest that male jealousy led ancient man to mimic female bodily functions at the cost of great suffering. Among some nonliterate peoples, men go through ceremonies that seem to imitate pregnancy, childbirth, and even menstruation. Some tribes require boys at puberty to enter some type of artificial womb from which they emerge as "newborn" *men*. In other tribes, men go aside to be ceremonially delivered of stones. Subincision (cutting the underside of the penis) and periodically induced bleeding are practiced by some tribes, and Montagu sees this as an imitation of female menstruation.

For him, even taboos imposed on women are rooted in male envy. Jealous over women's ability to have monthly periods and babies, men have reacted by forcing women into ceremonial regulations that are both handicaps and punishments.[8]

Taking issue with such views is H. R. Hays, whose studies in anthropology and social psychology cause him to doubt men's alleged envy of women's reproductive functions. Disagreeing with Montagu, Hays points out that periodic bloodletting occurs in only a few cultures, whereas the idea that menstrual blood is dangerous and to be avoided by men seems almost universal.[9]

Margaret Mead provides a balanced viewpoint by showing that either sex may envy the other. In Western cultures, man's achievements are praised and woman's role is depreciated. Anthropologists, however, have discovered other societies where woman's role is the one revered, envied, and imitated.[10] But where the role of woman is extolled, it is always her role as life-bearer that is meant.

Women and Reproduction in the Old Testament

In many respects, Hebrew customs surrounding women's sexual functions did not differ markedly from those of neighboring cultures. As Max Weber pointed out, marriage was viewed as a means of producing children and of providing economic security for women.[11]

However, Israel stood apart from other nations in that it had no fertility rites. There were times in the nation's history when it did slip into such practices and had to be called to repentance, but the people knew that Yahweh was a jealous God who would not tolerate idolatry. God commanded the Israelites to have nothing to do with "the gods of the peoples . . . round about" (Deut. 6:13-14). Who were these forbidden deities? Gods and goddesses common to agricultural societies where fruitfulness of fields, flocks, and the human womb is desired above all else. Phallic cults flourished, images of genital organs were set up, and ritual prostitution and ceremonial orgies were incorporated into pagan worship. But Israel was to stand apart and worship only Yahweh.

Motherhood Extolled

If followers of fertility religions revered woman as the giver of new life, what about Israel, where such worship was forbidden? Was a woman's childbearing ability viewed with wonder and appreciation there too? Very definitely. Large families were considered blessings from God (Ps. 127:3-5). To give birth meant honor and rejoicing for the mother. As Leah announced upon Zebulun's birth, "Now my husband will treat me in princely style, because I have borne him six sons" (Gen. 30:20 NEB). An abundance of children signified God's approval (Ps. 128:3-4). Conversely, sterility was seen as a disgrace—a sign that God's favor had been withheld. Therefore, when a woman conceived after long years of barrenness, she was apt to exclaim joyfully, "The Lord has taken away my reproach among men!" (e.g., see Gen. 30:23; Luke 1:25).

Yet woman's procreative abilities were not linked with strange, mystical female powers, as in the minds of fertility worshipers. Israel looked to God alone as the giver of life. Only God could bring the increase of "the fruit of your body, and the fruit of your ground, and the fruit of your beasts" (Deut. 28:4). God alone was trusted for bountiful harvests and flourishing fields (Ps. 104:14). It was to Yahweh that prayers were uttered for the fecundity of animals (Ps. 144:13-14). And it was God alone who could affect fertility in women, giving "the barren woman a home, making her the joyous mother of children. Praise the Lord!" (Ps. 113:9).

Thus, when Rachel echoed the cry of longing common to all Israelite wives, "Give me children, or I shall die!" her husband Jacob was understandably disturbed. "Am I in the place of God, who has withheld from you the fruit of the womb?" he replied (Gen. 30:1-2). Jacob himself and his twin brother Esau had been born in answer to their father Isaac's prayer for his barren wife (Gen. 25:21), even as Isaac too had been the child of God's promise, born to Abraham and Sarah in their old age.

Understanding of Reproductive Processes

Although the knowledge of the facts of reproduction were necessarily limited during this stage of human history, the Israelites did not think that women brought forth children magically through their own powers, nor were they unaware of the association between sexual intercourse and pregnancy. A husband *knew* his wife (had sex relations with her), and she conceived and brought forth a child. (Some writers have suggested that many ancient peoples did not see this connection, and this explains their awesome respect for the mystery of woman's fertility.)

On the other hand, there is no evidence that the Hebrew people thought of the child as the product of the father alone. This contrasted with the widespread ancient belief that a baby was engendered exclusively by the male, the wife's body being merely the "field" in which the husband planted his seed so that in time *his* child would be produced. Such a notion is seen in the sacred writings of Hinduism ("This woman has come like living soil: sow seed in her, ye men!"[12]) and Islam ("Your women are as fields for you"[13]).

Ancient Greek authors expressed the same idea. Sophocles describes the anguish of Oedipus upon discovering that he had unknowingly married his own mother. He cries out in horror about "this mother's womb, this field of double sowing whence I sprang and where I sowed my children!"[14] And in Aeschylus's *Eumenides,* when Orestes is brought to trial for avenging his father's death by murdering his mother, the god Apollo tells the jury that matricide is not so terrible a crime as they may think. Why? Because only the father is the actual parent; the mother is "but the nurse of the new-planted seed that grows."[15]

In Hebrew tradition, however, mothers were not viewed as mere incubators. There are references to *seed* to be sure, and in Genesis 38:9 the meaning is clearly "semen." But the usual meaning of the word is "offspring," "children," "descendants." There is no clear-cut agricultural analogy here as in the examples from other cultures. Most of the Scripture references speak of seed with regard to the father (since lineage through the male was emphasized in a patriarchal society), but Genesis 3:15 speaks of the seed of the woman. There are references to woman's conceiving seed (Num. 5:28 KJV) and to the "godly seed" of both husband and wife (Mal. 2:15 KJV). Israelite children were expected to give equal honor to both parents. Indeed, as the commandment is recorded in Leviticus 19:3, the mother is mentioned first.

God, in covenant with Abraham, said, "I will make you exceedingly fruitful; and I will make nations of you, and kings shall come forth from you" (Gen. 17:6). But Sarah's part was equally important, for God said, "I will bless her, . . . and she shall be a mother of nations; kings of peoples shall come from her" (Gen. 17:16). Eventually, there developed the tradition in Judaism that a child is not a Jew unless born of a Jewish mother, thus placing the primary stress on the *mother's* role in reproduction.

Commenting on Genesis 4:1, a rabbi of the last century describes how Eve might have felt when Cain was born. No doubt other Israelite women had similar feelings upon giving birth: *"And she said, I have gotten a man from the Lord.* I have gotten a child *with* God. God Himself created us, but now I and my husband have also a share in the child; for *three* have a part in a child; the father, the mother, and God, He gives the soul."[16]

The writers of the Old Testament did not understand the science of embryology, but they never ceased to wonder at the way a child was formed in the uterus. "As you do not know how the spirit comes to the bones in the womb of a woman with child, so you do not know the work of God who makes everything" (Eccles. 11:5).

> For thou didst form my inward parts,
> thou didst knit me together in my mother's womb.
> I praise thee, for thou art fearful and wonderful.
> Wonderful are thy works! (Ps. 139:13-14).

Taboos Associated with Woman's Sexual Functions

If a woman's status and worth were measured by her ability to bear children (cf. I Sam. 1:2, 6), and if childbirth was so highly regarded in ancient Israel, why then did such strict taboos, cleansing ceremonies, and sacrifices surround a woman's sexual functions?

We must keep in mind that the Israelite conception of ceremonial defilement was related to *cultic worship,* which in the words of de Vaux refers to "all those acts by which communities or individuals give outward expression to their religious life, by which they seek and achieve contact with God."[17] Cultic worship involved fixed rules, regulations, and rituals, and a rigid division between what was considered to be "clean" and "unclean."

The God of Israel was a *holy* God and must be approached in just the right way. To come before God while ritually unclean would be viewed as an affront to God's majesty and purity. Therefore, a person in a condition of defilement was cut off from the life of the cult and not permitted to participate in its worship until he or she underwent the prescribed rites of purification. Again, as de Vaux makes clear, ceremonial impurity should not be thought of as physical or moral defilement. It is rather a "state" or "condition" out of which a person must emerge in order to reenter the normal life of the religious community.[18]

Such ritual impurity was considered contagious and transferable to anyone or anything the affected person touched. It is interesting to note the states that were considered unclean: childbirth (Lev. 12), leprosy (Lev. 13 and 14), discharges from the sexual organs of both males and females, including not only disorders but also normal menstruation and emissions of semen (Lev. 15), and touching a dead body (Num. 19). Some Christian commentators see here an association with the idea of original sin and the Fall, since the states of ceremonial uncleanness relate to the propagation of human life in a sinful world, the ordeal of suffering and disease, and humanity's greatest enemy death—all of which could imply a connection with Genesis 3:16-19. Other scholars consider such interdicts to be vestiges of primitive beliefs and customs common to many ancient cultures.

Menstruation

Notice that two of the states of ceremonial pollution affected only women. Certain persons were forced to be set apart periodically simply because they had been born female. Every woman from the age of puberty onward would be considered unclean during her menstrual period each month and for seven days afterward (Lev. 15:19, 25, 28)—unless she were pregnant, in which case an even longer period of ceremonial uncleanness followed the birth of the child.

William Graham Cole warns against calling this discrimination against women, since an emission of semen from a man rendered him unclean also. A male, however, was considered unclean for only one day (Lev. 15:16), whereas female contamination lasted more than a full week. Why the disparity? The simplest explanation would seem to be the difference in duration of the two discharges. However, Cole suggests other possible reasons: (1) a patriarchal society's bias which would assign greater impurity to the sexual discharges of a female's body than those of a male, (2) the general awe, fear, and reverence of the Hebrews with regard to blood, or (3) a simple economic factor because a man couldn't afford to give so much of his time to purification rites.[19]

One might wonder how a woman could afford such time either! Probably she had a large family to look after. Yet, not only was *she* considered unclean all week, but so was anyone who touched her (even the tiny toddler clutching at her skirt?), as well as anything on which she had lain or sat. If someone happened to touch her bed or something on which she sat, that person was required to wash his clothes, take a bath, and even then was considered ritually unclean the rest of the day. (Similar rules were in effect for men who had certain kinds of discharges that were evidently infectious—Lev. 15:1-15. Possibly gonorrhea is being discussed here.)

Why did these customs regarding menstruation become part of Israel's religion? What was their significance? Were they mere superstitions similar to those of other peoples? Or did they mean something quite different? There are no easy answers, and opinions vary.

The phenomenon of periodic bleeding in women has been a source of wonder and mystery throughout history. In fact, even though the process is now well understood, there are still elements of mystery surrounding menstruation; and some physiologists are at present questioning its value—even going so far as to call it a "biologic failure." By this they mean that the reproductive processes of many animals are accomplished in a way similar to those of human females, yet without menstruation. Only among humans, monkeys, and apes is menstruation found.[20]

Be that as it may, women *do* menstruate. This has given rise to numerous beliefs and customs in different cultures. Some primitive groups associated menstruation with the moon's phases and the ebb and flow of the tides, even suggesting that the moon was female and was "having her sickness" when she waned. Many groups keep women totally isolated during menstruation. The ancient *Natural History of Pliny* attributes the blighting of crops, the rusting of iron, and the killing of bees to the presence of menstruating women. Some cultures forbid a menstruating woman to handle food, believing that her cooking would make food spoil and milk turn sour. Certain tribes associate menstruation with evil spirits.

The ancient Greeks took the idea of uncleanness literally and thought a woman's body needed periodic purging to be rid of impurities and poisons. They called the menstrual period "the katharsis." Similar ideas are found in the traditions of India.

No such beliefs surrounded Hebrew customs regarding menstruation. No explanation was suggested for this female bodily process; it was simply accepted as a given. The Talmud, however, does associate it with the curse upon Eve,[21] and the euphemism, "the curse," is still applied to menstruation by many women. *Why* God should demand the rituals surrounding this natural function is likewise not explained in the Bible. There is no indication of an association between these rites and notions of fertility, as in Hindu traditions where the ten days after menstruation began were viewed as the woman's *rtu* ("fertile period") and therefore called for sexual intercourse to take place immediately upon the cessation of the flow.[22]

Nor are the ceremonies of Leviticus 15 considered "magic cures" of some sort, as in other religions. Rather, purification ceremonies were performed *after* the unclean condition had ceased.

The Israelite taboo regarding menstruation seems to have been bound up with ideas of ceremonial purity as demanded by God and the concepts of holiness that God required. Anthropologist Mary Douglas suggests that the Levitical laws about pollution, taboo, and purification make little sense unless we try to grasp how the Hebrew mind conceived of holiness.[23] It meant much more than justice and moral goodness in this society. Kind and humane treatment of one's neighbor may have formed part of the notion of holiness, but the concept embraced a great deal more.

Although at its root *holiness* means "to be set apart for God," it also referred to wholeness—to the idea of physical perfection, completion. Sacrificial animals had to be blemish-free. Men with physical defects could not serve as priests. Even in the social sphere, completeness was important; tasks and schemes had to be finished so that a new totality could come into being.

In addition to holiness as "set-apartness" and "wholeness", Douglas mentions a third aspect—"right order." Certain classes of things must not be confused or commingled; there must be separation (cf. Deut. 22:9-11). Any deviation from wholeness or perfection, and anything that deviated from right order, fell into the category of "unclean." Defilement required separation; otherwise God's blessing would be withheld. However, when wholeness was restored, the separation ended. Special ceremonies reinstated the person into the religious community.

If we accept Douglas's explanation of the rituals of Leviticus, it may be that a woman's periodic isolation symbolized that her body was temporarily not whole and therefore could not properly mirror the holy. Blood flowing from her vagina seemed to signify something out of place, out of order.

Another possible key to understanding Israelite menstrual taboos lies in the Hebrew attitude toward blood. Other nations, in connection with fertility rites, ate and drank blood; Israel was expressly forbidden to do so. Israel was a separated people, and separation from blood—except in the sacred context of the sacrifice where it was sprinkled upon the altar of God—was one of the marks of such separation. Not that blood was considered vile and evil. It was viewed with awe and wonder as the source of *life* and the means of atonement (Lev. 17:11). Therefore, special taboos surrounded blood.

By extension, special taboos began to surround women. In later Judaism, for example, there arose a prohibition about touching women. If a merchant counted out money into a woman's palm, he must be especially cautious. She just might be having her period, and her contamination would pass on to him, making him ceremonially defiled.

Sexual intercourse during the menstrual period was especially singled out for condemnation under Israel's ceremonial law. Perhaps the mildest denunciation is given in Leviticus 15:24, where the man "defiled" by the woman's impurity must, like her, observe seven days of uncleanness. The message of Leviticus 20:18 is much stronger: "If a man lies with a woman having her sickness . . . he has made naked her fountain, and she has uncovered the fountain of her blood; both of them shall be cut off from among their people" (implying exile, possibly even death, according to some Bible scholars). In Ezekiel 18:5-6, one of the indications of a righteous man was his avoidance of a woman "in her time of impurity." These ceremonial rules do not imply that intercourse during menstruation and the specified days thereafter is *inherently evil* in God's sight. They must be viewed in connection with other Israelite rituals intended for a specific nation at a specific time. This particular rule may have even involved humane considerations, allowing Israelite women the freedom to say no to their husbands at a time of discomfort.

In this regard, it should be noted that among certain observant Jews today, the family purity rules are believed to contribute to marital happiness and stability. Rabbi Maurice Lamm, for example, has written:

"Absence makes the heart grow fonder." The laws of *niddah* [Hebrew word for "menstruating woman"], which demand total physical and sexual withdrawal from one another during twelve days following menstruation, impose a rhythm of passivity and activity, scarcity and availability, passionate fervor and disciplined withdrawal. After this period, there is almost a reenactment of the honeymoon, and the revitalizing of the pursuit and discovery of romantic love.

He points out that this is the reason observant Jewish homes have separate beds, rather than a double one, for husband and wives.[24]

Other Jewish leaders disagree with this viewpoint and point out the extremes to which the laws segregating menstruating women have been carried throughout history. Rabbi Roland Gittelsohn refers to the writings of the thirteenth-century Jewish scholar Nachmanides, who insisted on total avoidance of any kind of contact with a menstruating woman—not even walking on ground on which she had walked. Nachmanides prohibited a physician from even taking his wife's pulse during the woman's menstrual period. Gittelsohn believes that the *niddah* laws and traditions have no positive contribution to make to the modern world because they fail to treat menstruation as the natural bodily process it is. In counseling on love, sex, and marriage, Gittelsohn writes that the menstruating woman "is no more to be shunned or avoided than a person with a nosebleed."[25]

In the Old Testament, since the life of the flesh was considered to be in the blood, blood upon the altar was revered, "for it is the blood that makes atonement, by reason of the life" (Lev. 17:11). Blood upon a menstrual cloth, however, was an altogether different matter; such blood was despised. Again, perhaps there was the thought of something out of place. Blood lost from the body meant that the body was out of order and not in a state of wholeness (and therefore "holiness"). In another sense, menstrual blood may have symbolized *death* because it signifies the passing from the body of an unfertilized ovum which could have been a potential new life if pregnancy had occurred.[26] At any rate, the ceremonial uncleanness of menstruation became a favorite analogy for the pollution of sin—especially in the prophetic writings. Thus we read, "Ye shall defile also the covering of thy graven images of silver, and the ornament of thy molten images of gold: thou shalt cast them away as a menstruous cloth; thou shalt say unto it, Get thee hence" (Isa. 30:22 KJV).

Similar imagery occurs in Isaiah 64:6, although the English translations are usually less vivid ("All our righteousnesses are as filthy rags," KJV—or "like a polluted garment," RSV). The defilement of a menstruous woman was used to portray the revolting vileness of a sinful condition in God's sight. Ezekiel describes God's judgment on Israel: "Their conduct before me was like the uncleanness of a woman in her impurity" (Ezek. 36:17). In Jeremiah's lamentation over fallen Jerusalem, he describes the city as "a menstruous woman" (Lam. 1:17 KJV), with the idea being that of something "filthy" (RSV).

Modern women who think of menstruation as a normal bodily process are understandably disturbed in reading such passages. But we must remember what the Israelites were expected to learn from their ceremonial regulations, namely, that the people of God were to be holy as God is holy. They were taught through object lessons which emphasized completeness or perfection. A sinful nation that turned from God was like a diseased body—unwell, not whole. Isaiah described God's people as a sick and wounded human body in need of healing and cleansing (Isa. 1:5ff.). The nation could not know God's blessing unless it was in a state of health. (Our own word *health* comes from the Old English word *hale* which means "whole.")

Each time a woman menstruated and was required to go through the prescribed ceremonies, she was symbolizing this concept of holiness. The taboos meant a great deal of bother and inconvenience and were probably just as annoying to the Hebrew women as they are today in tribes with similar regulations, where women complain that the rules disrupt life and slow down work schedules terribly.[27]

Childbirth

Leviticus 12 describes regulations surrounding the second condition of ceremonial uncleanness for women, childbirth. Upon reading the chapter, we can't help asking two questions: Why did having a baby make a woman unclean and require a sacrificial offering? And why did giving birth to a *daughter* demand a double period of purification?

Purification for Mothers

Scholars have suggested many possible reasons for the placement of a postparturient woman in the category of uncleanness. Since the baby is not said to be unclean, but only the mother, the purification requirement may have something to do with bodily discharges associated with childbirth and a short time afterward. The taboos surrounding blood and the general cultic significance of ceremonial purity once again offer the most plausible explanation. The woman's body needed time to be restored to wholeness; until then, the state of ceremonial uncleanness prevailed.

Others have suggested that the long period of being set apart was simply out of consideration for the new mother's health—similar to the lying-in period for maternity cases which persisted in our own culture until comparatively recent times. However, the emphasis on not touching any hallowed thing and the prohibition against entering the sanctuary indicate that the reasons behind the ritual were primarily religious rather than hygienic.

Some commentators see something more here than ceremonial taboos connected with bodily discharges. They point out that the woman was commanded to bring a burnt offering and a sin offering (Lev. 12:6-8) and conclude that this refers to the doctrine of original sin. In this view, the sacrifice is necessary because a woman has brought another sinner into the world. However, such offerings were also required in cases other than childbirth where bodily health was somehow not in a normal state (see Lev. 14:10-32; 15:13-15, 25-30).

In Genesis 3:16, God told the woman, "I will greatly multiply your

151

pain in childbearing; in pain you shall bring forth children." The Talmud interprets this to mean that ten curses came upon Eve, menstruation and the travail of childbirth being two of them.[28] Rabbis explained the requirement of sacrificial offerings by saying that a woman was likely to sin in a specific way while bearing an infant, and this must be atoned for. What "specific way" did they have in mind? The regrets a woman might voice during the pangs of labor—perhaps similar to Rebekah's anguished cry when her twins were to be born (Gen. 25:22). In particular, argued the rabbis, a woman on the birthstool might swear impetuously that she would never again have intercourse with her husband if this is what comes of it! Thus, she would have to make a sacrifice for having spoken such a foolish vow.[29]

Among Christians who have interpreted Leviticus 12 to relate to the taint of humankind's ongoing sinfulness, transmitted through birth, was S. H. Kellogg, who wrote in *The Expositor's Bible:* "The extreme evil of the state of sin into which the first woman, by that first sin, brought all womanhood, is seen most of all in this, that now woman, by means of those powers given her for good and blessing, can bring into the world only a child of sin."[30] He went on to say that apparently childbirth shows the operation of the curse in its most conspicuous form, and thus women had to be barred from the tabernacle worship for an extended period.

There is one final interpretation sometimes suggested to explain the childbirth offerings. Could these sacrifices have been offered in thanksgiving to God for a safe delivery and for the gift of the child? Such a notion was incorporated into the old custom of certain segments of Christendom where "the churching of women" was required after childbirth, bringing women back into the fellowship of the church. (However, even the churching custom may merely reflect a later development of ancient taboos of restoration to community following a condition of uncleanness.)

Double Purification for Girl Babies

If a woman gave birth to a daughter, the purification period was twice as long as when a son was born. In a strongly misogynistic statement, S. H. Kellogg again saw the explanation in relation to original sin: "[The ritual] teaches us that not only has the curse thus fallen on the woman, but that, because she is herself a sinful creature, she can only bring forth another sinful creature like herself; and if a daughter, then a daughter inheriting all her own peculiar infirmities and disabilities."[31] The implication is that by bringing another female into the world, she has increased the likelihood of the continuation of the curse, because this child too will one day bear the uncleanness of menstruation and childbirth. "Because 'first in the transgression,' " Kellogg wrote, "[woman] is under special pains and penalties in virtue of her sex."

Others feel that the prolonged uncleanness after a daughter's birth was more a matter of social custom than of theology. Cole calls it "the prejudice of a patriarchal society."[32] And Hays points out that the longer period of purification after the birth of a female was a practice by no means confined to the Israelites. Such a custom has been practiced in India, New Guinea, within West African tribes, and among the Cree Indians of North America.[33]

Sons were clearly more highly valued and desired than daughters in Hebrew culture. As de Vaux notes, sons were wanted to "perpetuate the family line and fortune and to preserve the ancestral inheritance."[34] Girls, on the other hand, grew up, married, and joined their husbands' families. The strength of a household was measured by the number of sons.

The Apocrypha provides further clues to the Israelite preference for boys. Daughters seemed to be just too much bother!

> A daughter is a secret anxiety to her father,
> and the worry of her keeps him awake at night;
> when she is young, for fear she may grow too old to marry,
> and when she is married, for fear she may lose her husband's love;
> when she is a virgin, for fear she may be seduced
> and become pregnant in her father's house,
> when she has a husband, for fear she may misbehave,
> and after marriage, for fear she may be barren (Ecclus. 42:9-10 NEB).

The passage goes on to warn fathers that "headstrong" daughters could put the family to shame, and therefore girls must be closely watched. Added to the inconvenience of keeping daughters in line was the notion that females were inherently evil as compared to males. "Better a man's wickedness than a woman's goodness; it is woman who brings shame and disgrace" (Ecclus. 42:14 NEB).

No wonder the Talmud explains the prolonged period of purification for female births by referring again to a woman's probable rash vow to avoid future sex relations with her husband! The rabbis wrote: "On the birth of a male with whom all rejoice she regrets her oath after seven days, but on the birth of a female about whom everybody is upset, she regrets her oath after fourteen days."[35]

In addition to the *theological* reasons suggested for this custom (in particular, the idea of a woman's part in perpetuating original sin) and *cultural* reasons (the preference for sons in a patriarchal society), there was a third category—attempted *physiological* explanations.

According to one ancient notion, a greater physical derangement occurred within a woman's reproductive system if she gave birth to a girl, and the effects of this disorder took longer to pass away. Along this same line of thought, the Talmud suggests that the "fashioning" of a female occurred after eighty days in the uterus, whereas the male body was formed forty days after conception; the periods of uncleanness corresponded to this.[36]

Some rabbis also advanced a rather fascinating theory of obstetrics. They said that the mother's pain was much worse when giving birth to a female child. Why? Because "the female emerges in the position she assumes during intercourse and the male emerges in the position he assumes during intercourse. The former, therefore, turns her face upwards [the turning intensifying the pains of the mother] while the latter need not turn his face."[37]

Panos D. Bardis refers to an old Israelite belief that girls were inferior because they were thought to originate in the supposedly weaker and smaller left testicle, whereas boys were thought to come from the right one.[38] However, the Midrash indicates a belief that a child was produced by both parents, the infant's sex being determined by the parent of the opposite sex. "If the woman provides the seed," wrote the rabbis, "she bears a manchild. A female, on the other hand, is formed from the seed of the male."[39] Gittelsohn refers to an interesting variation on this point. Some rabbis taught that the sex of the child depended on whether the husband or wife *first experienced orgasm* during sexual intercourse at the time the child was conceived. If the wife was first to experience orgasm, a boy would result, whereas a girl would be born if the husband had been the first to reach sexual climax. While acknowledging the sexism in the preference for sons, Gittelsohn writes that this teaching had a practical effect that was positive for wives. "In short, if a man wanted a son," he explains, "he had better attend to the sexual needs of his wife!"[40]

Modern medical science, of course, explodes the attempted physiological explanations for the rules that considered women to be unclean for a longer period after a daughter was born. We are left then with the harshly misogynistic implications of the theological view that emphasizes female nature as the carrier of original sin—so that girl babies are seen as little Pandoras or tiny Eves who will bring more trouble to the world and must be "welcomed" with a longer period of ceremonial defilement. Or else we must simply accept the likelihood that boys were more desired in the patriarchy of Israel, and therefore the time of purification was cut in half out of joy that a woman had brought a manchild into the world.

Before leaving the subject of how the Old Testament viewed woman-as-childbearer, we must remind ourselves that despite many of the negative practices discussed, there was a real sense of wonder at the phenomenon of birth and a high estimation of motherhood. The overall picture of woman as the bringer of new life into the world is not one of degradation, but rather of appreciation. Despite the difficult and discriminatory passages examined (and there is the possibility that many of these customs, laws, and taboos originally reflected awe and reverence for woman's special place rather than attempts to put her down), it seems clear that the command to "be fruitful and multiply" was taken seriously in Old Testament times. The designation of Eve as "the mother of all living" (Gen. 3:20) was not considered an insult but a term of high esteem. To be a mother of many children was the highest honor known to the Old Testment woman. Reproduction, with all its attendant joys and sorrows, was regarded as her destiny simply by having been born a member of the female sex. In the culture of Israel, motherhood was both a divine duty and a happy privilege. It was the barren woman who was to be pitied, for she had no children to "rise up and call her blessed" (Prov. 31:28).

New Testament Attitudes Toward Motherhood

We notice a shift in attitudes when we reach the New Testament. Some theologians explain it by the fact that the Child—the Savior, Redeemer, Messiah, the One whom Jewish mothers had hoped to bear—had already come. The seed of the woman had already entered the world to crush the serpent's head (Gen. 3:15).

At any rate, there was a gradual move away from the implication that reproduction is a woman's most important contribution to the world. A woman's status and self-worth no longer depended upon the number of children she produced. The emphasis changed from physical birth to spiritual birth—entrance into the family of God through faith in Jesus Christ. Membership in God's household, the church or community of believers, was valued above human family ties. Even singleness for the sake of the kingdom of God was highly regarded. This had special significance for women because, under traditional Israelite cultural norms, to be unmarried (or married but childless) was a deep misfortune if not an actual disgrace.[41]

Thus, the New Testament has little to say about woman as womb-man. There is neither the awe nor the mixture of both revulsion and reverence observed in portions of the Old Testament as well as other cultures. This aspect of woman's life is largely ignored in the New Testament, with but a few exceptions.

Perhaps the verse with the most difficulties is I Timothy 2:15: "Yet woman will be saved through bearing children, if she continues in faith and love and holiness, with modesty." The un-Pauline view of salvation here (by childbearing rather than through faith) is one reason some Bible scholars conclude that this epistle was not written by Paul but by his later followers. Even if one attempts interpretations other than the idea that having babies is efficacious for securing eternal salvation, the passage continues to be obscure and puzzling.

Some Christians interpret the verse to mean that a woman is saved "through *the* Childbearing," that is, the Savior's entrance into the world through a woman (Gal. 4:4). To others, the verse means that a faithful Christian woman will be delivered through the ordeal of giving birth to children, despite the effects of the curse pronounced upon Eve. One problem with this last view has to do with the committed Christian woman who dies in childbirth. Is the verse implying that she has not continued "in faith, love, holiness, and modesty"? Should others conclude that God has punished her by failing to deliver her through the anguish of giving birth? Such a notion hardly fits with New Testament theology and would offer little comfort to the grieving husband.

Another passage in the same epistle (I Tim. 5:14) also stresses childbearing as a worthy activity for women, with the context in this case hinting that having babies would keep troublesome, meddlesome women at home and out of mischief.

Interestingly, in discussions of the marriage bed (Heb. 13:4) and sexual relations between husband and wife (I Cor. 7:3-4), there is no reference to procreation. There is, of course, no negation of the Jewish idea that children should be regarded as gifts of God. And the New Testament epistles provide exhortations on nurturing children in the fear and discipline of the Lord, instructing them in the faith (e.g., Eph.6:1-4). Children born of a mixed marriage (between a Christian and a nonbeliever) were not considered unclean, but holy, by virtue of the believing partner (cf. I Cor. 7:14). Spiritual analogies to childbirth and child care are made in the New Testament, just as in the Old Testament (e.g., Gal. 4:19; I Thess. 2:7).

The Gospels record the births of John the Baptizer and Jesus, and the customs and attitudes of Old Testament Judaism are seen in their mothers. Elizabeth speaks of God's goodness in "removing her reproach" (childlessness). The cousins visit together during pregnancy and exult in the joy of their approaching motherhood (Luke 1:39ff.). Neighbors and kinsfolk gather to celebrate John's birth, circumcision, and naming (Luke 1:57ff.). Mary, the mother of Jesus, fulfills the Levitical law of purification after childbirth, bringing the sacrifices of a family able to afford only the simple offering required of those in poverty (Luke 2:22-24; cf. Lev. 12:8).

Although Jesus certainly honored his mother and cared about her welfare (even as he was dying on the cross), he was never sentimental about the virtues of childbearing. When a woman yelled out from one of the crowds, "Blessed is the womb that bore you, and the breasts that you sucked!" (Luke 11:27), Jesus did not seize upon the occasion as a unique opportunity for a Mother's Day sermon. Instead, he showed that a woman is not honored in God's sight according to her possession and use of reproductive equipment, but rather by her performance of the will of God.

A similar thought is expressed in Matthew 12:46ff. There, when Jesus is told that his mother and brothers are seeking him (presumably because of spreading rumors that he had taken leave of his senses), Jesus replies that his *followers* are his family. Again, the shift is away from the human family unit to the larger family of God.[42]

Jesus empathized with mothers, having deep compassion for those who would be pregnant or nursing infants at their breasts during the prophesied destruction of Jerusalem (Matt. 24:19). And as he walked the painful steps of the Via Dolorosa, he turned to the weeping women who watched and said, "Daughters of Jerusalem, do not weep for me, but weep for yourselves and for your children. For behold, the days are coming when they will say, 'Blessed are the barren, and the wombs that never bore, and the breasts that never gave suck!' " (Luke 23:28-29).

Jesus loved children, and when mothers brought them to him he welcomed them warmly. But the many unmarried women who followed him were just as warmly appreciated and honored.

Earlier in this book, we looked at Jesus' compassion and concern for the woman who by faith touched his garment because she believed he could heal her from the vaginal bleeding that had plagued her for twelve years. It took courage for her to disregard the fact that the Levitical law called her unclean. Yet Jesus did not shrink from her, as would have been the normal reaction of the rabbis of that day. The entrance of Jesus Christ into the world brought an end to the ceremonial laws that applied to women, just as his coming brought about the end of dietary laws, other rules, and the rituals of animal sacrifice (Heb. 9:9-11; 10:1, 9).

A concluding indication of Jesus' attitude toward the childbearing function of women is seen in John 16:21. There Jesus used the analogy of childbirth in speaking of his disciples' sorrow in view of his coming departure. He wanted them to know that their sadness would give way to greater joy than ever before, for they would see him again as the risen Lord! "When a woman is in travail she has sorrow," Jesus said, "because her hour has come; but when she is delivered of the child, she no longer remembers the anguish, for joy that a child is born into the world."

The statement is realistic (there *is* pain), but it is positive. No negative statements are made about the curse of Eve, the punishment that childbearing is supposed to be, the evil natures that women have, the awfulness of bringing new sinners into the world, and so on. Rather, there is a note of great joy.

Interestingly, the Greek word for "child" used in the last part of the verse (in some Bible versions translated "man") is *anthropos,* meaning "a human being." It is not a designation of a person of the male sex. Thus Jesus is speaking of the thrill of bringing into the world a new *person*—a human being, whether a girl or a boy, with all the potential that little child may have as a member of the family of God and a disciple of Christ. Nothing is said here to indicate a preference for sons or a longer purification period for daughters. Only joy is mentioned—joy over the birth of any baby, regardless of its sex.

Female children and male children are *equally* valued by Christ as human beings made in the image of God—and so are their mothers.

10.
REPRODUCTION AND THE MODERN WOMAN

The majority of American woman are mothers by the end of their childbearing years. In 1980, for example, only about 6 percent of all ever-married women aged 40 to 44 remained childless, but there have been significant changes in the timing of births. The proportion of ever-married women in their twenties who have not had a child rose dramatically between 1960 and 1980. . . . In the 1960's, there was a move from having children before age 25 to having them between 25 and 30. In the 1970's, a significant group of women . . . delayed childbearing until after age 30. By ages 30 to 34, the proportion childless drops considerably and by ages 35 to 39 only 8 percent of ever-married women in 1980 were still childless. In other words, 92 out of every 100 ever-married women in 1980 were mothers by age 40.

—U. S. Bureau of the Census[1]

I came to terms with motherhood when one of my plainspoken daughters asked me the ultimate question. . . . *No one* was paying attention to her. When would *somebody* have time to play with her? . . . I had an article deadline to meet and would be at my desk all afternoon with the door closed. . . . That was when she asked, "Did you ever wish you never had us in the first place?" I think I became partially paralyzed. Guilt flooded my cheeks with blood . . . I've scarred her, I thought: I've made her feel like a burden—unwanted, unloved, rejected. . . . I sorted my ragged thoughts and took her onto my lap. Gentleness wrapped around us like a fog. "Sometimes my life is a little too full because I have you children," I said. "But, for me, it would be much too empty if I didn't."

Letty Cottin Pogrebin[2]

AT ONE TIME IN OUR SOCIETY, MOTHERHOOD SEEMED SACROSANCT. Politicians supported popular issues because not to do so would "be like coming out against apple pie, the flag, or motherhood." Women who gave birth to large numbers of children were praised highly and presented with Mother of the Year awards. Children and grandchildren made a woman's life seem worthwhile. Why should she worry about personal aspirations when she could bask in the reflected glory of her offsprings' achievements? Her son the statesman or the doctor would one day pat her wrinkled hand and say, "Everything I am

today I owe to my dear mother who sacrificed everything for me."
She could end her days with a warm, contented feeling, knowing she
had contributed something important to the world—children. She
had performed the task society expected of her. And society was well
pleased.

But then things began to change. The population explosion
throughout the world caused politicians to wonder if it might not be
wise to come out against motherhood after all! Some even suggested
changes in income tax laws to discourage couples from having large
families. Research on better contraceptive methods moved ahead,
and efforts at wider dissemination of birth control information were
made. The notion of planned parenthood and limited family size
came to be, with few exceptions, accepted with little debate in
contemporary American society.

How Women Are Affected

At this stage in history, as never before, a woman need not accept
the life-bearing role that was once considered her natural and
inevitable destiny. She may choose to have only one or two
children—or none at all. Modern contraceptive technology makes
this possible, and society's present mood makes it easier.[3] At one
time, a husband and wife were considered selfish if they chose not to
have children; now it is not unusual to hear praise for such couples.[4]
Those now labeled "selfish" are couples who insist on having a large
number of children, thereby aggravating societal problems because
of population growth pressures. Bringing children into the world has
come to be seen as a luxury rather than a duty or necessity.

Where does that leave woman? We have long since moved from
the stage where agricultural prosperity was associated with woman's
fertility, and quite likely that change of emphasis lowered woman's
"self-image" long ago. Yet, there was still the sense of worth attached
to woman's role as a baby-producer. Early societies longed for
children to replace the many persons who died. In modern industrial
societies, the worry is reversed. There are fears that too many new
people will enter life upon a planet with limited resources, and
concerns that the quality of human life could be severely affected by
overcrowding. Today it is becoming as out of place to praise woman
as a baby-producer as it is to praise her as a good-luck charm for
fertile crops! Does the deemphasis on her childbearing role bring
woman new freedom? Or does it threaten to take away her whole
purpose for living? It can do either.

Traditionally, societal pressures have influenced women to believe that childbearing and childrearing should be the main focus of their lives. Marriage and motherhood *are* a woman's career, according to this viewpoint. Why should she want any other career?

The church has reinforced this idea with its Mother's Day awards to women who have given birth to the largest number of children, as well as its sermons and religious writings about the unique contributions a woman can make by devoting her life to home and family. Seldom are awards given to women who have contributed to the church and society through their brains rather than through their biological makeup. Occasionally, of course, women missionaries are honored for spreading the gospel and alleviating human misery, but those are considered to be the exceptional women. The traditional assumption has been that most Christian women will serve God through motherhood. Many clergymen tell women that the Bible teaches this is God's will.

However, this is Old Testament thinking. Already we have observed the shift of emphasis as Christianity came upon the scene. In the New Testament, it is not the propagation of the race that matters so much as the propagation of the gospel message. Kinship ties—blood relationships—are valued less than spiritual ties. The tie that binds men and women together as brothers and sisters in Christ is their common membership in the community of faith, the family of God, the church. In this setting, virginity came to be seen as a positive good. A woman (or a man) did not have to enter marriage and have children in order to experience God's blessing and a sense of usefulness.

By the same token, childlessness came to be viewed as not "sinful" or a social disgrace. Couples without any children or with small families could exhibit the virtues of Christian home life just as well as large ones. A shift from a material emphasis to a spiritual one also changed attitudes toward property. This affected attitudes toward having sons to perpetuate the family name and inherit the family wealth. The emphasis was no longer on laying up treasure for one's sons but on laying up treasure in heaven.

Seeing the total picture, rather than the Old Testament emphasis alone, can help the Christian woman rethink the matter of motherhood. She can come to see that being a physical life-bearer is not nearly so important as being a bearer of spiritual life—the kind of life-bearer Jesus was (see John 10:10). She can share herself, her energies, her service, and her time in ways that heal and help and challenge and bring new life to humankind. She can learn that there are other gifts she can offer the world besides children, gifts that are every bit as important. No Christian woman should feel that being a member of the female sex somehow requires her to have many (or any) children, and that she will be displeasing God and failing as a woman otherwise.

Most Protestant religious leaders encourage the use of birth control in our day so that children are planned for and wanted, spaced in ways most beneficial to the family, and limited in number. However, what is often overlooked in discussion of limited family size is woman's role and purpose. Often the same religious leaders who recommend small families are telling women at the same time that their destiny lies in wifehood and motherhood. Young girls have not been strongly encouraged to think in terms of other goals.

Many Christians would quickly praise the following statement written by a young woman in a letter to a friend: "I've heard it said that everyone is put here upon this earth for a reason. . . . I like to feel (right or wrong) that my purpose is to be a good wife and mother. If I can help my children to grow into useful, responsible citizens, with a sense of duty to God, their fellow humans and their community, then, I will feel that I have completed my task."

Although there is much to be commended in this attitude, the problem arises because the completion of that task comes upon a woman much sooner than she expects. Most women have their last child before reaching age thirty. That means that all her children will be in school by the time a woman is in her mid-thirties. It is then that many women find that time is heavy on their hands. As the children grow older and develop other interests, and as her husband becomes more deeply immersed in his career, a woman who has invested herself totally in her family begins feeling less needed and less fulfilled. Thus, it isn't unusual at this stage for a woman to suggest to her husband that they have another baby. Once again, her life-bearing function seems to promise the most rewarding path to meaning, fulfillment, and an enhanced self-image.

A Woman's Choice

Ideally, the time to think about these matters is before marriage. Many young women today say they are learning to think about long-term goals and to plan their lives accordingly, just as men have always been encouraged to do.

All too often, marriage and children "just happen." Women who are serious about pursuing further education and commitment to a profession know they don't dare risk haphazard, indecisive, careless planning. And they realize that they must seriously and wisely face the issue of marriage and children. Otherwise, it will not be easy to arrange one's life with definite goals in mind—goals that will allow maximum utilization of talents and training.

Such women find themselves asking many hard questions: Should I marry at all? If so, when? What kind of man would I want for a husband? Would we want to have children? If so, would it be best for me to take out a few years from my career and have them early in the marriage, then go back to my profession when they reach school age? Or would it be better to have children later, after many years of getting established in my career? How do I feel about baby-sitters and child-care centers?

All of these questions and many more are of great import with regard to a woman's career aspirations as well as to her family life. They are the kinds of concerns she and her husband-to-be will want to discuss thoroughly before the wedding takes place. A woman seriously committed to a career may choose to have only one or two children. Some may choose to postpone parenthood for a number of years. Others may choose to remain childless in order to devote their total energies elsewhere. Christian women may prayerfully decide on any of these options, and they should not be judged by other Christians who can only see woman's role in terms of the childbearing function.

Many egalitarian couples feel that the outside careers of both husband and wife are equally important, but at the same time they do not want to deny themselves the experience of parenthood. They thus view it as a cooperative venture, determining that child care should be the task of *both* partners in the marriage. Such couples can find ways to work this out so that neither family life nor career will be sacrificed. This takes planning, patience, and a willingness on the part of both spouses to make adjustments and pay some prices. It is not easy. Yet it can be well worth the effort.

Contraception, Abortion, and Sterilization

In many ways, it's hard to believe that in this very century clergymen were denouncing birth control as sinful in the sight of God. Politicians were expressing fears of "race suicide." States had laws banning the sale of contraceptives. Condoms were spoken of as "rubber articles of immoral use." Diaphragms for Margaret Sanger's birth control clinic were illegally imported from Germany via Canada and smuggled over the border in oil drums.[5] Abortion was a crime. Hospitals refused to perform sterilizations for other than "valid medical reasons."[6]

All of this has changed. The Pill, IUD, and other contraceptives are easily available. The 1973 Supreme Court decision on abortion overthrew restrictive state laws, leaving the matter of abortion up to the woman concerned and her physician; the state would only be permitted to step in with regulations regarding the later stages of pregnancy. And by 1970, the National Fertility Study was able to report the dramatic finding that voluntary sterilization has become the most popular contraceptive method used by older couples. One-fourth of couples in which the wife was in the thirty to forty-four age group had been surgically sterilized. Among these couples there was an almost equal division as to which of the partners had undergone the operation.[7] By 1982, close to two-thirds of couples who intended to have no more children had chosen either female or male sterilization.[8]

Obviously, these matters relate directly to how a modern woman thinks about her reproductive capabilities. Other kindred matters both present and future are also difficult to evade—questions regarding artificial insemination, surrogate mothers, frozen sperm banks, fertilizations of a woman's ova by her husband's sperm which are carried out in a laboratory and then replaced in her uterus (in efforts to help couples with infertility problems), the possibility of growing babies in controlled conditions outside the uterus from conception to full term, so that a woman might have her own baby without the necessity of giving birth. Then there are the experiments in "cloning," in which nuclei cells containing genetic material would be transferred from one person to the ova of another. Resulting embryos would be expected to develop as genetic carbon copies of the donor. Another related issue is the possibility of one day choosing the sex of our offspring.

In view of such research, a statement by Dr. Richard Bube (in connection with other achievements of medical science) seems appropriate. He writes, "More and more, God is bringing man to the place where man must make the decisions that in previous years he felt justified in leaving in the hands of God."[9] This can be frightening, or we can accept it as a challenge—a further step in carrying out the creation mandate to subdue the earth and have dominion over the works of God's hands (Gen. 1:28; Ps.8:6).

Controlling our own fertility seems to be one part of this great responsibility that God has placed in our hands. If we accept this responsibility with a sense of stewardship and accountability to God, we can surely trust God for wise guidance in the many decisions we must make.

Some of these decisions are easier than others. The method of birth control, for example, can be decided according to the individual couple's preferences, after talking with a physician and studying the matter thoroughly with regard to effectiveness and health factors, such as safety, side effects, and so on.

The choice of permanent birth control by means of a vasectomy for the husband or a tubal ligation for the wife may be a bit more difficult to make. Christians who have elected voluntary sterilization emphasize the need for husbands and wives to talk the matter over thoroughly beforehand with each other, with physicians, and with trusted friends, and to be absolutely sure that they do not want more children. This includes facing the possibility of the death of a child or the death of a spouse and later remarriage. Once the decision has been made to go ahead, however, the couple should determine that there will be no regrets, assuring each other that they have made the *right* decision and need not feel guilt or remorse. Christian husbands and wives who believe God intended sex not only for procreation, but for communication and recreation as well, testify to the tremendous freedom they experience in their sexual relationship after sterilization. No longer fearful of an unwanted pregnancy, they are free to enjoy each other and express their love to each other with a new spontaneity that enhances their marital union often to a greater degree than ever before.

No doubt the toughest decisions related to reproduction concern abortion. Christians differ widely in their views on the subject, with some calling it nothing short of murder and others saying it can be a humane, merciful act fully in accord with Christian principles. There is no denying that questions about abortion are agonizing ones. Theologians have never settled the issue of when a fetus "receives a soul" or becomes a human being.[10] Thus, perhaps the Supreme Court was wise not only with respect to asserting a woman's right to privacy and leaving the choice with her, but in interpreting the constitution to refer to postnatal life only with regard to the right of individuals. "The unborn have never been recognized in the law as persons in the whole sense," wrote Justice Harry Blackmun in the majority opinion. In Genesis, the first human being became a living soul when God's breath provided the breath of life. R. F. R. Gardner, who is both a practicing gynecologist and an ordained clergyman, writes, "My own view is that while the fetus is to be cherished increasingly as it develops, we should regard its first breath at birth as the moment when God gives it not only life, but the offer of Life."[11]

Even so, decisions about terminating a pregnancy are not to be taken lightly or casually. Yet, at the same time, is abortion entirely out of the question for a Christian couple faced with an unplanned pregnancy at a time and under circumstances when it would be detrimental to the whole family? Or what about an unmarried junior-high-school student who lacks basic sexuality information and yields to a boyfriend's pressure, only to find herself pregnant later? What about a Christian couple who learn through genetic testing that their offspring will suffer from a severe genetic disorder? Or the wife who contracts rubella early in her pregnancy and knows her child is likely to be malformed? Does Christian morality insist that these pregnancies be carried through, even though bringing the child into the world may cause extreme emotional distress and financial hardships for the family? We think not. A decision to have an abortion in such cases can free the couple to have another child, a healthy, normal child that might otherwise never be born.

It is one thing to discuss these matters theoretically; it is quite another to face them in real life. Perhaps that is why the title of Gardner's book is so apt—*Abortion: The Personal Dilemma.*

So much of the oversimplification, arrogant dogmatism, and emotional sloganeering associated with certain spokespersons in the right-to-life movement has obscured the complexities and ambiguities inherent in the topic. To support a woman's right not to be coerced into bearing a child is not to be against life. "Those of us who favor availability of choice are at a disadvantage concerning semantics," writes attorney Sarah Ragle Weddington, who served as a White House aide during the administration of President Jimmy Carter. "Those who oppose availability of choice emphasize being pro-life. All of us would affirm the sanctity of life, the joy of life, the value of life. The points on which we divide include the definition of human life, the weighing of concerns for the pregnant woman and for the fertilized ovum, and the implications of constitutional law."[12]

As one religious scholar has written, "It may be possible to justify abortion in some instances precisely for the sake of a greater reverence for life in a deeper and fuller sense."[13] Another theologian suggests that our discussions of abortion-related questions would be aided by a new look at the two Greek words the New Testament writers used for "life"—*bios* (biological life, the "mere sustenance for moral existence") and *zoē* (the "sanctity, reality, and qualitative dimension of human living"). Thus, the abortion question as a conflict of life with life might be seen in a clearer light.[14]

Christians who have had to face this issue in the concrete reality of their personal lives or the lives of those who are close to them have agonized intensely over the decision. Abortion is not to them an abstract issue of theological/moral/legal debate or a settled absolute that allows no room for questions. Those who have chosen abortion have done so after much prayer, counsel, and soul-searching.[15] Christian love, compassion, and sensitivity demand that we recognize their struggles and their desire to do what they believed to be the right thing, regardless of our own feelings about abortion. As Christian ethicist Roger Shinn reminds us, "One part of any morality, in situations of moral conflict, is the grace to recognize that people who oppose us may be acting out of a moral concern as authentic as ours."[16]

Those persons who have claimed divine guidance to bomb abortion clinics (to use an extreme example) and those Christians so quick to judge and label any woman "selfish" and "sinful" (to use a less extreme and more common example) have no idea of what it means to live that woman's life. They have no knowledge of the painful situation that lies behind her decision. They have no understanding of the stress she undergoes as she walks in to have the abortion, flanked by sign-carrying protesters who picket and scorn her and then humiliate her with the mock funeral, complete with a tiny casket, which they stage as she leaves the clinic.

In one community, an antiabortion letter writer to the local newspaper blasted amniocentesis as a "search and destroy mission" because its use in diagnosing abnormalities in fetuses could mean the pregnant woman might exercise the option of having an abortion so that she could try again with another pregnancy. A mother of a severely handicapped daughter wrote a response that was also printed in the paper. She asked if the original letter writer had "profound and intimate knowledge of what it's like to be prospective parents in the high risk category." She told of the frightening experience of learning that her newborn might not live through the night and must be transported by ambulance to a major medical center. She asked if the unempathic critic of amniocentesis was there when the child turned blue from trying to take nourishment and then collapsed in sheer exhaustion many times because of persistent projectile vomiting. The mother told of the countless medical procedures the child had to undergo: eye operations, ear operations, cardiac catheterizations, casts, braces, trips to the emergency room again and again. Where was the letter writer, the mother wondered, when the parents were told the child was also mentally retarded?

"Was he listening," she asked, "as the doctor continued by saying that any future children born with this same genetic defect would probably not live past one year of age? If they did survive that first year, they would be blind, deaf, severely retarded, a complete invalid and probably ultimately succumb to a severe congenital heart defect."

The woman ended her letter by asking if the man who opposed amniocentesis had any idea of "what it's like to eagerly await the birth of your first child and come home with empty arms to face what I've just described." She went on: "What then do we do with amniocentesis? Do you dangle it in front of us and give us hope, then snatch it away because you feel we are 'abusing' it? Share with me and my family, Mr. ___, the emotional trauma. Walk a mile in my shoes and then tell me what you would do."[17]

Beverly Wildung Harrison, a professor of Christian ethics, calls attention to the attitude of anti-choice politics that "intent as it is on eliminating all elective abortion, is so suffused with the implicit judgment that women are *not* responsible decision makers."[18] It is assumed that women need others to guide them and determine their own best interests, laws to make sure they carry pregnancies to term regardless of their own circumstances or wishes.

Many of those who oppose women's right to choose abortion would like to see legislation that would rule out *all* abortion, even in cases of rape and incest. "Why should an innocent unborn baby have to suffer and pay for the crimes of its father just because it was conceived through rape?" some argue. There is no consideration for the suffering of the *victim* of the rape who would be forced to carry for nine months this reminder of the horror of the rapist's invasion of her body. True, some say they would "help the young woman as much as possible through her pregnancy and the birth." But, *unless she chooses* to carry the pregnancy to term, their "help" is only an implement of their coercion and control and is not a measure of true compassion. A comment by James Kraus is appropriate here. "If it is a terrible thing to play God by terminating physical life," he writes, "it is also a terrible thing, in another sense, to play God by imposing as a divine absolute a prohibition that may cause immense suffering both to individuals and society."[19]

Sociologist Kristin Luker sees the current abortion controversy as a clash over two different world views focused on the roles of the sexes and beliefs about the centrality of motherhood to a woman's life. Her careful study of the polarization over abortion has led her to conclude that "while on the surface it is the embryo's fate that seems to be at stake, the abortion debate is actually about the meanings of *women's* lives."[20] This is not to deny that countless Christians have a genuine concern over the fetus and believe abortion is the taking of a human life and is somehow linked with undervaluing other human life (such as the elderly and physically and mentally disabled persons).[21] But undergirding basic attitudes toward abortion to a great extent are convictions about the nature and purpose of women's lives. Certitude over "woman's role" can mean disregarding woman's reality.

The rhetoric often used paints a simplistic, distorted, negative picture that ignores the concerns and complexity of women's lives. Thus, an advertisement by a group called Heartbeat Ministries was headlined "Mother's Day 1985: The End of Abortion and Feminism . . . The Beginning of Motherhood." The ad went on to say that "one root cause of abortion is the ethic in our society that depreciates and destroys the beauty and honor of motherhood." The root is said to originate in feminism, "and it is a root to which the axe must be laid." The ad quoted the president of the March for Life, Nellie Gray, as saying, "I consider the feminist movement to be, unfortunately, a very hate-filled group of women who hate babies, and families, and men, and God, and Church, and Country, and Society."[22]

Men have enjoyed procreative freedom and the ability to plan and control their lives in a way that women could not until comparatively recent times—a way made possible through improved contraceptive technology and, in certain necessary or emergency situations, through the availability of abortion. To tell a woman that under no circumstances could she ever have an abortion is to place a burden on women that men have never had to bear. To brush over this fact by saying that she *chose* to become pregnant and now that the time of choice is over, she has no further options except to give birth is both unrealistic and unfair. As Roger Shinn points out, "To the woman, trapped in an unwanted pregnancy, this course of action seems to victimize her. Whether pregnant because of ignorance, accident, error or sin, she is not the sole cause of her pregnancy; but she is solely pregnant."[23]

Many women, even under the most difficult circumstances, would never feel right about having an abortion. Others would. But the choice must be theirs.

Adoption and Foster Care

Adoption and foster parenthood also relate to a woman's life-bearing function. One can bring life to children in ways other than giving birth to them. Some couples today look upon adoption or taking in foster children as excellent ways of giving their love to little children while at the same time having a small part in easing population pressures. Rather than bring a new child into the world, the reasoning goes, why not give love to some child already here? It would seem in keeping with the spirit of Christian teachings on self-expending love to take into our homes children who might otherwise never know the love of a family—especially children who are hard to place for adoption, such as older children, handicapped children, or children of racially mixed parentage. An unmarried woman can also experience the joys of motherhood in this way.

Parenthood in the Total Scheme of Things

We have seen that all through history woman has been praised, worshiped, feared, and criticized for her reproductive capabilities.[24] From her body new generations come forth. Because of her, life continues upon the earth.

Yet the body is not the woman; it is only part of her. And motherhood is only one aspect of a woman's life, just as fatherhood is but one aspect of a man's life. A woman is not a baby-machine. She is a total person, with mind, heart, will, and a multitude of talents and abilities. Never must she think that she has nothing to offer the world except the fruit of her womb. She can also bring to the world the fruit of the Spirit (Gal. 5:22-23) and the fruit of her mind. And if God calls her to motherhood, she can realize that it is quality more than quantity that matters. She can give her best to her family, trusting God for wisdom and strength to enable her and her husband as partners together to "train up a child in the way he [or she] should go" (Prov. 22:6).

When motherhood is perceived as drudgery, duty, and inevitable destiny, it can limit a woman's potential and cause feelings of restlessness and even resentment. But motherhood freely chosen and creatively implemented can be one of the most exciting and joyous experiences a woman can know.

11.

THE SINGLE WOMAN

Virgins follow the Lamb, because the flesh of the Lamb is also virginal.

—Augustine (referring to Rev. 14:4)[1]

There are two ways of life: . . . marriage is the more moderate and ordinary; virginity is angelic and unsurpassed. Now if a man choose the way of the world, namely marriage, he is not indeed to blame; yet he will not receive such great gifts as the other. For he will receive, since he too brings forth fruit, namely thirtyfold. But if a man embrace the holy and unearthly way . . . he grows the perfect fruit, namely a hundredfold.

—Athanasius[2]

Everything wrong in life has its beginning in marriage, which distracts one from the true life.

—Gregory of Nyssa[3] (who was married)

"WHO'S YOUR BOYFRIEND?" IS A QUESTION A GIRL IS ASKED FROM THE time she is old enough to answer. If she manages to graduate from college with a B.A. and no Mrs., the question becomes, "Aren't you married yet?" After she has worked for several years, the question turns to a pitying, "Why isn't a nice girl like you married?"

Our language has no polite word for an unmarried woman past thirty. We can be thankful that all but the most thoughtless have given up "old maid," which usually connoted rigidity and wretchedness. Some use "bachelor girl" or "career girl," but who wants to be called a "girl" all her life as though she were still twelve? Indeed, many consider marriage the rite of passage into adulthood and the unmarried as perpetual children. "Spinster" is making a comeback and still may prove acceptable, but at the moment "single woman" is about the best we can do. It serves as a constant reminder that society still considers pairs the norm.

As though another reminder of the "Noah's ark syndrome" were necessary! At the supermarket the bargains are all in the family size. At work a memo from the president concerning a company dinner offers the options: "Yes, my spouse and I will be able to attend"; "I can attend, but my spouse cannot"; or "Sorry, we cannot attend"! At church one has a choice of the younger marrieds' class or the older marrieds' class. I once received a mailing from my church advertising a class being offered by a child psychologist in the congregation. The mailing said, "Limited to married people." Certainly, divorced and widowed single parents needed the class as much as anyone else, and I as an unmarried teacher could surely have benefited from it. One book for teens concerning marriage puts it bluntly: "The plan of the Creator is *marriage,* not singleness. . . . The plan of God is marriage. Singleness for religious service is a cultural tradition and not the plan of God."[4]

Singleness Preferred

The writer of this statement obviously had studied neither Scripture nor church history well. Ironically, until the Reformation in the sixteenth century, the single celibate life was considered the ideal Christian life-style; married life was definitely second-class. As Augustine put it, "Continence from all intercourse is certainly better than married intercourse itself which takes place for the sake of begetting children."[5] The ideal was based first of all on the fact that Jesus is portrayed in the Gospels as a single person, though that was unusual for a young Jewish male of his day. Surely one would not say he was incomplete or he had not fulfilled his potential or he had deviated from the plan of God by remaining single. (And to consider him as an exception is to deny his full humanity.)

While Jesus spoke positively at times about marriage, reluctantly honoring the marriage at Cana with his first miracle, he never recommended it. Siblings Mary, Martha, and Lazarus were among his closest friends, and he does not appear to have suggested that they marry. Anna, who had been a widow for many decades, was the first to proclaim Christ's coming in Jerusalem (Luke 2:36-38). A discussion of divorce in which Jesus affirmed marriage (Matt. 19:3-9) was followed immediately by an equal affirmation of singleness (Matt. 19:10-12). In the parable of the wedding guests, he implicitly condemned the one who put his wife before an invitation to join the kingdom of God (Luke 14:20-21).

The apostle Paul spoke of marriage, not singleness, as a limitation to serving God. How many positive sermons have you heard on these texts: "To the unmarried and the widows I say that it is well for them to remain single as I do" (I Cor. 7:8); or "An unmarried woman, like a young girl, can devote herself to the Lord's affairs; all she need worry about is being holy in body and spirit. The married woman, on the other hand, has to worry about the world's affairs and devote herself to pleasing her husband" (I Cor. 7:34 JB)? Preachers today, depending on their inclination, explain these verses away by saying that they were only given because the early Christians thought the Great Tribulation and Second Coming were at hand (two thousand years later they are farther away?) or that the author's thinking was tainted by body-denying Gnosticism. Why can we not just admit that Paul, like Jesus, saw real virtue in devoting one's life to God without the encumbrances of married life, pleasant as those may be?

Certainly the church for a millennium and a half took these words very seriously. For some, particularly the Latin fathers, marriage was to be avoided because sexual involvement was defiling for both men and women. For the Greek fathers the stress was more on the transient nature of earthly relationships. A true Christian was to be detached from earthly family ties and fixed on love for God alone.[6] Indeed Cyprian called virgins "the flower of the ecclesiastical seed, the grace and ornament of Spiritual endowment . . . the more illustrious portion of Christ's flock."[7]

Although some today argue that women and perhaps even single men cannot be ordained because the writer of I Timothy said that a bishop and a deacon must be "the husband of one wife" (I Tim. 3:2, 12), as though this mandated marriage for clergy, the early church usually interpreted this reference to prohibit remarriage after widowhood (rather than to prohibit polygamy). From earliest times in the church, there were revered orders of virgins (male and female) and widows ("having been the wife of one husband," I Tim. 5:9). Justin Martyr boasted that "many, both men and women, who have been Christ's disciples from childhood, remain pure at the age of sixty or seventy years."[8] The Council of Elvira in the early fourth century declared total celibacy appropriate for all clergy.[9] Ambrose, the great bishop and preacher of Milan, devoted seven complete works to the elevation of the single life.

Single Christians, then, should not have to be defensive about their state; indeed, in terms of the Christian tradition, married people are the ones who should be defensive. Yet with psychiatrists, ministers, media, and meddling acquaintances continually warning single people that life without a spouse is meaningless, the Census Bureau tells us that 34.7 million Americans over 30 are unmarried (8.6 million Americans over 30 have never married; 9.5 million are divorced; 12.7 million are widowed; another 3.9 million are technically still married, but their spouses are absent for one reason or another). Nearly 30 percent of the American population do not currently live with a spouse. More and more young people are postponing marriage—men until age 25.4; women until age 22.8

(compared with 23.1 and 21.1 in 1974; 22.8 and 20.5 in 1963). In 1983 there were 114 divorced persons for every 1,000 married persons (compared with 47 in 1970 and 35 in 1960).[10] The average woman is widowed at age 56 while her life expectancy is nearly 80.[11] Virtually all women are or will be single during their lifetimes.

Why Are Some Unmarried?

The most obvious answer to the question of why some are unmarried is that some people are just lucky. Yet some people, singles included, seem to think that any woman single past thirty is frigid, neurotic, or man hating—the assumption being that males are the grand prizes in the female game of life. One woman working in a church was asked by a parishioner if she planned to get married. When she replied that it was not a priority item on her agenda at the moment, he rebuked her, "Don't ever say that. Every normal woman wants to get married, and the church wants normal women!" (which may reflect more of his homophobia than his high regard for marriage). In David Reuben's best-seller *Any Woman Can!* (get married, that is), case studies "showed" how any unmarried woman can be cured of her disability by his psychiatric help.

Strangely, society's stereotypes of the single woman do not seem to correspond with reality. Psychological studies have found that single women are second in happiness only to married men (married women and single men are far less happy). Studies comparing personal and social adjustment of groups of married and never-married women have found no significant differences. Several studies have found that single women have fewer emotional problems than married women. Singles are also physically healthier. Ninety-one singles die of cirrhosis of the liver for every one hundred married women; sixty-one single women die as a result of homicide for every one hundred married women.[12] More than one-third of the wives filing for divorce complain of physical abuse.[13] Marriage is definitely hazardous to a woman's health!

Another suggestion single women hear is that they are afraid of marriage. Given the statistics on wife abuse and divorce, fear would seem to be a healthy response. Many people do come from homes where their parents had loveless and abusive relationships, where their parents were too wiped out on alcohol and drugs or too devoted to business to pay any attention to them, where they were physically, emotionally, or sexually abused. Many have been so harmed by their families of origin that they do not choose to marry. Many young people, victims of divorce, are disillusioned by the marriages they see. Some churches teach such a repressive view of marriage that no self-respecting woman or sensitive man would want to participate in so oppressive a relationship. Many have tried marriage once and had a bad experience. Many widows simply enjoy living their own life at last. As Letha's mother said of herself and her friends in Florida: "When we were married, we lived our husbands' lives; now we live our own."

Those who do not marry are often accused of being choosy, as though even a rotten marriage is preferable to singleness. Popular wisdom has it that "anyone who really wants to can get married." Yet the Census Bureau tells us that currently in the United States, there are only 90.8 men for every 100 women over 18 (only 70.7 men for every 100 women over 62). The life expectancy for white men is 71.5 years and for black men 64.9 years, but for white women it is 78.8 years and for black women 73.5 years. Obviously the older a woman becomes, the less opportunity she has to find another spouse.

For the woman with above-average talents, the marriage market is even more restricted. As sociologist Jessie Bernard outlines graphically in the *The Future of Marriage,* men tend to marry women less intelligent, educated, or socially prominent than themselves. Thus single women tend to be the "cream of the crop" while single men are the "bottom of the barrel," those in prison and those unable to hold a steady job.[14] Feminist Germaine Greer has asked, "If men are content to spend their leisure time with their intellectual inferiors, why cannot women be so?"[15] Certainly many women have made this choice and their patience and tolerance should be respected, but some women would rather be single than settle for less than the type of soul-companionship described in our chapters on marriage. The Christian woman, particularly, searches for a partner with whom she can truly share a one-flesh relationship that includes spiritual as well as physical and intellectual communion. I once rejected a marriage proposal from an otherwise charming and intelligent man who offered to support me in a course of psychoanalysis so that I could get rid of my "religious hang-ups." Is waiting for God's best being too choosy?

Some people are simply in between single and married. They are cohabiting, or they are involved in a long-term relationship. Some are young people planning toward marriage. Others are older people who have tried marriage and are gun-shy, or they may be senior citizens whose meager pensions would be lost if they married. As we all are aware, the institution of marriage is in a state of change, but the church is one of the last institutions to begin to grapple with those changes. Many Christians are forced to lie or to leave their churches when they find themselves in an experimental relationship.

Another reason that some people are single is that both society and the church deny them the opportunity to be and say what they truly are: lesbians and gay men. Sociologists and historians estimate that in every society about 5 percent of the men and 2 percent of the women are predominately or exclusively homosexual in their sexual orientation.[16] Researchers suggest that between four and six million Americans are gay. There is evidence that biological and prenatal factors influence this; it is clear that orientation is set at an early age, usually before puberty, though many only realize their orientation much later, sometimes after marriage. Indeed in previous centuries, homosexuality has been obscured by the fact that most marriages were arranged by parents for their children, often before puberty.

Today the church remains one of the institutions most oppressive to gay people, sometimes opposing their basic civil rights to jobs, housing, and legal protection. Within the church, many gay people are given the message that their souls are beyond salvation, even though God's criterion for salvation according to John 3:16 is a commitment to Jesus Christ, not a reorientation of one's sexuality. Other Christians acknowledge the persistence of sexual orientation but demand that gay people live celibately if they are to save their souls; again forgotten is the assurance that all salvation is a free gift of God's grace, not of works lest anyone should boast (Eph. 2:8-9).[17]

Many gay Christians are in long-term relationships to which their commitment is as strong as to any marriage, but most churches refuse to sanction or even acknowledge such relationships. Many gay relationships would last longer if they had the support and nurture from church and society that marriage affords heterosexual couples. The demand that gay persons remain celibate may actually encourage brief affairs (which can then be "forgiven") rather than encourage the hard work necessary to the success of a committed relationship. The Metropolitan Community Church and the Unitarian-Universalist Association now offer gay couples the opportunity to make public commitments to each other and to receive spiritual affirmation of their unions. Other religious bodies are in the process of rethinking this issue. Despite all of the pressures, many gay relationships are based on a lifetime covenant: Dot and Joyce have been together for nearly forty years; Bill and Anthony more than twenty years.

A number of older women who have never married were forced

into that choice by their churches; some groups urge the same choice today upon women who wish to serve God in the church, on the mission field, or in a demanding career. Many women take Paul seriously; they feel that they should forego marriage in order to devote themselves fully to God's service. Born and reared on the mission field, one woman returned to the United States for college, enjoyed her education, and got on well with other students, but never found a man who understood her background or shared her call to return to the field. So she accepted her single state and found fulfillment in her vocation. Within the Roman Catholic Church the religious life has been an honored profession for women; Protestantism has often demanded the same sacrifices but withheld the honor.

Choosing Singleness

For those who have not chosen singleness but have found it thrust upon them by circumstances, handicap, divorce, or widowhood, it can be a painful journey. Some (usually married) write glowingly about the "gift of singleness." Certainly, as Christ implied in Matthew 19:11-12, singleness, celibacy, can be a gift from God.

Not all . . . can receive this saying, but only those to whom it is given. For there are eunuchs who have been so from birth, and there are eunuchs who have been made eunuchs by [other people], and there are eunuchs who have made themselves eunuchs for the sake of the kingdom of heaven. [The one] who is able to receive this, let [that one] receive it.

But I am here to testify—as can many of my sisters and brothers—that not everyone who prays for it gets it! And many are in no mood to ask for it; if it arrived, they would probably say, "Why me, God?" and return it unopened and marked "No Thanks!"

We perpetuate a very cruel hoax on our young people when we tell them all as teenagers that God will provide a marriage partner for them. For my fifteenth birthday my aunt gave me a booklet titled *How to Get a Husband for Christian Girls*, which stated bluntly: "Your Heavenly Father has a plan for your life. . . . But you must want it earnestly, every fiber of your being. . . . In this plan is to be found the Mr. Prince Charming Husband whom God has selected for you. . . . He is planned to perfectly fit your need."[18] The author was certainly presumptuous in making promises for God that God did not deliver, at least to me!

That kind of thinking is a perfect setup for disappointment and bitterness. As the writer of Proverbs said, "Hope deferred makes the heart sick" (Prov. 13:12). For the gay young person who is also told that responding with love to a mate would be sinful, God becomes a cruel despot. Not a few people have simply turned their backs on the church and on God in order to survive. In many churches, proud of their "family orientation," such people are unwelcome anyway.

The spiritual conflicts set up by this contradictory teaching are enormous. Homilies on such texts as "My God will supply every need" (Phil. 4:19), "Ask, and it will be given you; seek, and you will find" (Luke 11:9), and "No good thing does the Lord withhold from those who walk uprightly" (Ps. 84:11) ring hollow indeed when God apparently chooses not to supply one's most basic need and desire for love and companionship. How can one believe that God answers prayer when one's most fervent petition has been ignored? How can one believe in God's love and goodness when the yearnings God implanted lie unfulfilled? How can one believe that God intends the best when one is denied what Christians have said *is* God's best? One is tempted to blame God, to become bitter and depressed.

Another alternative is to blame oneself. Perhaps God is punishing one for some sin. Perhaps God has deemed one accursed. Many people indeed feel that they have no hope of happiness or reconciliation with God because someone has told them that being gay or divorced or an unwed mother or an adulterer or whatever is the unpardonable sin. For those who have confessed all the sins they can think of and pleaded for forgiveness and still not found a mate, the result again is despair. Yet Scripture tells us that whatever our sin is, "if we confess our sins, [God] is faithful and just, and will forgive our sins and cleanse us from all unrighteousness" (I John 1:9). Being single is not God's punishment for anything (nor would God ask anyone to stay in an abusive marriage as a punishment for marrying the "wrong" person).

When one asks a pastor or a Christian friend for counsel, one is usually told to blame oneself. I have been told by several well-meaning, mature Christians that I am not married because I am overweight (despite the fact that many married people are also overweight). Twice I lost considerable poundage, and I still am unmarried. I have also been told that my intelligence is a discouragement to marriage. While it is true that many men are not too intelligent and prefer women even less intelligent than themselves, some of my very intelligent women friends have found intelligent (or at least secure) male companions. The anti-intellectual bias within the church, compounded by the prejudice in society against intelligent women, do make the role of the intellectual Christian woman a sometimes difficult and lonely one.

The single woman who buys the myths of society and the church may try an exhausting regimen of self-improvement—therapy, plastic surgery, diet, exercise, new wardrobe, cosmetic makeovers, job change, and so on. She may frequent singles' bars even when she does not drink or dance, or go to Parents Without Partners even when her only dependent is a dog. Ann Landers once reported on a sober woman who joined Alcoholics Anonymous to meet men. Such a frantic quest only leads to lower self-esteem and more despair.

A woman may settle into a life of fatalistic resignation. After all, it is just more of the same numbing waiting she has been doing since kindergarten when she was taught to sit quietly. During her teens she learned to wait for the phone to ring, wait for a boy to ask her out, wait for him to kiss her. At church she has been told to wait on God. So she waits—and drifts from job to job, or floats in the same low-level position, rents a furnished apartment, visits organizations here and there, and dabbles at hobbies. Or she tries to escape through drugs, alcohol, exhaustion, or promiscuity. After all, what else is there to do "until I get married"?

Is there an alternative? Most books and articles for Christian singles are written by people who have "solved" the "problem" by getting married—which leaves still-single readers feeling more like social failures—or by such "victorious Christians" that most ordinary readers feel like spiritual failures. But like most of life, living the single life is an ongoing, up-and-down struggle.

Every person—single, married, divorced, widowed, gay—must eventually come to terms with her or his life. It is impossible to change anything one does not first accept. No amount of denying, crying, complaining, cursing, or counseling will alter the facts of one's life. Contrary to popular myth or Protestant theology, marriage is not what every person needs to live a complete and fulfilled life. All people need loving relationships and a sense of purpose that make living worthwhile. For some people, establishing a marriage and rearing a family constitute that relationship and purpose. But having babies is not every person's calling, every woman's vocation. Most everyone has reproductive organs, but in addition God has clearly given each person unique capabilities. Finding one's own talents and developing them for God's glory is every Christian's task. As Dorothy Payne says in *Women Without Men,* the single woman must "pick up her option to choose her own lifestyle."[19]

The maturing Christian takes responsibility for her own life.

Confident in God's love and providence, she can get on with her life. One of my favorite mottoes is incorporated in a serigraph by artist Corita Kent: "To believe in God is to know that all the rules will be fair—and that there will be wonderful surprises."

Taking responsibility for your life means letting go of the victim stance and no longer blaming any and everyone else. Granted that your ex-husband was a bum, that your late mate should not have overworked himself into a heart attack, that you didn't ask for a homosexual orientation, that your mother should have fed you cantaloupe instead of cake, broccoli instead of bagels. What are you going to do with your life today? That is the question only you can answer.

Taking responsibility means setting priorities and being willing to answer for them. Every woman knows in this culture that higher education limits the chances of marrying, yet for some of us graduate education is reasonable stewardship of God's gifts and we choose to go forward. Certainly a woman makes choices in terms of her physical appearance and fitness. Does she want to attract the sort of people who prefer a high-fashion model or an earth mother? She must make choices accordingly.

At the center of taking responsibility is self-esteem. The individual must value who and what she is, the gifts God has given her, rather than try to bend herself out of shape and into society's or her church's expectations. Finding self-esteem is a particularly difficult issue for many women and for many Christians who have been taught that God (read, their parents) will love them only if they are "good." That is why it is important to remember that God created us and that God loves us individually, "just as I am." That is why books like this are important in telling women that God did not create us to be second-class citizens, that women are fully human, that we are not the source of sin nor the cause of men's temptation and fall. Each of us, women and men, are in God's image. We indeed may sin, but we are no less loved by God. We are valuable to God as human beings.

We feel like victims, and sometimes we are victimized because we have very low self-esteem. One of my reasons for desiring marriage was to bolster my self-esteem with the knowledge that I had been chosen by another person and with a ring that I could display as a social "stamp of approval." Many times society does seem to esteem married people more highly—from the break they get from the Internal Revenue Service to the better mental health ascribed to them. I wanted a mate to tell me that I was a good person, a worthwhile human being. I also wanted someone to take care of me.

That is how our society defines marriage. The husband takes care of his wife by providing materially for her and the wife takes care of her husband by making a comfortable home for him and meeting his sexual needs. Now I have learned to take care of myself. Self-esteem is knowing I can do that adequately.

The Need for Relationship

All of us—married or single, man or woman, gay or straight—need relationships. Sometimes single people are told (most often by a married person) that "God is sufficient," implying that if the single person's relationship to God is solid enough no one else is needed. If that were true, God would not have created a second human being. Even the most devout mystics in the history of the church have lived in community. We have defined the need for relationship as part of what it means to be created in the image of God. We were made to be in relationship with God and with other people, as God is in relationship within the Trinity (which is not a dyad or a nuclear family, incidentally) and with us, God's creatures. Because it is such a central part of our being, it is little wonder that relationship is an area of our lives where we experience difficulty.

To say that some of us remain single or become single again because we have had difficulty with relationships is not to blame ourselves but simply to face reality. Some people have both great desire for and fear of true intimacy, primarily because they experienced some pretty dreadful things in their families of origin—abuse, addictions, neglect, messy divorce, or suffocating togetherness. Others want to find satisfying relationships, but since they never experienced that in their families of origin, they simply do not have the skills to achieve a healthy relationship. For various reasons some people dislike themselves and thus fear others. Women with low self-esteem sometimes project their self-hatred on other women and cut themselves off from friendship. Those with bad relationships with their fathers sometimes cut themselves off from relationships with men or choose husbands who abuse and/or abandon them as their fathers did.

Other people seek relationships—and sometimes find them—in a neurotic way, latching onto others in attempts to escape themselves, their loneliness, their fears. Rather than deal with their own problems, they find someone with problems that need attention. A person might choose an alcoholic partner so that he or she can focus energies on the "sick" person. As we said before, some people marry in order to bolster their own self-esteem. After all, "I must be a good person because he chose me!" We are all aware of the classic Don Juan or the nymphomaniac who compulsively seeks sexual partners. Many more "respectable" people seek friends and deeper relationships out of the same need for a "fix." Some gay people have been told that marriage would "cure" them.

Another reason why so many of us screw up the relationships we do attempt is that many of the messages we get about "love" from music and the media are less than healthy, such as "love is never having to say you're sorry," "love conquers all," "you're all I need," "love is suffering," and so on. I recently heard a song that said, "I'd lie to you to get your love"! We are led to expect that the person we love will meet all our needs. We expect to become totally dependent on that loved one. We expect to suffer and be hurt. Women, especially Christian women, are told that they are to give up their own lives and pour all their talents and energies into the husband's career and the children's lives—which sometimes leaves them feeling used up and angry, particularly when the children have left the nest and the husband has left the marital bed for that of some younger woman.

So what can we say about healthy relationships, especially for the single person? First, we need to be brutally honest with ourselves. Do we avoid serious relationships in order to avoid true intimacy? Have we had a series of bad relationships because we are playing out our parents' scripts rather than writing healthier ones for ourselves? Do we know how to relate in a healthy way? Those who have survived the breakup of a relationship need to analyze carefully why it happened. It is much easier to blame other people than to accept our own part in the failure and try to do something about it.[20]

I personally have found psychological counseling helpful in this regard. In choosing a counselor, the most important elements are their skill and one's compatibility with them. I have worked with both Christians and non-Christians and do not think that makes a big difference as long as the counselor respects one's religious convictions and helps one to examine them. Working through deep psychological problems or very difficult things in one's past can probably best be accomplished in individual therapy, while social skills can be learned more quickly in a group therapy situation. After praying for God's guidance, I have found my therapists usually through the recommendations of friends or other therapists. County mental health facilities, women's counseling centers, and some church-related counseling centers offer a sliding scale for payment. Women therapists are often able to understand women's issues better.

Healthy relationships are born out of self-respect and choice. When we are happy in and with ourselves, we are ready to give ourselves to other persons. When we like ourselves, others will like us. When we are happy in our own company, we will find solitude rather than loneliness, and relating will become a choice rather than a neurotic compulsion. When we know we can depend on ourselves, dependence on others and by others will not seem so overwhelming. We will also realize that meeting our needs is our own responsibility, not the responsibility of a partner in relationship, and not a magical result of relating. We will be confident and patient in working toward healthy relationships, whether they be friendships or marriage.

One myth of society is that marriage is the only and the total "relationship." Most single people have experienced losing good friends once they become "coupled." The tendency is to let one's friends drop by the wayside the moment one "falls in love." Yet married people need a variety of relationships, and certainly single people do too. We need casual friends with whom we can see a movie, go to a concert, work in an organization, share an athletic contest, or discuss our work during coffee breaks. Each offers us opportunities to learn, grow, share. We also need deeper friendships, someone to depend on when our cars break down, when we need an emergency sitter, a shoulder to cry on, or temporary housing. We need friendships with members of the same sex and with those of the opposite sex, with other single people and with married people—if for no other reason than to learn that nobody has it easy.

And we all need at least one or two very deep and intimate relationships. For some this will be in marriage or a committed union. For others it will be in special friendships. Such relationships are not easy to find and take constant attention to survive. No relationship is static. As individuals and as a couple, we must continue to grow, adapt, challenge, change. One of the best things friends and lovers can do for each other is nurture each other's growth toward wholeness. This is not easy; all of us fear and resist change in ourselves and those we depend on. Yet we either grow or die.

Sexual Needs

We are sexual persons—single or married, young or old, gay or straight. We are all embodied, incredible, delightful, integrated organisms, created by God who said, "It is good." One of the most devastating dualities the church has fostered is the duality of body and spirit. This division has caused and continues to cause the world untold grief. Added to the duality of male and female, it has brought pernicious dimensions to sexism. Defining ourselves, human beings, as spiritual beings with a heavenly home has led to the rape of the physical earth, our embodied environment. Always identifying ourselves with mind and spirit while projecting sexuality and physicality onto others has multiplied the horrors of slavery, racism, homophobia, nationalism, and militarism.

Yet we are all sexual people. As Christians we can accept that fact, indeed glory in our sexuality as one of God's most gracious gifts to us. Whatever our situation in life, being fully aware of and accepting our sexuality is a giant step toward wholeness.[21]

Many parents choose to ignore the developing sexuality of their children. Fortunately, it does not wither away or die without their attention. My parents told me very little, which worked out nicely because I did not get any of the negative messages they might have felt duty-bound to deliver, as so many of my contemporaries' parents did. Some parents and some churches do great damage to people with their negative view of all sexuality and the enormous guilt with which they surround it.

Some single people and homosexual people want to stifle or ignore their sexuality. Divorced or widowed people are often surprised by their sexuality, since they assumed that it died along with their former relationship. Too often the church's only response to sexuality is "Don't!"—which is not particularly helpful. Here again, self-esteem, acceptance, responsibility, and choice are crucial.

Some people use sexual conquest as a means of bolstering their self-esteem. The result is usually the opposite—guilt, frustration, and lower self-esteem. One gets the same results when one tries to deny one's sexuality or to repress it. *Sublimation* has been called "God's message to the unmarried." It is usually defined as "channeling one's sexual energies into other activities." That works for some people perhaps; for others such a suggestion is a mockery. The capacity for sublimation is developed comparatively early in life and is largely an ability to tolerate the frustration of instincts and unconsciously redirect them. For many, it is simply another way of saying "repress your feelings." To say to a person who did not develop this in childhood and who is now suffering from sexual need, "You must sublimate," as if one could do so on the spot, is futile.[22] The result is someone who usually ends up seeking much more from work or hobbies than such activities were ever intended to give. This person becomes compulsive, perfectionist, demanding. There is no substitute for physical intimacy and relationship with another person. God made it that way. As one artist commented, "The idea that creative work, such as painting or writing, is a substitute for sex is hogwash. It meets a different kind of need."

The first step is to accept one's sexuality. God made sexuality and it is good; God made me and I am loved by God. All of my feelings are a part of me and known to God. One of my favorite prayers begins, "O God, unto whom all hearts are open, all desires known, and from whom no secrets are hid. . . ." God knows us completely and still loves us. Thus we can also explore our own sexuality, experience all of our feelings, get in touch with our bodies. Too many people, too many Christians are only in touch with their heads; they think but cannot feel. When we block sexual feelings, when we block those feelings like anger that we label as negative, we lose access to all of our feelings, even those we would welcome. So we need to welcome and nurture and accept all of our feelings, including our sexual feelings. We can delight them without ever choosing to act on them. We can accept our feelings and thank God for them as indications that we are alive and whole, even when we may have no present opportunity to express them with another person.

We can love ourselves, emotionally and physically. Some readers were shocked by my discussion of masturbation in the first edition of this book. When I explained to one older woman that masturbation was stimulating oneself to orgasm, she told me it was impossible. A man told me that masturbation was what homosexuals did. I reminded both of them that studies have found that a high percentage of men and women, married and unmarried, gay or straight, do masturbate. Even babies do it. One survey of unmarried evangelical Christians found that 27 percent did it more than once a week.[23] Masters and Johnson found that most women have more intense orgasms through masturbation than through intercourse.

Many enlightened Christians still feel guilty about masturbation, however, because of all the myths about it in society. Teenagers used to be told that it caused acne and insanity. Freudians warned women that if they learned to achieve orgasm through "childish" clitoral stimulation they would not be able to switch in marriage to a "mature" experience of vaginal orgasm. Masters and Johnson, of course, found that there is only one type of orgasm, and physiologically it is produced in the same way whether one is masturbating or having intercourse.[24] Masturbation, however, can be a celebration of one's sexuality. One can enjoy it and thank God for it as an indication that one is alive and functioning.

Christian writers have been taking a new look at the subject.[25] Some have argued that it is wrong because it is self-centered rather than other-centered, body-centered rather than person-centered, even though we are commanded to love ourselves and that includes our bodies (Matt. 22:39). Some have even agreed with Thomas Aquinas who said that masturbation was worse than fornication because at least in the latter two people were involved as "God ordained." Aquinas never explained why God made masturbation possible and pleasurable without "ordaining" it. Moreover, the Bible clearly condemns fornication (see I Cor. 6:9–7:2; I Thess. 4:1-8; Eph. 5:3-6) but says nothing about masturbation. Some have suggested that masturbation is condemned in the story of Onan in Genesis 38. Indeed some dictionaries define *onanism* as "masturbation." However, Onan's sin was not that he "spilled the semen on the ground" in solitary pleasure, but that by doing so he defrauded Tamar of his obligation to father her child because he did not want it to inherit family lands. God killed him in punishment for his greed, not for his sexual activity! (It is interesting how in any number of biblical stories we have labeled the sin as sexual whereas God was really concerned about other sins closer to those we regularly commit!) Other Christian writers consider masturbation at least morally neutral, if not a positive good. It offers a way of dealing with sexual tensions without "using" another person, and may well be "the wise provision of a very wise Creator" who "gave it to us because he knew we'd need it."[26] The only harm caused by masturbation is the guilt produced in those who have been taught it is wrong.

In the light of Jesus' warning about guarding one's sexual thought life in Matthew 5:28, some Christians worry that masturbation is linked with lust. Some people fear that having any sexual thoughts about a person other than one's mate constitutes lust. I personally think that appreciating another person's body visually and mentally is simply enjoying God's good gifts, as one enjoys a beautiful sunset or the sound of a tumbling mountain stream. However, if our thoughts involve conquest, violation, or degradation, we need to ask ourselves why something like that is part of our sexual desire. Do we really respect and appreciate the other person as one of God's creations, or are our feelings angry, hostile, abusive, violent? And if so, why? On the other hand, if our thoughts are positive and pleasurable, why not just enjoy them? We have millions of thoughts that we do not choose to act on. Fantasies are a natural part of being playful, of relaxing, of being a sexual, embodied creature of God.

Sexual mores concerning activity outside marriage have undergone considerable revision in the past several decades, due in large part to the accessibility of inexpensive and reliable contraception. The injunction many of us heard as teenagers—"Don't do it; you'll get pregnant!"—no longer holds a lot of water. True, too many teenagers still get pregnant, but more and more teenagers, even Christians, are having intercourse. Two-thirds of all teenagers have sexual intercourse before they reach age twenty. Of never-married women in their twenties, 82 percent have had sexual relations.[27] Many of those who remain single and those who have been widowed or divorced consider sexual activity an acceptable part of a deeper relationship, whether or not it is headed toward marriage. Thus the matter of appropriate sexual activity for Christians is under revision.

The whole wait-until-marriage rationale is now largely ignored. It never was very useful to those who never married or to those who had already been married and were no longer. We need to talk more about what my friend Lauralyn Bellamy calls "responsible stewardship of our sexuality." Here again, a crucial factor is responsible choice. The old prohibitions simply built up a wall of "shouldn'ts" and "don'ts." They threatened a truckload of guilt on our heads if we did not conform. So people refrained from sexual activity because they feared the consequences, not because they made responsible decisions. For me that seemed to be a victim stance, victimized by all of the moral prohibitions and expectations of my subculture.

An authentic celibacy is based on accepting one's sexuality and then making responsible decisions about it. There is nothing wrong with saying no when that is one's choice. Young people who understand their sexual feelings and are comfortable with them will not feel pressured by their peers to prove anything. When self-esteem is intact, one does not need sexual activity to prove attractiveness or desirability. When one learns to take care of oneself, one does not need to exchange sexual favors for caretaking from others.

On the other hand, as each of us knows and accepts our sexuality, we become more aware of how much it is involved in every area of our lives. We can enjoy the sexual energy we feel with certain people without feeling any loss at not being able to act on those feelings if it is inappropriate. We can enjoy the feelings and know that we can act on them if we so choose. That sense of choice often results in less activity, since we have nothing to prove or rebel against. On the other hand, when love and respect deepen between two people, they may choose to express those feelings physically at whatever level feels right to both people. Rather than being bound by a set of moral legalisms and cultural expectations, many people are now making their own individual decisions based on prayerful dialogue with God about what is best for them in their situation.

Another aspect of this issue is touch. Unfortunately our society's focus on genital sexuality has made all bodily contact suspect. In many countries men hug and kiss one another upon meeting, women hold hands walking down the street; but our homophobia often limits such behavior. We permit touch only under highly ritualized conditions. Man have invented all sorts of athletic mock-combat situations where it is perfectly acceptable to tackle one's opponent, roll around together on the ground or a mat, put an arm around a teammate, or pat his behind. Women have various kissing and patting rituals of greeting and parting.

Jesus often touched those he met, even those considered untouchable by his society.[28] Reaching out and touching have been hallmarks of saints through the centuries. And his hands, their hands, have brought healing both physical and spiritual. The church has traditionally laid hands on new members, on the sick, and on those sent out to minister, as a sign of the Holy Spirit's presence and power. Christians were urged by the apostle to greet one another with a holy kiss (I Thess. 5:26), and many churches have reinstituted the "kiss of peace."

All of us need physical as well as verbal expressions that we are accepted, appreciated, valued—a pat on the back from our boss or a hug from a friend. Researchers tell us that we all have deep needs for touching, stroking, caressing, in addition to sexual need for orgasmic release. Psychologists call it "skin hunger." Children who receive no physical touching—even though they are fed, washed, and kept warm—will wither away and die.

The single person observes the married couple embracing or a parent cuddling a child and feels very much left out. Dr. Marc Hollender studied what he calls "the need to be held," and found that in some women (and men) the need for cuddling was even stronger than the desire for sex. One woman described it as "almost a physical feeling . . . an ache."[29] Cuddling represents security, protection, comfort, contentment, and love. Without it the women in Hollender's study became tense, let down, rejected, hurt, and lonely. Many felt they must make sexual advances or give sexual favors in return for being held. Although some would wrap themselves in blankets or fuzzy sweaters or rock themselves as a substitute, none found satisfaction for their longings outside of actual holding.

Ann Landers learned the same thing when she asked readers if they agreed with a letter writer who said, "If you were to ask 100 women how they feel about sexual intercourse, I'll bet 89% would say 'Just hold me close and tender. Forget about the act!' " More than 90,000 women answered the challenge, and 64,000 said yes!—40 percent of whom were under forty.[30]

When the single person reaches out for touch, the overture is sometimes mistaken for a sexual advance. The person is either rebuffed or propositioned. Sometimes the message is mixed for both parties. We say we want to be hugged, when in fact we would like sex, though perhaps not from this person. Part of this confusion can be avoided when we really stay in touch with our feelings, accept those feelings, all of them, and then choose deliberately how we will act on them. Here again self-esteem plays a large part.

Although skin hunger is primarily for the touch of another, it can also be somewhat satisfied in solitude. We can take care of ourselves with bubble baths, silky robes, soft linens. Our bodies need to run, dance, sing, and shout. In our sedentary society, we need to find ways to unwind, to use our bodies fully, through aerobics, running, tennis, swimming, skiing, bicycling. Pets also offer an opportunity to stroke and cuddle, to be warmed by another living body. I seldom sleep alone—my cats Phoebe and Fletcher sleep on either side of me, my dog Ben at my feet.

Finding a Sense of Purpose

A therapist once reminded me that in the end all that we can hope to depend on is ourselves and meaningful work. Despite all of his very helpful work on adolescent development, Erik Erickson suggested that young men find their identity in career while women find it in the men they relate to. Women today are realizing that that is a crock. Women too must find their self-worth in their own meaningful work, whether that is rearing their own children or teaching others' children, cooking creatively at home or in a restaurant kitchen, painting their walls or building houses, writing letters or books. Each person has been given unique gifts by God, and each is responsible for using those gifts.

Women today have many more opportunities and much more encouragement to continue their education and get the training they need to pursue the work that they find most meaningful. Some members of the Evangelical Women's Caucus have been critical of the educational credentials so prominently listed in conference programs and publicity. Yet a decade ago education was only a dream to many of these women. It has been through the support of the women's movement, in the church and in society, that many women have found the courage to make their dreams come true.

Yet many women, single and married, have depersonalizing and boring jobs. Locked into the lowest, most meaningless, least remunerative positions, they often express their frustration in inefficiency, pettiness, and bickering. It used to be said, "Oh, she's just a cantankerous old maid." Since her vocation is often the center of a single woman's life, she must not allow herself to be trapped in a hopeless position. Part of the panic of being single is being caught in a situation where marriage appears to be the only form of salvation. Getting married, however, to "someone who will take me away from all this" is no formula for success. The single woman must again take responsibility for her own life, get up, and get out of her rut.

A single woman's future financial security and independence rest solely on the development of her vocational skills (so does that of a married woman, as so many divorcees and widows have learned so abruptly!). Yet younger women are often counseled away from advancement programs because "with a Ph.D. or as an executive, you'll never find a husband." So a woman ends up at thirty-five, without a husband anyway, and still at the lowest level of her profession or in a field she does not enjoy. But it is never too late to go after one's goals. The older single woman may find it frighteningly risky to change jobs or cities or to give up a job in order to return to school for further education, but the sacrifices are worth the rewards in self-esteem, enjoyment, and advancement. Unhampered by family and/or a less-than-supportive husband, the single woman is freer to take the risk. She has no one to blame but herself if she is stuck at the bottom. If she is discriminated against because she is a woman, she can seek legal redress. Today as organizations become aware of women's potential, she can often move ahead quickly if she has the necessary credentials.

To anyone who piously questions if she should be striving for financial reward, she can reply that her tithe will be larger. The single woman must also be concerned with her own insurance and retirement finances. Some single women have a tendency to drift through life, always thinking that someday they will have husbands to make all of those financial plans. Many married women assume their husbands have made such plans. Both may be sadly mistaken. Those who do not make their own plans may well end up old and poor and alone—a very difficult situation.

A single woman certainly should not deny herself the comforts of home and children, if she desires them. Many Christians feel somehow that having possessions is sinful, and tend to project this guilt onto single people. They enviously eye the single person's new car or wardrobe. Christian organizations in particular seem to feel that women should work for significantly lower salaries and effect a poverty-level life-style. Although no Christian should be covetously enslaved by possessions, Christ did once say that the laborer is worthy of his hire (Luke 10:7). This also applies to laborers who happen to be female and single. Since her job is one source of her self-worth and worth is measured in our society in terms of pay, a decent salary for a single woman is very much a part of her affirmation, to say nothing of justice.

Given our tax situation, a home is one of the best investments anyone can make. Some singles think of their apartments as simply places to live until they get married. They view buying a house as an admission of defeat, a clear indication that they plan to be single forever, or at least until the thirty-year mortgage is paid. Taking on the obligation certainly does feel like the assumption of real, adult responsibility. Royalties from the first edition of this book provided a down payment on a condominium when I moved to Atlanta. The day I signed the contract, I did have a major anxiety attack, but I have never regretted the decision. There comes a time when one is ready to "settle down," to make a home of one's own, a time to open the "hope chest" and enjoy the silver and linens.

Enjoying one's home and being comfortable with one's possessions also often open up opportunities for hospitality and ministry. I drive a large, four-door car because as a single person I have too often ended up having to crawl awkwardly into a cramped backseat. I enjoy being able to give an elderly friend a ride to church or take a gang of people along to dinner or an outing comfortably. In Deerfield, Illinois, I had a wonderful friend, Doris Roethlisberger, a former missionary and now professor of English, who has a marvelous gift for hospitality. I was often the recipient of it and I learned much from her, lessons that I try to practice. I learned that hospitality is not a matter of having the best furnishings and the finest food but a matter of loving people and being willing to share whatever one has.

Some single people are also single parents. Many divorced or widowed women have children to cope with. A lot of never-married women feel the urge of the biological clock in their late twenties or early thirties, just as their married sisters do. Having survived my thirties, I have cautioned younger friends that it is a phase one goes through. Thus one should not make any hasty decisions on the basis of hormones. I am certainly glad that I did not adopt a child when I wanted to so strongly. Laws in most states, however, do allow single persons to adopt children or to become foster parents, particularly to kids with a handicap or mixed racial ancestry. One parent who really loves a child is better than institutional care. Many single women, many lesbian couples, have intentionally borne children, usually through artificial insemination.

Those women who have tried it have found their lives enriched. One woman who became guardian to her mentally retarded younger sister after the death of their mother commented:

I suppose some people pity me when they see us together, but they shouldn't. She gives me so much. The advantages far outweigh the disadvantages. I don't think I could love my own child more—in fact she seems like my own child now that Mother is gone. Although others in the family may spend more of the waking hours with her, she comes to me now as her authority and security. She's a bundle of sweetness in my life.

In her early forties this woman found a man who was happy to have both of them in his life. Another woman took a seven-year-old girl from an orphanage to the zoo as part of a volunteer project. When the woman asked the child what she would like to call her, the child replied, "Mother." A year later a judge made it official. The fact that this affirmation grows out of choice and affection rather than simply the natural processes of biology makes it a very special one.

On the other hand, just because one does not marry or does not have children does not mean one is bereft of family. One of the burdens so many single people—never-married, gay, divorced, or widowed—bear is the myth that only the nuclear family (a father, a mother, a boy, and a girl) qualifies as "family." One would be extremely hard pressed to find that definition of family in Scripture. Up until the last century, even biological families have always been much more extended than they are today. Sociologists now speak of "families of origin" and "families of choice." While many single people of all ages are choosing to live alone, we need not. And even if we choose to live alone, we can still build support networks, "friends as family," as one book on the subject is titled.[31] Some builders are constructing houses specifically for singles who choose to invest and live together, houses with two master bedroom suites. Christians all over the country have experimented with various types of living in community. *Sojourners* magazine is published by such a community and regularly highlights various other groups.

The Church and the Single Adult

The church should be one place where a person can feel loved and accepted. After all, did not Jesus say, "Come to me, all who labor and are heavy laden, and I will give you rest" (Matt. 11:28)? Was not the mark of the early church the way they loved one another? Yet the single person often feels most isolated at church. "It's the place of my deepest loneliness," admitted one woman. Another explained, "I'm tired of singing in the choir or teaching a Sunday school class, but it's hard to always have to sit alone in the congregation amid all of those families. There's just no place for us." Many singles just drop out of the church, particularly in the city where no one attempts to get to know them if they do attend, so no one misses them if they do not.

What should the church do to make singles feel welcome? In the past decade many churches have instituted all sorts of "singles programs." Most seem to view this ministry as a way of segregating singles and getting them matched up appropriately. And certainly some singles do want that—a decent place to meet decent people. Some churches supplement that with informative programs, small Bible studies, subgroups for single parents or those coping with addictions, rewarding community service projects.

Personally, I prefer to be incorporated into the general life of a church which does not advertise itself as family-oriented but welcomes all sorts and conditions of people. My pastor, a single man, uses a variety of sermon illustrations from single and married life. All of the church's programs are open to all of its members. Women and single people are welcome at all levels of service and administration. Women usher and men are on the altar guild. Even the traditional "women's activities" are not segregated by age or marital or employment status.

Single people have a great deal to offer the church, and the church has much to offer them. However, some churches also turn them away by overloading them with work. Erroneously assuming that single persons have more time than married persons, some churches wear single persons out by heaping too much work on them. This is particularly true of younger professional people. Single people need to be aware of their own needs and limitations. We all need to take care of ourselves and not accept more obligations than we can comfortably carry, no matter how flattered we may feel to be asked.

Ask any single person what is the greatest problem of being single and the response will undoubtedly be, "Loneliness." One side of the coin is the freedom not to have to consider anyone else in making one's decisions. The other side is the fact that no one else has to care about the single person. One can break out of one's isolation, but it takes effort. Once we have discovered essentially who we are, we long to share that self in an intimate relationship with another. For many people this intimate relationship is marriage. Yet this is not automatic. Many marriages know no bonds of intimacy beyond physical coupling, while many single persons, aside from sexual union, have found the deepest sharing within friendship.

How can the single person break out of her isolation? It is not easy to love without knowing that one is loved. As Christians we know theologically that God loves us, that through the death of Jesus Christ we are reconciled to communion with God. It is not a love that we can buy or that we must earn. God loves us freely, completely, steadfastly. Christ offers us daily, moment-by-moment companionship and promises never to leave us.

Love is not to be found in being attractive, being dependent, or being in control. The "art of loving" is learning to express love, to exercise one's capacity to love. As Erich Fromm says, "Love is not primarily a relationship to a specific person; it is an attitude, an orientation of character which determines the relatedness of a person to the world as a whole, not toward one 'object' of love."[32] Loving is not something that goes on only between marriage partners or parents and children. Christ constantly encouraged his followers to love others as he had loved them. The early church was characterized by love for one another.

The source of our love, single or married, is God's love. The one "who loves is born of God and knows God. . . . If God so loved us, we also ought to love one another. . . . If we love another, God abides in us and [divine] love is perfected in us" (I John 4:7, 11-12). God calls us and enables us to love. The Christian single woman will find many God-given opportunities to perfect the art of loving.

God's love will radiate in her eyes and smile. One of the delightful things about children is that they will not flinch if one stares at them but often will return a steady look of curiosity that sometimes ends in a smile. It's sad that growing up often means that we learn to avert our eyes, to restrain the smile that might become the first bridge to friendship. A steady gaze, a warm smile can be ways of saying to another person that she is accepted, taken seriously, loved. Sometimes a single person needs to receive such reassurance before she is able to give it—but when God enables her to give first she often finds her openness rewarded.

In order to meet her needs to share her life, the single woman must reach out. She will find that even though she may not have one with whom to share everything, she can find many with whom she can share much. It's often easiest to find someone to share her troubles because people need to feel needed. When my father first suffered a heart attack, I found it difficult to share my burden with my co-workers out of fear that they would not care or that they would be embarrassed by the necessity of responding. Yet when I was able to tell several, I found them eager to support me and my family in prayer and concern.

Surprisingly, it is more difficult to find someone with whom to share our joys. Yet when there is no one with whom to share a tribute, savor a compliment, or rejoice in a job completed, life seems empty and meaningless. If someone is in real difficulty, we will listen and help because it makes us feel important and superior. But if someone shares a small triumph, we immediately say, "How nice . . . but listen to what happened to me!" Or we make a perfunctory response and then find some way to deflate the other's joy. Why are we jealous of others' happiness or threatened by their advancement? A single woman particularly needs to know that what she is doing is worthwhile. She needs people to share her joys and reinforce each contribution to her self-esteem. Paul speaks of the church as Christ's body in which "if one member suffers, all suffer together, if one member is honored, all rejoice together" (I Cor. 12:26).

German theologian Dietrich Bonhoeffer once said that true community is characterized by three gifts of God: sacrificing for one another in love, praying for one another, forgiving one another's sins and lifting the burden of guilt.[33] As Protestants we are sometimes hesitant to exercise that final gift. We reject the idea of absolution, yet it is just the giving of a verbal reminder to the penitent that God will always forgive and heal. Confession is essential to human relationships. Deep love can never grow until we are willing to open our lives and get rid of the sins we have kept hidden.[34]

There comes a point in any relationship where, if the two people are to go on to intimacy and communion, they must be ready to let each other see their faults and weaknesses as well as their virtues. Each must be ready to accept the other's faults and forgive any shortcomings. This involves great vulnerability and risk. Some have taken the risk and been hurt. Some have developed scar tissue so thick no one can get close to them again. But Christ can also dissolve that tissue and heal those scars if we are willing. And we can find true community, even outside marriage.

12.

WASTING THE CHURCH'S GIFTS

Caller to radio talk show: "What do you think of Philip's four daughters who prophesied?"
Guest minister: "It just means they witnessed for Christ."
Caller: "But why can't women preach and teach?"
Minister: "That ministry is for men only and I can give you a very good reason: God made roosters to crow and hens to lay eggs."[1]

THIS STORY MAY ILLUSTRATE IN MORE WAYS THAN ONE WHY THE church today is in trouble! Christian poultry farmers tell us they keep roosters on their farms and call pastors to their local church to do a lot more than crow. Christian women tell us they want to do more for the church than bring children to Sunday school, warm the nursery nest, and fry eggs at pancake breakfasts.

Despite the varied ministries that women exercised in the early church, women have been systematically excluded from the ordained ministry and the power structure of the church. Today the issue is being raised in many churches, Protestant and Catholic, evangelical and liberal, but the response is still often akin to Archie Bunker's on television's "All in the Family." In a theological debate with his wife one night, he summarized the issue with his usual pungency: "Stifle yourself, Edith. God don't want to be defended by no dingbat!"

Most churches do permit women a variety of lay ministries—making pies for the church supper, doing macrame for the bazaar, redecorating the social hall, collecting clothes for missionaries, teaching the toddlers, and even leading a housewives' Bible study. But these ministries are usually limited to the domestic sphere and are seldom integral to the church's mission to the world. For example, the church bulletin one Sunday advertised a "Men for Missions" breakfast coming up at a special restaurant. Men were also invited to visit a seminary in another state to discuss possible calls to the ministry with a leading theologian. A third announcement simply stated: "Women are needed to help make Raggedy Ann dolls for the nursery."

Women have been permitted a wider role, on a semiclerical level, if they promise to do it elsewhere! Many women with leadership and evangelistic gifts have volunteered for missionary service overseas or in "underprivileged" areas of this country. One evangelical denomination which would not consider allowing a woman to pastor an established church has let an outstanding woman, and those women she has been able to draw around her, carry on a difficult work in Appalachia. Yet the work of these women is downgraded by repeated statements that God uses them only because men refuse to answer God's call.

On the level of officially ordained clergy, women are scarce. Though some eighty Protestant denominations around the world do ordain women, not more than 5 percent of the ministers in these churches are women—though in every denomination about two-thirds of the members are. And these denominations comprise a small minority of all Christians. The largest groups, which rely heavily on tradition—Roman Catholicism, Orthodoxy, and parts of the Anglican Communion—do not ordain women. Nor do many evangelical and fundamental groups.[2]

These churches' understanding of the ministry and the reasons they raise for denying ordination to women affect the role of women throughout the churches. In the Catholic tradition, priests are sacramentally commissioned to pronounce absolution and to celebrate the Eucharist. Their powers have been passed down from Christ and the apostles, and they serve as dispensers of God's sacramental grace to the people. Protestant ministers are commissioned more as preachers, teachers, guides. Their essential function is the ability to publicly proclaim the gospel, to correctly interpret and teach the Word of God. Organizing and directing congregational activities are also important to their role. Why then are women generally excluded from the "ministry"?[3]

Scriptural Prohibitions

Many people simply assume that the statements "women should keep silence in the churches" (I Cor. 14:34) and "I permit no woman to teach or to have authority over men" (I Tim. 2:12) automatically rule out women pastors. As we have seen, and as the vast majority of denominational commissions which have analyzed these Scriptures have concluded, there is no basis here for denying women ordination.[4]

The issue is usually approached more broadly, if more bluntly. A contemporary Roman Catholic theologian put it this way: "The reason . . . for denying women the right to teach is a reason that is absolute and universal, based on the natural condition of inferiority and subjection that is the position of women."[5] The history of theology is strewn with such statements. Scriptural justification is usually sought in terms of the order of creation which we considered earlier. This is often buttressed by psychological arguments that women are by nature less apt at reasoning, less capable of handling doctrine objectively, more easily deceived, less assertive, and less capable of public speaking.[6]

In Roman Catholic circles women have traditionally been told that they are incapable of receiving the "indelible character" which orders confer. This conjures up an image of paper or cloth so highly sized or glazed that God's indelible ink won't mark on it and simply washes off. Theologically this is not what the phrase means at all. The "character" of the priest is the spiritual power given by God at ordination and used to perform the sacraments through which God acts. "Indelible" simply means that a sacrament cannot be repeated, that it is once and for all (baptism and confirmation are also considered so). Thus, to say women are incapable of receiving the indelible character is to say that, first, God refuses to endow women with divine power and, second, women are incapable of being validly baptized or confirmed either.[7]

Protestants speak more in terms of "the keys" or "ruling authority." They argue that "the New Testament evidence thus requires, in the present age, that the ruling-teaching office be restricted to the man and that the woman be restricted from it because she is a woman." Or as a Reformed pastor declared: "The whole of Scripture witnesses with one accord that to man is confided the heavy task of ruling, to woman the beautiful task of serving."[8]

The Orthodox variant on this theme reaches back into the Old Testament teachings on woman's periodic "impurity."[9] This comes close to pagan beliefs that women simply have bad mana and should not be allowed to participate in mystery or magic. In the Christian tradition women have been the ones most often labeled "witches." Yet if a woman was allowed the most intimate functions of bearing, nursing, and nurturing God Incarnate, should not women today be able to handle Christ's body and blood?

Overall, it is clear that while many people feel they are arguing on the basis of scriptural prohibitions, they are simply standing on theological tradition based on cultural prejudices. What they are saying is that for one sex, half the human race, sexual differentiation is a handicap so crippling that no amount of personal talent, intelligence, piety, or even divine enabling can make them fit ministers of the gospel.

Lack of Scriptural Example

On the whole the Bible is a masculine book and reflects patriarchal cultures. God is frequently spoken of in masculine terms; the Old Testament highlights patriarchs, priests, and male prophets; Jesus and the Twelve were males. These precedents are often used to bar women from Christian leadership.

If God is male, then women cannot be ordained to represent "him."[10] As we have seen, the attribution of sexuality to God is a misunderstanding of the divine nature. The Old Testament priesthood was all male, based on patriarchal lineage, but its function was to represent the people to God. The word of God to the people most often came through the prophet. Throughout Scripture women were given the gift of prophecy and used by God to convey God's message. Christ himself was outside the Old Testament priesthood, a member of the tribe of Judah rather than Levi, "a priest for ever, after the order of Melchizedek" (Heb. 5:6). His self-sacrifice was the culumination of the old covenant and the termination of the priesthood.[11]

Jesus was a male. Few people would dispute that. The question is, So what? We have discussed why Jesus came as a male and how New Testament writers reacted to it. If his humanity did not incorporate all of us, then only half of us were redeemed by his sacrifice. Christ was both fully human and fully divine. In the 1977 "Declaration on the Question of the Admission of Women to the Ministerial Priesthood," Pope Paul VI declared that "Christ himself was and remains a man" and that "there would not be this 'natural resemblance' which must exist between Christ and his minister if the role of Christ in the eucharist were not taken by a man."[12] However, if one of the criteria for being able to represent Christ is to be like him (i.e., male), is this not elevating masculinity above divinity? Christ came to be the Jewish Messiah, the sacrificial lamb to take away the sins of the world, the king to reign on David's throne—for these reasons he was male. But "the Christian priest is not ordained to be another Christ and do again what only he could do and has done."[13]

A variant on this argument is a reference to Christ as the bridegroom, the church as his bride. The tacit assumption again is that ministers represent Christ and thus only men can be bridegrooms. Not only contrary to New Testament teaching, this is presumptuous! In the Gospels Jesus speaks of himself as the bridegroom, but his disciples are the guests (Mark 2:19-20), at least some of whom are women (Matt. 25:1ff.). The priest or minister is always part of the church, part of the bride, as are all Christian men and women. We are all the sons of God! We are also all the daughters of God![14]

Jesus' twelve apostles were all men—and all Jewish. This fact raises a pertinent question: Why are we so selective about what in the New Testament we emulate? As Krister Stendahl notes, Jesus ordered his disciples to walk, staff in hand (Mark 6:8). Is that our biblical paradigm for ministerial travel? Jesus himself said his disciples were sent only to the lost sheep of Israel (Matt. 10:6). Is this normative today?[15] What was the point of Jesus' choosing twelve male apostles? He tells us that they represent the twelve tribes of Israel which they will judge in the kingdom (Matt. 19:28). If the New Testament church could make the radical innovation of allowing Gentiles to become leaders of the church and heirs to apostolic authority, could not the church today take the less radical step of ordaining women?

And while the Twelve all answered to masculine names, Jesus did commission and send out the Seventy (Luke 10:1-20). They were given the same instructions and powers. Women traveled with Jesus (Luke 8:1-3). Paul says some wives traveled with their apostle husbands (I Cor. 9:5). So who is to say that pairs of women or married couples were not among the Seventy?

Were there any women at the Last Supper? If only men were there, theologians presume that only men can reenact the scene today. Several reasons can be offered as to why only men were there. Some say in Jesus' day women were never included at the Paschal meal. Others say they were present in family groups, but would not have been invited by a single man dining with male guests. Another suggestion is that Jesus knew of the imminence of his arrest and so did not include women. Jesus also ties it in with the New Israel (Luke 22:28-30).

And what about the meal referred to in Mark 14:1-2 and John 12:1-3? Many have suggested that Martha, Mary, and Lazarus were Essenes, a Jewish sect which followed a different calendar and celebrated the Passover earlier. This may well have been a ritual meal which included women.[16] And after all, if Jesus meant to set an example by not inviting women to the Last Supper, how did the church presume to do so?

Nowhere in the New Testament are any of these reasons used to prohibit women from ministry in the church. Paul does not allude to the Last Supper in his instructions to women even though he discusses it in the same context (I Cor. 11–14). Paul, who considered himself an apostle, never uses his own example, or the Twelve, or Jesus as grounds that women could not hold office.

There is one rather cogent case that could be made from New Testament evidence—though we have yet to see theologians make it. Matthew and Mark clearly record that the Great Commission was given to the "eleven disciples" only (Matt. 28:16-20; Mark 16:14-15). If male theologians would like to absolve women of all responsibility for fulfilling this command, then perhaps women could simply devote themselves to other pursuits. All the evangelism and missionary sermons we have ever heard, however, leave the distinct impression that women too are under God's command to spread the gospel.

Tradition

The church never has ordained women to leadership positions, it is often asserted, and therefore should not now. (Paul did not use a microphone either!) However, the case is not that clear-cut. For one thing, the New Testament is certainly not definitive about church order or we would not range from highly democratic congregations to strictly hierarchical churches all claiming scriptural basis. While some see clearly defined orders of bishop, priest, and deacon, others see nothing of the kind.

Second, despite their subordinate social status, some women were ordained in the early church, complete with the episcopal laying on of hands. Both the New Testament and historical evidence show women deacons until about the tenth century. Church history is a record of what women were successively stopped from doing. No one ever said they could not be martyrs, but Tertullian told widows to stop teaching and baptizing. The Council of Laodicea in 381 said no more women presbyters could be appointed and women should henceforth not "approach the altar," indicating liturgical functions of some kind. The Synod of Orange in 441 forbade the ordination of women, but the second Council of Orleans in 533 spoke of women deacons.[17]

Throughout history women have distinguished themselves in Christ's service. Paula (347–404), a wealthy Roman noblewoman, helped Jerome translate the Vulgate in addition to founding a monastery, convent, and hospice. Pulcheria (399–453), regent for her brother Theodosius and empress of the Eastern Empire for forty years, instructed her brother's bride Eudocia in the faith and helped her in a poetical paraphrase of the first eight books of the Old Testament, plus Daniel and Zechariah. She summoned the Council of Chalcedon and was influential in its defense of orthodoxy against several heresies. Other women founded religious orders and in the "Dark Ages" ruled as abbesses over huge double monasteries for both men and women. They held great authority (in tenth-century England four were peers) with the right to ban persons from their domain, send out knights, give judgment in court, mint coinage, and attend the imperial diet in Germany.

Despite its emphasis on the laity, the Reformation did little for women, but among the anabaptist groups women played a great part. Lysken Dirks, for example, was imprisoned for her faith in Antwerp in 1551. Monks questioning the pregnant woman asked why she was meddling with Scripture instead of sewing. She answered, "Christ commands us to search the Scriptures and Christ is to be obeyed rather than man." They drowned her. First Quaker missionary Elizabeth Hooten, on her second mission to America, was whipped at age sixty to "improve" her theology. Women in the nineteenth century helped found and fund the great missionary movement.[18]

To paraphrase John, there are also many other things women have done in the church's history; were every one of them to be written, the volumes would probably fill library shelves equal to those already devoted to the history of men's work in the church. Women have proven that God does call and empower them and that they are equal to the task. Their record has simply been ignored.

Social/Cultural Considerations

Deprived of scriptural and historical arguments, those opposing women's full ministry in the church often turn to cultural considerations. Women just could not combine the ministry as a career with marriage, critics warn. Only the pope, however, raises this objection in regard to men. We laud male evangelists, missionaries, and denominational executives who spend a great deal of time away from their families. And yet we say families would disintegrate if women were to serve God outside the home.

From a biblical standpoint God did not seem too concerned that Deborah and Huldah were married when they were chosen as prophets. Priscilla seems to have had a hand in every letter that is considered genuinely Pauline, probably having them copied and distributed to the churches, yet Paul apparently did not worry that it would hurt her marriage to Aquila. What about all the married women today who very successfully combine "secular" careers with marriage? And how does this argument apply at all to single women, divorcees, or widows seeking ordination?

A corollary is the assertion that a woman could not handle some aspects of a pastor's job, such as counseling, confession, certain visitation, and so on. Men in the congregation just would not work with a woman pastor, some claim. The experience of ordained women in parishes has disproved all of these contentions. They find men do respond well to their leadership, that they can shepherd the flock in ways a man cannot. For any man who feels ill at ease counseling with or confessing to a woman, there have always been women who hesitate to discuss personal problems with male ministers. Women in secular counseling jobs have the same problems and have been able to successfully meet them.[19] Besides, not all people ordained are called to the local church—some serve as chaplains in the military, prisons, hospitals, colleges, and similar institutions.

Other foot-draggers note that seminaries are currently turning out more ministerial candidates than the churches can hire and that women entering the profession would drive men out. Does that mean that God is confused, calling too many people into divine service? Perhaps it is the church which should have a broader vision.

"Society just isn't ready for women ministers" summarizes these arguments. The rapid changes in our society in the past two or three decades already give the statement a dated ring. In this area society seems far ahead of the church in permitting women full development of their talents. And even if it were not, since when should the church wait to proclaim the truth until society is ready for it? Should the church cater to prejudices that society at large or its own members have?

Is Ordination Relevant?

Many people today, women among them, feel that the whole issue of ordination is passé. They argue that the church is moving into a new era when clergy-lay distinctions are being weakened, when the concept of ministry is changing from an authority figure to a servanthood model, when the priesthood of all believers is becoming more of a reality. True as that may be, Luther also said it four hundred years ago. And women are a bit suspicious when denominational men's and women's boards are abolished in the name of egalitarian reform and the result is a new board made up of all male executives and women administrators are suddenly out of a job. As long as the church does maintain some sort of hierarchy and power structure, women should be admitted to it.

Ordination does have advantages. Whatever their theology, all churches consider ordination at least symbolic of God's empowering an individual for service. On a sociological level ordination is a sign that the recipient has been tested and found capable and worthy, just as a doctor's license certifies that she or he is trained and competent. A minister will be readily admitted into many areas of service such as hospitals and prisons where a lay Christian will not. Ordination is also a commitment by the church to stand behind and support its ministers, something women need and deserve as much as men.

Ordination has advantages not only for the person ordained but also for those to whom she ministers. Refusal to ordain women has deprived thousands of Christians in remote areas of this country and on the mission fields of services that the church allows only ordained people to perform. Women missionaries have not been allowed to baptize, confirm, perform marriages, or celebrate Holy Communion for their converts. Thus the church has willfully denied important aspects of the Christian life to these people just because of basic prejudices against women.

Ordination is relevant to women who feel called to the official ministry, and many women in all branches of the church do feel this call of God upon their lives. Can the church continue to deny them opportunity to respond to this call?

A Talent Buried

The Bible makes it clear that God has given each of us specific, unique gifts to be used to glorify God and to serve one another (I Pet. 4:10). As members of the body of Christ we have a variety of gifts—wisdom, knowledge, faith, healing, miracle-working, prophecy, discerning of spirits, tongues, interpretations. We are equipped by the Holy Spirit for many tasks—to be apostles, prophets, evangelists, pastors, teachers, helpers, administrators, speakers (I Cor. 12:4-31; Eph. 4:4-16).

None of these gifts is labeled "for men only." Scripture nowhere indicates that men alone are given the gifts of leadership and women those of following and helping. Quite the contrary. First Corinthians 12:11 emphatically states that all gifts "are inspired by one and the same Spirit, who apportions to each one individually as [the Spirit] wills." Although Ephesians 4:8 is sometimes cited to prove God intends only men to be apostles, prophets, evangelists, and pastors (v. 11), the word in Greek is *anthropos,* the generic term for all people, not just males. When a woman tried to get Jesus to affirm motherhood as "woman's role," he said, "Blessed rather are those who hear the word of God and keep it!" (Luke 11:28). Another time he commented, "Whoever does the will of God is my brother, and sister, and mother" (Mark 3:35). To do the will and work of God in the world is the task of all Christians.

"To each is given the manifestation of the Spirit for the common good" (I Cor. 12:7). The decision to use or to squander our gifts is not a purely personal one, but something that has ramifications for the entire Body. If anyone hides her talent or uses it for purely selfish ends, the Body is weakened, handicapped. But if each uses her gifts to build up the Body, then all benefit.

Shortly before his death, Jesus instructed his disciples with an interesting series of parables about servants, wise and foolish virgins, talents, and do-gooders (Matt. 24:45–25:46). He warned all his followers that they were expected to be faithful, diligent workers. Those who were not would be cast out of the kingdom. The parable of the talents is particularly applicable to our subject. Two servants, given gifts by their master, went out in his absence and doubled their worth. On his return they were praised and rewarded. The third had this to say:

"Master, I knew you to be a hard man . . . so I was afraid, and I went and hid your gold in the ground. Here it is." "You lazy rascal!" said the master. ". . . You ought to have put my money on deposit, and on my return I should have got it back with interest. Take the bag of gold from him, and give it to the one with the ten bags. . . . Fling the useless servant out into the dark, the place of wailing and grinding of teeth!" (Matt. 25:24-20 NEB).

How could God be so harsh on the poor timid soul, who did after all return the original gift in mint condition? Will God be as harsh on the woman who confesses:

I heard your call to preach your word, but when I sought advice from my pastor he ridiculed me.

I applied to a seminary, but they told me women were not permitted to enroll in the master of divinity program.

I requested ordination from our denomination, but they told me women were not called to ordained ministry.

I asked to candidate at a local church, but they said people in the congregation would not accept a woman pastor.

I applied to a mission board, but they turned me away when they learned my gift was evangelization, not nursing, secretarial work, or teaching children.

So I just gave up, got married, and had kids like everyone had been telling me to do all along.

We think rather that Christ's judgment will be turned on those who have denied women opportunities to develop and use their gifts—with words akin to those in Matthew 25:41!

The church does actively discourage women. If they report that the Holy Spirit has given them gifts for changing diapers, corralling seven-year-olds, baking cakes, or rolling bandages, the church has a place for them. But if their gifts are administration, accounting, theological investigation, or public speaking, forget it. A century ago a young woman of the Church of England wrote, "I would have given the church my head, my hand, my heart. She would not have them. She told me to go back and do crochet in my mother's drawing room."[20] Florence Nightingale had to go to another church in another country to find training to serve God.

In her teen years, Letha was invited into a wide variety of churches to play the trombone, present Bible studies, and give her testimony. Some Baptist deacons took her aside and scolded her for her public speaking. Nancy as a teenager felt called to missionary service but visiting missionaries constantly discouraged her by saying, "Get married, and we'll be happy to see you on the field." Clearly they did not want her; they wanted her husband. Young women today still report similar experiences.

The church's pattern of discrimination leads to absurdities. Women are permitted to teach women and children. Yet if women are as weak-minded and prone to error as theologians say, does this mean we do not care if women and children are led astray? And at what age does a boy become a man? Why should it be all right for women to teach men in universities, even in Christian colleges, and yet not in church? Why do we hire women as directors of Christian education? (The observation that churches now tend to hire a man in the same capacity with the title "minister of education" and a higher salary is no sign of enlightenment!) One well-known woman missionary once was permitted to speak only to the women of a certain church. But her speech was recorded and immediately played for the men assembled elsewhere in the building! At the time she was furious!

If women are supposed to keep silence in the church, why do we let them sing solos, play musical instruments, and even lead choirs? After all, does not Colossians 3:16 link singing with teaching? If the church really took seriously the charge that women were unfit teachers, many fine hymns which teach doctrine and which were written by women would be ripped from our hymnals.

And why are women allowed to write Bible studies, Sunday school quarterlies, magazine articles, and books which instruct men as well as women?

Young women at an international youth organization's missionary convention responded to a call for volunteers to help distribute the elements at the climactic Communion service. They were told that "biblically" only men could do so. Women can serve family suppers in the church, but not the Lord's Supper.

What are the results of these large and small discriminations? Many women take the easy, acceptable way out. After all, Christ's instructions not to hide one's light under a bushel must have been for men only too. The pious woman is supposed to be retiring, self-effacing, always ready to offer her husband's opinions rather than her own, to step aside from any position when a man becomes available for it, to make suggestions which male superiors can offer as their own. Women soon get the message and hide their gifts. Pride is often proclaimed as man's primary sin. For women it seems to be irresponsibility.

And manipulation. The church not only allows but also encourages women to be devious, to exercise influence behind the scenes. Women in the church are often pacified with the assertion that they wield immense power. But it is irresponsible power. We condemn such corruption in government and yet condone it in the church.

Many women cannot accept the circumscribed roles the church offers them. They become frustrated, depressed, and sometimes bitter. "The unfulfilled potential, the unlived experience, haunts consciousness, for deep down in every [person] lives the knowledge that the sin of unfulfillment is a sin against the Holy Ghost, the spirit of life whose breath is the Awakener."[21] Such women struggle to find avenues within the church through which they can serve God only to be met with suspicion and resistance. One seminary handbook warns the young minister that women in *his* congregation will want to work because they are neurotic, lonely, status seeking, and guilt-ridden. They are usually unqualified for what they want to do, divisive, jealous, resentful, given to gossip, and their husbands may

207

use their work as an excuse to stop giving. The young minister is cautioned to structure women's role in the church into a women's organization represented by one woman on the official board and responsible for domestic tasks.

Sometimes women simply conclude, as many women have told us, "The church has no place for me." A seminary wife commented, "I've been put down so many times in churches. For example, prayer is requested for someone and so someone comes up to three men around me and says, 'Let's pray.' They ignore me like I'm not there or like my prayers wouldn't do any good. I can't go into a local church and witness to a gospel that is not Good News for women as well as men." A woman seminarian with an established ministry expressed fears that those who have supported her in the past will discontinue their gifts when she marries. Despite the fact that her husband is a student, they will expect him to support her and her ministry or expect her to quit her ministry and devote her energies to supporting him.

Some of these women continue to attend church but invest their talents elsewhere.[22] Others, like the young convert at a major university who was excited about Christ until campus Christians began telling her that Christ opposed women's liberation, simply leave the church. Women who felt called into the ordained ministry have often had to leave the church of their birth and change to a more open denomination.

To deny one's own gifts or the gifts of others is to quench and grieve the Holy Spirit. Dietrich Bonhoeffer once warned, "A community which allows unemployed members to exist within it will perish because of them. It will be well, therefore, if every member receives a definite task to perform for the community, that he [or she] may know in hours of doubt that he [or she], too, is not useless and unusable."[23] Women are not asking to take over the church as many seem to fear. Instead their cry echoes the instruction of Paul (Rom. 12:6): "Having gifts that differ according to the grace given to us, let us use them"!

13.

WORKING WOMEN:
AT HOME AND BEYOND

As they passed the rows of houses they saw through the open doors that men were sweeping and dusting and washing dishes, while the women sat around in groups, gossiping and laughing.

"What has happened?" the Scarecrow asked a sad-looking man with a bushy beard, who wore an apron and was wheeling a baby-carriage along the sidewalk.

"Why, we've had a revolution, your Majesty—as you ought to know very well," replied the man, "and since you went away the women have been running things to suit themselves. I'm glad you have decided to come back and restore order, for doing housework and minding children is wearing out the strength of every man in the Emerald City."

"Hm!" said the Scarecrow, thoughtfully, "If it is such hard work as you say, how did the women manage it so easily?"

"I really do not know," replied the man, with a deep sigh. "Perhaps the women are made of cast-iron."

—From *The Marvelous Land of Oz*[1]

IN WHAT SEEMED A STRANGE ITEM OF BUSINESS AT THE 1970 AMERICAN Political Science meetings, conferees were asked to try to solve the following riddle: a father and his teenage son were involved in an auto crash that killed the father and critically injured the boy. At the hospital, the surgeon called to perform emergency surgery took one look and said, "I can't do it. That's my son!"

The riddle stumped most persons. Had its source not been so carefully concealed (a group of women concerned with equality in the professions), no doubt its answer would have been guessed more quickly. But as it was, the incident underscored how deeply ingrained are gender-role stereotypes in our thinking.

Because of cultural reinforcement, such attitudes form early— even in the most liberated families. Psychology professor Matina Horner tells of being startled when her small daughter expressed amazement upon learning that a female family friend happened to be a physician. The three-year-old's first question was, "Is she still a girl?" which was quickly followed by a second query. "Is she still Eric's mommy?" Then the child concluded, "She must be all mixed up." Dr. Horner was astonished, since the little girl not only had a mother actively engaged in a profession but had also known other women physicians. Even so, society's expectations and gender-role stereotyping had implanted the notion that doctors are men. And women are mommies.[2]

Traditionalists see the matter simply. Woman's place is in the home. It is *man* whose place is in the world. And if women venture into that world (except temporarily while waiting to get married, or in cases of dire financial necessity), it is called "undesirable," "dangerous," "harmful to the family," "unfeminine," and much more.[3]

Societal attitudes have conceded a place in the world for certain kinds of "women's jobs"—clerks, secretaries, domestics, waitresses, schoolteachers, and nurses, for example. But it is this very segregation of the job market that accounts in large part for the disparity between women's and men's earnings, with women's overall wages being about 40 percent lower than men's. Women who find themselves in occupational "ghettos" which keep them apart from the achievement opportunities and financial and prestige rewards provided in male-dominanted sectors of the labor market are increasingly becoming aware of the inequities in the world of work. Thus, the debate over *pay equity* (sometimes called "comparable worth" or "wage comparability") has become one of the hottest public issues in recent years. It confronts systemic sex discrimination at its roots and puts the spotlight on one of the main contributing factors to the feminization of poverty.[4]

Sociologist Peter Rossi has observed that women's lower status in society has the effect of depressing the status of occupations in which women make up a high proportion of the work force. "Those occupations in which women are found in large numbers are not seen as seriously competing with other professions for personnel and resources," he points out.[5] No doubt the attitude he describes lies behind the failure to treat highly trained professionals such as schoolteachers, social workers, and nurses with the recognition, respect, and pay they deserve. It also accounts for the division of labor that has often occurred *within* such professions, with males traditionally being granted the greater opportunities and benefits.

The idea that women should even *attempt* to equal men in a desire for leadership, involvement in the world's serious issues, and genuine commitment to a career has been considered a laughing matter. This in itself is a symptom of how society feels about woman's place in the world. As one sympathetic business executive put it: "When you talk about equal employment of blacks, you no longer have Amos and Andy jokes. But you still have jokes on the woman's issue. Society hasn't taken the issue seriously."[6]

For many religious leaders, the matter of women in the labor force is nothing to joke about. On practical grounds alone, women out earning a paycheck means having fewer women available to do volunteer church work. Who will cook the church dinners, arrange flowers for the sanctuary, conduct fund-raising projects, or even teach in the Sunday school? Publishers of religious literature point out that one reason traditional two-week vacation Bible school courses are now offered in abbreviated, one-week editions is because so many churches complained that the "working-mother problem" makes it more difficult than ever to staff VBS. Shorter courses or evening sessions seemed the only workable solution.

Most churches have trouble adjusting to employed women, whether single or married, because they simply cannot fit into the traditional mold and schedule that is built around the housewife ideal. Thus, all too often, the woman who works outside the house is resented, if not frankly criticized. Without realizing it, many Christians are very close to Hitler's ideology which spelled out woman's "proper" and limited sphere: *Kinder, Küche, Kirche.* The children, the kitchen, and the church comprise her domain—and even there, she must be careful not to step out of place.

Should Women Be Involved in the World?

Perhaps a better question than, Should women be involved in the world? would be this: Should human beings have a choice about what they will do with their lives? Most people are quick to say *yes* to that. After all, freedom is a highly esteemed value in our society. Yet, they contradict themselves by encouraging one kind of choice for males and another for females. Girls are expected to choose marriage and motherhood. If a little boy answered a question about his future plans by saying, "I just want to be a husband and father when I grow up," someone would quickly set him straight. "Oh yes, of course, but you'll also want to be something else. You'll want to have a job like your daddy so that you can take care of your wife and children. You'll want to do something important in the world—like being a doctor or lawyer or astronaut. Or maybe a great scientist." How many little girls would hear a response like that? Few indeed. They would probably hear. "That's nice. You'll be a good mommy someday. Now run along and play with your dollies and toy dishes."

This dichotomy of woman-in-the-house and man-in-the-world

was not always so rigid. In agricultural societies, women are involved in economic production along with household duties. In our own Western society, it was traditional (before mechanization) for farm families to work together. Father alone wasn't considered the breadwinner. Family businesses utilized all family members, and often the home was located on the same premises as the store or mill. Working with their husbands in various crafts and trades, women played important roles in the bustling world outside the home. The notion of "full-time mothering" was unheard of.

We have already seen that the Bible speaks of many women who were active in the outside world—Deborah, the political leader; religious leaders such as Phoebe, Priscilla, and Philip's daughters; and Lydia, the businesswoman; to name only a few. If such examples explode the myth that women who love God shouldn't be involved in the world, the ashes of that myth are driven underground by Proverbs 31:10-31. Somehow, when the passage is used for Mother's Day sermons, it comes through quite differently from the way it does when we go directly to the Bible. The picture in Proverbs 31 is not that of a "clinging vine" or "helpless female," but rather of a mature woman of good business sense, capable of wise thought and management, resourceful, responsible, and highly esteemed by her husband who places his whole trust in her (see v. 11).

Ministers often use this passage to describe an ideal wife and mother. After all, the woman in Proverbs knows how to cook and sew and dress tastefully (just like the ideal homemaker in the women's magazines). And "like a ship laden with merchandise, she brings home food from far off" (v. 14 NEB). In other words, she does a good job with the weekly shopping and takes advantage of supermarket specials. She gets up early and goes to bed late (woman's work is never done!). Her children turn out well. Her husband thinks the world of her and is successful in his own career. And to top it all off, she is spiritually minded (v. 30). What more could anyone ask?

But many women *are* asking for more. So does the woman in Proverbs 31. She needs the sense of worth and achievement that comes from interests and activities outside the home. There are two main ways for women to become involved in the world: through voluntary, unpaid service (e.g., charitable, religious, or political work), or through an actual occupation with monetary earnings. The woman in Proverbs chooses both. "She opens her hand to the poor, and reaches out her hands to the needy" (v. 20). But she also has a wise head for financial management and investment. "After careful thought she buys a field and plants a vineyard out of her earnings"

(v. 16 NEB). Furthermore, she sets up her own weaving and garment business and supplies merchants with her goods (Prov. 31:17-18, 24, 31). The fact that she has servants indicates that she is not fearful that delegating certain household and child-care tasks to others might be detrimental to her family.

Yet, this dynamo of energy is not presented as an "unfeminine," "emasculating," scheming, aggressive female. She speaks kindly and wisely and seems to convey to her family a spirit of tranquillity, confidence, and happiness. Her husband isn't the least bit threatened by all her capabilities and activities. In fact, he is delighted. "He sings her praises: 'Many a woman shows how capable she is; but you excel them all' " (vv. 28b-29 NEB). Her children likewise commend her.

This is not to say that all women must be involved in the world beyond home and family and that all women should be gainfully employed and career-oriented. We are only suggesting that women be given the *choice*—just as men are given choices. And we are pointing out that there is nothing "unchristian" or "unbiblical" in the decision of a woman who opts for an outside occupation instead of, or along with, family responsibilities. It is really the freedom to choose that the women's movement is all about.

Such freedom is not contrary to the Christian faith, which also lays much stress on the matter of choice. We are to *choose* to serve God, to *choose* to receive the offer of salvation, to *choose* to follow Christ. Individuals are encouraged to say, "*I* will follow God wherever God leads *me*." Yet at the same time, we contradict ourselves by implying that we *know* where God will always lead women (into traditional domestic roles)—as well as *how* God leads women (by leading their husbands and asking that the women follow).

Why Women Want Involvement in the Outside World

Many Christians, brought up to consider the traditional mold as the "normal" order of things, have difficulty understanding the discontent of so many modern women. What is it that women want?

Much of it has to do with the issue of freedom to choose one's destiny, as has already been mentioned. Increasingly, such freedom is thought to be a human right. A caste system is thoroughly out of keeping with the values we espouse today. It doesn't seem rational to assign whole groups of people to a certain place or sphere simply because of characteristics received by the accident of birth. Blacks and other groups have rebelled at the way society has blocked freedom of choice and opportunity for no reason other than a difference in pigmentation over which they had no control. And women too are awaking to the fact that they also have been forced into a particular mold, regardless of individual aptitudes and talents, simply because of having been born female rather than male. They too are asking for "freedom now."

The desire for self-fulfillment—finding what one really wants to do with one's life and then doing it—is not some phenomenon confined to women. Growing numbers of both men and women are returning to school, learning new skills, or changing careers in their middle years. Sometimes the reasons are financial; but often they are attempts to find something meaningful—a way to use one's gifts and talents to make worthwhile contributions to the world. More and more individuals no longer are willing to accept passively "what fate has handed them." They see the possibility of rational control and manipulation of many of life's circumstances. They can envision second and third chances, rather than feel they must continue in a dull rut or a dead-end job. And they are willing to take risks and put forth great effort to make their dreams come true.

Behavioral scientists point out the linkage between occupational achievement and a sense of self-esteem. One of the first questions we ask someone is, "What work do you do?" And the answer to that question influences our opinion of that person. With women, the question usually centers on what her husband does. Men are expected to define themselves in terms of their jobs, but women are expected to define themselves in terms of roles and relationships.

Yet, given society's value of occupational achievement and the rewards of money, prestige, and power, the items expected to comprise woman's self-image count for little. What kind of man has chosen her? How spotless does she keep her house? How attractive is she? How do her children behave? Women are sensitive to the low rating society places on their domestic endeavors; hence the apologetic statement, "Oh, I'm just a housewife." We may decry such self-denigration as wrong and unfortunate, but it is a fact of life.

Ann Oakley, who has researched and written widely on the sociology of housework, describes four characteristic features of the role of housewife in the modern industrial society: (1) its exclusive *assignment to women*, (2) its association with *a wife's economic dependence*, (3) its *status as "non-work"* as opposed to what society considers "real" or "economically productive work," and (4) the *expectation that the housewife role will take priority* over other roles in a woman's life.[7] Homemakers know how hard they work and find it very painful to be contrasted with "working women."

Actually, the work of housewives has been calculated to be equal to at least 25 percent of the gross national product (GNP), although such work is not included in that economic indicator. One writer, concerned about the lack of recognition for "women's unpaid contributions to the economic well-being of the nation" through both voluntary community service and homemaking and childrearing tasks, has written of the unfairness of the statistical basis for the GNP. "I find it interesting," writes Dee Dee Ahern, "that the work of a maid or housekeeper is counted in the Gross National Product, but if the maid or housekeeper marries her employer, she is no longer counted."[8] Even if a couple decide that a wife will be paid for her housework and work out their own contract to seal their agreement, the courts would not be likely to honor such a contract. Traditional family law considers it to be a wife's duty to provide domestic services to her husband.[9] She has neither the satisfaction and sense of worth that comes with earning her own income nor the recognition that her hard work is important and valuable to society.

As psychology professor Judith Bardwick expresses it: "In our masculine-oriented culture a person is worth the market value of his skills and personality. One's esteem depends not on the human qualities one possesses but on success in the competitive market place."[10] Therefore, many women feel that they should also have the right to achieve in the way that will allow maximum utilization of talents and bring the rewards that society gives for successful accomplishments, including the reward of enhanced self-esteem.

Some Christians may ask at this point, "Isn't that letting ourselves be squeezed into the world's mold? Isn't that what the apostle Paul warned about in Romans 12:2? Why should we be influenced by society's values? Why shouldn't we measure self-worth in terms of relationship to God rather than in relationship to the economic system?" There is much truth in this. To know that we "are of more value than many sparrows" and that the hairs of our head are numbered by our loving God, to know that God created each of us as a unique and special person, to know that Christ died and rose for us—surely all of these assurances bolster self-image.

However, we must not lose sight of the fact that a Christian's sense of worthwhileness and self-esteem comes not only from awareness of the individual's importance to God but also from the knowledge that we were created in God's image. One aspect of that image, as we've already seen, is the capacity human beings have for relationship—both with God and with one another.

In addition to the "relation side" of God's image in male and

female, there is also a "creation side." God made human beings to
share in the ongoing work of creating—to be like God in producing,
achieving, subduing, controlling, and the like. In the Genesis
account, there was the manual work of caring for the garden and the
intellectual work of naming the animals. God has given us the ability
to think, discover, create, explore, compose, make, cultivate, mold,
and build. Such an ability is a reflection of what God is like and is thus
an aspect of God's image in humankind. Psalm 8:3-6 catches the
wonder of this truth.

God intended that both men and women should reflect this aspect
of the divine image by exercising dominion over the earth (Gen.
1:26-31). Yet, traditionally it has been considered a man's job to
produce ideas and goods, while a woman's job is to produce babies.
These verses from Genesis knock down that notion. God knew the
women couldn't be fruitful and multiply alone. Obviously, then, that
statement wasn't intended for her only! Why should we think that
God gave the commandment to subdue the earth to the man alone, as
some Bible study guides suggest? It's foolish to say that half the
human race, made in God's image and possessing God-given talents,
should have no part in the world God has placed in our hands.

This is the crux of the issue. All too many Christians label women
"selfish" if they desire to work outside the home, or choose not to
marry in favor of a career, or elect not to have children. It's assumed
that women are materialistic and intent only on making money for
luxuries. Such critics have difficulty understanding that not only do
many income-earning women *have* to work, but many women also
desire to work outside the home in order to use their talents and
training creatively, in a way that brings meaning to their own lives
and benefits society as well. Woman, made in God's image, should
want to be a good steward and exercise the gifts God has given
her—just as a man should. Perhaps both men and women together
need to rethink the matter of vocation and formulate a theology of
work that views all of us as being in charge of God's world and
responsible to our Creator for what we do with it.

It's wrong to criticize women for desiring to be a part of the world
beyond marriage, home, and family. Many women want to work not
for what they can get but for what they can give. They want to
serve—in politics, in medicine, in scientific research, in business, in
education, and much more. And the world needs them. Why should
it be denied their talents simply because God chose to place those
talents in persons whose bodies are female?

Many Christians remain unconvinced, believing a woman's

greatest contribution to the world is to become a good wife and mother. She is to be the family's haven from the cares and pressures of the outer world, the coordinator of family life to keep things running smoothly, the one who guides, trains, nurtures, and supports. Shouldn't this be enough for a woman? Isn't such a role sufficient to provide a woman with a sense of achievement and of having made a worthwhile contribution to the world? True, a homemaker doesn't get paid, but money isn't everything.

Those who reason this way like to point to examples of the past. Again, a favorite illustration is the life of Susanna Wesley. Sermons have been preached to show how this mother of nineteen children devoted her whole life to her family. "Think how tragic it would have been for the Christian church if Susanna Wesley had practiced birth control," announced a minister as he introduced a Charles Wesley hymn to his congregation, pointing out that Charles was the eighteenth child to whom she gave birth.

But another question arises. There is no denying that the world would have been poorer without Charles Wesley; but as matters now stand, might it not be true that in a sense the world is also poorer because Susanna Wesley was withheld from it? She was a very talented and brilliant woman, "indeed superior in mind and ability to her husband," writes Bishop Gerald Kennedy. "Born in a later time, she would have made a mark for herself. In the eighteenth century, she found fulfillment through her children and especially in the lives of her two famous sons, John and Charles."[11]

Mrs. Wesley poured her energies wholeheartedly into the task of rearing her children with strict but loving discipline, training them in both Christian doctrine and academic subjects (each child learned the alphabet on his or her fifth birthday and was expected to begin learning to read Genesis 1 the very next day). She wrote her own curriculum materials, including poems and books on theology to be used by her children, and she methodically sought to instill character-building habits in each son and daughter. Ten of her children died during infancy, but a strict regime was followed for the remaining nine so that all of them received individual instruction and time alone with her, talking things over with her, praying with her, and learning from her.

Susanna Wesley felt that this was the trust given her by God. She began her systematic plan of instruction out of a desire to do something more for God, saying that since she was not a man nor a minister, perhaps this would provide a way of serving the Lord.[12]

But even this did not seem enough. Mrs. Wesley was disturbed that the assistant curate failed to hold evening services while her husband, the Reverend Samuel Wesley, was away. To correct this, she began inviting neighbors in on Sunday evenings for a time of Christian instruction. Soon more than two hundred began attending regularly and more were turned away due to lack of standing room. Through this ministry of leadership and teaching, Susanna Wesley experienced a wonderful sense of achievement, fulfillment, and service to God. Yet, as has been the case with so many talented women, she felt a nagging guilt and uneasiness about what she was doing. Her husband disapproved for one thing, and there were the traditional interpretations of certain Scripture passages to contend with. Was she usurping the place of a man? Yet the people needed her ministry and she felt compelled to help them. Like so many of her modern sisters, she was pulled two ways.[13]

If even Susanna Wesley felt a need to utilize talents in ways other than child care exclusively, how much more is this true of a woman today with only two or three children? She is likely to see her youngest go off to school while she is in her early or midthirties. Her husband is reaching the best years of his career. Her children grow increasingly independent and reach out to new worlds opening up through school, friends, and outside activities. Suddenly a woman feels alone and not so needed any longer. She begins to yearn for something more. Betty Friedan termed these feelings so common among housewives, "the problem that has no name."[14]

An observation by pyschologist Judith Bardwick is pertinent here. She points out that most attempts to define and measure achievement "derive from the academic-vocational-masculine model," but suggests that this should not be the *only* model used with regard to women. At certain times of their lives, according to Professor Bardwick, women desire achievement along other lines—particularly in matters relating to social success, internal development, and interpersonal relationships. If this is so, one kind of model (the internal-interpersonal achievement model) may be more salient for women at one stage of life, whereas what has been considered the "masculine" model that emphasizes vocational achievement may be more applicable at another stage.

Dr. Bardwick says that this may explain a finding in certain psychological tests which has shown that, among wives with some college training, there occurs after ten to fifteen years of marriage an increase in motive to achieve. At this stage, it isn't unusual for women to return to universities to complete degrees or to undertake graduate training. Or they may resume a career abandoned years before. Some may begin an altogether new type of occupation.

Behavioral scientists find it significant that this "motivation to achieve" appears at this particular point in life—especially in view of traditional achievement-motivation theories which have emphasized that the motive to achieve must develop during childhood or it will never develop. Bardwick suggests two possible explanations. Possibly an internalized motive to achieve develops later in women than in men and requires the security of having affiliative needs met first, thus reducing anxiety about achieving. "A stable marital relationship may permit the development of a secure and independent sense of self and the motive to achieve." Or, on the other hand, it may be that the women mentioned in the psychological testings above *did* develop strong motives to achieve during childhood but did not act upon them behaviorally. Achievement motivation may have been suppressed because of anxieties about failing or because of fears of alienating other people (by not fulfilling traditional feminine roles, for example).[15]

Either possibility, of course, underscores the effects of how girls are socialized in our culture. But the point is that, even if the internal-interpersonal kind of achievement (success in social relationships) does seem to satisfy many women at one stage of life, there still appears to be a need—at least in the lives of women who have had some higher education—for achievement along the lines recognized and rewarded in our society, that is, academic and vocational achievement. Women who have not married have had more encouragement from society to act upon achievement needs and aspirations earlier. Traditional expectations for married women have made it harder.

Combining a Family and Career—Problems and Rewards

Sidney Callahan points out that "developing a new theoretical approach to women is one thing, living it another." This is true for all women, but especially so in the case of a wife and mother. Callahan (herself the mother of six children) writes that society supports a *single* woman in her career, expecting her to be seriously committed to her work and to be a responsible, active, and growing person. In contrast, societal norms for a married woman discourage rather than support her stepping outside traditional feminine roles.[16]

In candidly describing her own personal struggles and conflicts,

Callahan has shown herself to be a loving wife and mother who immensely enjoyed the rich family life she and her husband had worked together to build. Yet, she reached a point at which she experiences increasing boredom, frustration, and confusion about her role. "Ten years without formal intellectual work or study was all that I could bear," she writes. "During those years I had helped launch my husband and created a family and functioning household. Now I had to put myself first for awhile or sink."

But should a Christian woman ever put herself first? Doesn't the Bible say that the person who wants to be first should be the servant of all? It was precisely her commitment to such Christian ideals that intensified Sidney Callahan's conflict and forced her to do much soul-searching. She goes on:

My Christianity held up the ideal of self-sacrifice and service for the sake of love. Why could I no longer love enough to give up intellectual pursuits and intellectual work? The upheaval and inner questioning caused me suffering of a new kind. Out of that agony I was finally able to come to some decisions. I decided there was a fine line between sacrifice and suicide. I could not live without intellectual function and some systematic nondomestic work in the adult world. To try to live the traditional feminine role would be suicide and a betrayal as well of the ideals and equality of our marriage.[17]

Callahan's personal solution resulted from her decision to write and to attend graduate school. Other women deal with the problem in other ways, but it's important for them to know they are not alone in their struggles. Nor do these struggles automatically disappear never to return again. "I still have many, many conflicts and problems in combining work and family life," says Callahan, "but they are better conflicts than my old self-destructive embittered conflicts born of frustration and boredom. I chose them freely."

What many deeply dissatisfied and frustrated housewives consider to be self-sacrifice really *is* "suicide," as Callahan pointed out. They are destroying themselves. Witness the numbers of married women, with husbands busy in their careers and no more small children at home, who stream into physicians' offices with varied complaints. They may hope the doctor will prescribe tranquilizers or antidepressant drugs or will suggest an operation (a way of being the center of attention and something to talk about afterward). Some such women wonder if having another baby might not bring new zest to life and make them feel useful again.

Tired, bored, lonely, some women turn to alcohol or get involved in an extramarital affair. Some have "nervous breakdowns" and require hospitalization. Others take out their frustrations on their families; they nag, whine, complain, interfere, dominate, and in general try to live through their husbands and children. As a result, the whole family often feels sapped and trapped. It is not a healthy situation.

Such women may think of themselves as martyrs, sacrificing everything for their families. In actuality, they are committing mental-emotional suicide, hurting both themselves and others. Such mothers are not really giving themselves to their families. They are denying their families the real personality, the richly fulfilled woman, the true self that could have been (and still could be) if only they would be willing to face up to the problem.

Poet and author Maya Angelou likes to quote an African adage: "Be careful when a naked person offers you a shirt."[18] We cannot love others as ourselves until we first learn to love *ourselves* and be all we can possibly be. We cannot reach out to others' needs or care for them until we have learned to take care of ourselves so that we have something to give them. If we are naked, we have no shirt to offer. If we are intellectually and emotionally starved, we can't feed the spirits of those we love.

A Woman's Options

Voluntary charitable, political, and church work provide avenues that may meet the needs of some women. At the same time that they are being "ministered unto," they are also "ministering" through performing helpful services. Other women find this solution insufficient—especially when mere busywork crowds out opportunities to develop and use talents, training, and intellectual abilities.

A return to school is another possible solution. Interest in adult education is growing in today's world. No woman should feel it is ever too late to learn, to grow, to train or retrain for some career that interests her. A magazine survey once endeavored to discover the major regrets of adults in looking back over their lives. Heading the list was the statement, "I regret that I didn't get more education." But a missed opportunity at one stage of life needn't mean there can be no second chances. Sometimes opportunity *does* knock twice.

Yet often women are afraid to open the door. It takes courage and means hard work, sacrifices, and inconveniences for both the woman and her family. But it's well worth it. Many women have found that a return to school invigorates them, opens up a whole new world of ideas and interests, brings to light talents and abilities they never knew they had, and helps them better understand themselves, their families, and life in general. They find themselves better able to relate to their husbands and children and to converse with them. The whole family's life can be enriched by mom's venture into the classroom. Her children may tease her about having to do homework right along with them in the evenings, and they will be the first to ask what grade she received on a test. But they will be proud of her and do all they can to help. Some women say their return to school helped bridge the "generation gap" with their teenagers. A thirty-two-year-old Sunday school teacher says that since her return to college she understands her students as never before.

There are difficulties in resuming formal education—particularly if there are still young children in the home. Mothers who have returned to school warn that there is a real temptation to take a course load that is simply too heavy. They suggest that in most cases a woman who wants to combine student life with family responsibilities should seek wise counsel and only take a reasonable amount of course hours at a time. What is reasonable will vary with the individual, but realistic planning is in order in any case.

No woman interested in further education should be afraid to try. A dean at a major university says the fact that a woman has been out of the classroom for years needn't deter her. "Our experience shows us she can achieve. The good student remains a good student. The mediocre student often becomes a good student because of a different motivation."[19] Many universities have adjusted their programs to accommodate the mature student who can only attend part-time or who needs great flexibility in scheduling classes. Some universities offer evening courses and correspondence courses that may be applied toward university credit. Community colleges are springing up in many areas. All such programs are worth investigating.

In addition to becoming involved in the outside world through voluntary activities or further education, there is always the option of paid employment. Some women are interested in "just finding a job" so that they can get away from the house or earn some extra money—often to supplement family income for some specific purpose, such as travel, house payments, or the children's college education. For other women a mere "job" isn't challenging enough. They aren't interested in becoming secretaries or supermarket cashiers; they desire a professional career that can utilize their present training or the training they hope to get.

Working Women: At Home and Beyond

The problems of combining family and outside work are similar in both cases. But they seem to be intensified in the case of a woman who is totally immersed in a profession—something that cannot be conveniently laid aside after an eight-hour day. A scientist, for example, may feel a need to spend twelve or more hours at the laboratory as she works on an important experiment. Knowing there is a family at home—a husband and children who need her—can't help producing conflict in her mind.

But the woman who works from nine to five in a clerical or sales job has her anxieties too. She finds that in essence she has two jobs, because in most cases she continues to do all the cleaning, laundry, mending, and cooking, in addition to her outside occupation. Her husband comes home from work and grabs the evening paper. She comes home from work and grabs an apron and a skillet. Even at that, her husband may complain that she is still doing housework long after he has gone to bed.

Some women have found that part-time work, where possible, is a workable solution. One variation on this theme is the arrangement one team of authors call "the tandem job."[20] Where cooperative employers can be found, two women take the same job, but divide the hours, responsibilities, and pay. The authors cite such examples as the two housewives who share a bank teller's job, with one working mornings and the other afternoons. Other women alternate days on their shared job. In some cities, special teaching partnership programs even permit tandem teaching arrangements. This would seem to work out quite well in nursery schools and kindergartens, for example.

Without ever hearing of such things as tandem jobs, some husbands and wives have worked out similar systems out of sheer necessity. One registered nurse, with preschoolers still at home, accepted an offer to work afternoons in a physician's office. Her college professor husband arranged his class schedule so that he could arrive home shortly after lunch to take over the household when his wife left for work. He did his reading, writing, and lecture preparations while the children took their naps; and he even prepared the evening meal. Another couple split a forty-hour work week at a bookstore into two twenty-hour jobs, so that either the mother or the father was taking care of their children while the other worked.

In her book, *Academic Women,* Jessie Bernard predicts many more such arrangements in which husbands and wives will cooperate with regard to both outside occupations and home and child-care responsibilities. She cites examples of couples who feel that both their professional lives and their family life are benefited by their being husband-wife teams at work and at home.

One woman, now in her thirties, makes the observation that the schedule juggling and concerns over child-care arrangements that are so much discussed today were common in her childhood. She grew up in a southern, working-class neighborhood where both her parents worked long hard hours in the textile mills. "The dual earner family isn't anything new," she told us. "It just seems that way because it has been discovered by the middle class. When I was growing up, a full-time housewife was the exception, not the rule. My mother and the mothers of my friends couldn't choose to stay home any more than my father could. Everybody had to work to make ends meet. My dad pitched in with the housecleaning, laundry, dishwashing, and child care; and we kids were expected to do housework and learn to take care of ourselves (and often younger siblings) as soon as we were able. It certainly helped us learn self-sufficiency!"

Husbands' Attitudes toward Wives' Employment

An understanding, considerate, cooperative, and supportive husband is essential when a married woman is involved in the world outside the walls of home. Otherwise, there will be endless frustration and turmoil. Dr. Bernard tells of a college student who asked a married woman, just back from a trip to India, what advice she had for someone who wanted to specialize in Indian studies. The student was outraged by the reply: "Think about the kind of man you might marry who would make a career in Indian studies possible." The advice seemed so irrelevant at the time. But later, married to a professor whose area of specialty complemented her own, which not only meant support and encouragement but also opportunities for collaboration, the young woman who had asked the question saw the wisdom in the advice she had been given.[21]

Eli Ginzberg and Alice Yohalem make the same point: "The fact that many men are willing to accept certain conditions at home—a less than spotless house, a limited amount of entertaining, the necessity to help with household chores and the care of children—frequently represents the margin of difference between whether women can or cannot work."[22] A husband who sees the importance of the wife's career and encourages her makes it possible for her to pursue her occupational endeavors without feeling guilty and overburdened.

How does one get such a husband? In a speech at Wellesley College, sociologist Alice Rossi said it is important for young women to *look* for such a man and not to marry anyone who isn't willing to stand with his wife and to encourage her in her career pursuits.[23] An unsupportive husband can be a millstone, dragging a woman down and holding her back from all she could otherwise be. A woman should determine *before marriage* what kind of husband can work together with her rather than against her. If such a man can't be found, a lifetime of singleness would seem preferable to a marriage in which a woman's gifts would be stifled and in which the husband and wife could not share fully their total selves.

Ginzberg and associates, after calling attention to the facts of high female employment in recent years and the various factors that encourage women to enter the labor force, list three counterforces pulling in the opposite direction. These are the rising standards and expectations for child care and mother-child relationships, the problem of finding competent domestic help, and the difficulties posed by residency in suburban areas from which husbands commute to the cities but which leave wives cut off from work opportunities.[24] However, there are signs of change as many firms move out to the suburbs—a fact which aggravates inner city problems at the same time that it leaves the suburban wife a little less stranded.

For women with certain skills, working at home seems to offer an ideal solution. Free-lance writers, certain copy editors, and artists may find they can mesh their occupational and home responsibilities well. They are at home to greet the children after school (or keep an eye on preschoolers). They are able to put the laundry in the washer or the casserole in the oven during coffee breaks. And yet, they are "at work" all day. They are available to care for a sick child who unexpectedly wakes up with a fever and can't go to school that day. They can arrange their schedule to take a child to the dentist or attend an afternoon school program with a minimum of difficulty. Some women enjoy this work-at-home system, as do some men. Others find it impractical and especially resent interruptions. One free-lance artist and mother of five has her studio in her home but nevertheless hires a baby-sitter several hours a day so that she can work undisturbed.

Music teachers provide another example of women who can earn money without leaving their homes. Imaginative women have found other ways as well. One mother who didn't want to leave her baby during the day came up with the idea that she could put her cooking skills to use. She makes hors d'oeuvres and pastries and provides a catering service for private parties. Her business is booming.

But for most women, working at home is not feasible. Their professions, like those of most men, require that they be present somewhere else—perhaps in a classroom or office or hospital. How, then, does a woman work out conflicts resulting from the demands of home and career? Ginzberg and Yohalem in their book, *Educated American Women: Self-Portraits,* described four basic categories of women with respect to the home/career dilemma.[25]

There were first of all those whom the authors called the "planners"—women who have had clear goals from a young age and who directed their efforts toward their goals without allowing other things to interfere or deflect them. Second, there were the "recasters"—women who shift their interests, plans, and goals when something else is perceived as more desirable. Perhaps they had original dreams about what they wished to do with their lives, but obstacles and barriers have blocked them and they have settled for something else. Or maybe they simply changed their minds about what they once thought they wanted and purposely chose another way of life that seemed better.

The "adapters" are a third category described by Ginzberg and Yohalem. These women are highly flexible. Convinced that their adult lives will require many adjustments and changes, such women are prepared to adapt themselves—particularly to the different situations that arise at different stages of their marriages. They tend to resolve conflicts in the direction of the family and its needs and at the same time use their resourcefulness to find fulfillment in their outside work.

Last of all, there is the category of women whose self-portraits show them to be among what Ginzberg and Yohalem call the "unsettled." These are women who may have been at one time in any of the other three categories but for whom plans have gone awry. They are now fumbling and searching and often experiencing much discontent.

How a woman resolves the problem of home and career demands depends to a great extent on which of these four categories describes her. But even within the categories, the problem is handled in different ways. People and circumstances vary, and what works well for one family may be highly undesirable for another. In trying to develop a workable pattern, women can read about ways other women have met the challenges and coped with problems in relation to home and career. In recent years, books and magazine articles in abundance have permitted women to speak for themselves about the joys, challenges, and problems of attempting to excel in both family and career.

Once again, the husband's cooperation (or lack of it) cannot be overstressed. For example, would a husband be willing to pass up an opportunity for advancement if it required relocating in another city that would take his wife away from her law partnership or medical practice? Traditionally, wives have followed husbands, but would a husband be willing to reverse this custom if his wife were offered greater opportunities in another location—even though his own career would be affected? These are the kinds of decisions increasing numbers of couples are being forced to face as more and more wives desire to use their talents and contribute to the outside world.

Some couples make diligent efforts to find positions in the same area before *either* considers a job relocation. For example, a prominent theologian placed a classified ad in a national periodical in an effort to find a university where he could teach in his field and where his wife (also a Ph.D.) could teach literature. In still other cases, the husband and wife may choose to work in different locations and maintain apartments in two cities, commuting on weekends to be together. If there are no children, some couples report that this arrangement can be quite satisfactory. Their emphasis is on the quality rather than the quantity of their time together. (Christians who are critical of such couples are often the same ones who heap praise upon evangelists and missionaries who are away from their families for weeks at a time.)

Wives who are committed to achievement goals and who have career aspirations just as their husbands do never seem entirely to escape anxieties, doubts, occasonal feelings of guilt and role conflict, and an ongoing questioning: "Am I doing what is right in regard to my family?" "Am I doing my best in my profession?" "Am I investing myself as I should in both areas of life?" Judith Bardwick points out that some women worry about their own normality when freedom of choice replaces rigid definitions and cultural norms are no longer clear. Some women become uncertain about their femininity, especially when they choose professions atypical for women.

According to Dr. Bardwick, women who have trained for a profession suffer various anxieties regardless of how they seek to resolve the family/career dilemma. Those who leave their professions while their children are small worry that they may become

227

intellectually rusty and fail to develop their full potential or fail to keep abreast in their fields. Those who try, on the other hand, to combine the traditional mothering role with professional commitment often feel guilty because their working "evokes obvious, surface changes in the family." These changes, according to psychologist Bardwick, are occasioned by the mother's being too busy to take part in activities that her children and community consider to be normal responsibilities—leading a Scout troop, working with the PTA, and so on. Not being solely preoccupied with her children, she may wonder if she is harming them.[26]

Income-Earning Mothers and Their Children

The question of how a mother's working outside the home affects her children is a salient one. This is particularly true in the case of Christians who have a strong commitment to family life and a conviction that God wants them to rear children "in the discipline and instruction of the Lord" (Eph. 6:4). Because of alarmist articles and sermons, the usual picture conjured up in the minds of many is one of crumbling homes, divorces, juvenile delinquency, emotional disturbances in youngsters, and visions of dirty-faced tots with runny noses and tattered clothing playing in the streets because their mothers are neglecting them in order to earn a paycheck.

There is no disputing the fact that such tragedies do occur; but as with most other social problems, the blame cannot be attributed to one cause alone. It is unfair to blame everything on "working mothers." Mothers who *don't* work at paying jobs but who rule their children's lives, nagging them and stifling their development with smother-love, also lie behind such problems. Likewise, fathers who show no interest in their children because they have shifted all responsibility onto their wives in order to devote all their energies to advancement in their careers must share the blame. Then there are the many cases where both parents are simply too wrapped up in other noncareer interests—church meetings, clubs, community activities, and organizational responsibilities. In the rush and busyness of everyday life, such parents have no time (or take no time) to share deeply with their children and to interact with them on a warm, personal, human level. They feed them, clothe them, scold them, tuck them into bed—but they never get to really know them.

Actually, studies are contradictory and uncertain with regard to the effects a mother's employment has on her children. So much depends on such factors as social class, the reasons for her working, the financial situation of the home, where a family lives, the kind of work a woman does, the type of child-care arrangements available and what kind of mother-substitute is provided, and so on.

In general, it seems that mothers who feel intensely guilty about being employed, or who dislike their jobs, will have somewhat negative effects upon their children. On the other hand, mothers who are committed to a profession and who thoroughly enjoy their work may find that their children are better off than if they weren't working. One teenager whose mother returned to college and became a schoolteacher says his life is better than ever. The mother is so happy and not bored and discontented as before, he points out. And besides, she has become a fascinating person and is able to share the interests of her husband and son as never before.

Much is being discussed today about competently staffed child-care centers that can release mothers for employment while at the same time providing enrichment experiences for children. For many mothers, this may provide an excellent solution. Some churches see a real opportunity for ministry along these lines by putting Sunday school classrooms to use during the week as day-care centers, providing not only physical care for youngsters but also spiritual guidance under Christian teachers.

Even so, many mothers prefer to stay at home during their children's preschool years to be on call when their children need them. They want to be the ones to train their sons and daughters and to answer their questions about God or sex or death or any other deep issues for which children seek explanations—often unexpectedly during the course of a day. Such mothers want to be there to take part in the once-in-a-lifetime experience of watching their children grow from babyhood to school age.

Other mothers think differently. They feel they are better mothers if they have been away from their children part of the day and have been intellectually stimulated through working in their professional careers. To remain at home all day cut off from the adult world, they feel, would be stultifying and boring and they might end up "taking it out on the children," by acting annoyed and irritable. However, after a day on the job, they find they come home eager to be with the children and to relax with them and enjoy them. Such mothers feel that either a trustworthy baby-sitter (when one can be found) or good day-care arrangements can assure care for their youngsters that is just as good as what their own mothers could offer them.

Another solution is a commune setup. In this arrangement, several families live together sharing household tasks and child-care.

229

Actually, it is just a new form of the old extended family idea in which various relatives lived together in a large home or on a farm or nearby so that someone was always available to take care of the children. No one worried if a baby or small child wasn't with mommy constantly; the youngster received plenty of love, attention, and care from aunts, uncles, grandparents, older siblings, and others. Some Christian couples are experimenting with such a system, which not only gives mothers freedom for outside interests but also provides children with opportunites to know deeply and lovingly a variety of adults—each of whom can contribute much to their development.

All of this is a matter of individual choice. There is no one and only answer. Some women choose to marry and have children after they have had several years in a career. Other couples choose not to have children at all so that a woman's commitment to her profession can continue without interruption. Some women manage career and pregnancies and small children concurrently without too much apparent difficulty. Others find it too physically exhausting and emotionally taxing; they prefer to take out a few years from their professions and return later. If such is the case, it's crucial that they keep learning, reading, and growing during that time-out period. Again, the choice must depend upon the individual couple involved.

There is no denying that women are concerned about being part of today's world with all its problems and challenges and opportunities. To judge them as straying from Christian principles because of this desire for involvement is unwarranted. There is the matter of stewardship of talents to consider—of using what God has given in order to benefit others and to serve the world in Christ's name. Related to this is the matter of the world's needs. Can we afford *not* to utilize the talents of women?

There is also, as we have seen, the fact that woman bears God's image; like man, she too desires to create and build and discover. And there is the matter of self-fulfillment. A woman must love and respect herself and must experience the self-esteem that comes from successful achievement. This can, in turn, release her love and creative energies in new ways so that her positive contributions to her family and to society are greatly enhanced.

Jesus told us to love our neighbor as ourselves. The woman who is not being true to herself finds it extremely difficult to love herself. Until she learns to do this, she may never know what it really means to love others, even her own family, in spite of all her talk about sacrificing and living for them alone.

14.

WHERE DO WE GO FROM HERE?

Confusion has seized us, and all things go wrong.
    The women have leaped from "their spheres."
And instead of fixed stars, shoot as comets along,
    And are setting the world by the ears!
In courses erratic they're wheeling through space,
In brainless confusion and meaningless chase.

Oh! shade of the prophet Mahomet arise!
    Place woman again in "her sphere,"
And teach that her soul was not born for the skies,
    But to flutter a brief moment here.
This doctrine of Jesus, as preached up by Paul
If embraced in its spirit, will ruin us all.

                                        Maria W. Chapman[1]
                        (Nineteenth-century feminist humorist)

"CHRISTIANITY HAS DONE MUCH TO RAISE THE STATUS OF WOMEN"
is a persistent shibboleth. The infinite worth of all human beings and
the possibility of their redemption *are* basic tenets of the faith.

But Christians must honestly face the historical fact that the
church has erected many barriers—social, legal, spiritual, psychological—against women's advancement. By propagating the notion
that God ordained women to be passive and dependent, lacking
initiative and assertiveness, confined to kitchen and pew, the church
has hampered growth and fostered low self-esteem in women. It has
not challenged women to recognize their God-given gifts, encouraged them to fully use their talents, or helped them to gain a
mature sense of personhood. In fact, objective outside observers
have concluded that "churches are one of the few important
institutions that still elevate discrimination against women to the
level of principle."[2]

Change is taking place rapidly, and the church cannot afford to lag
any further behind the world in implementing the gospel we profess
to believe. We should have learned from the history of slavery and
racism. Those who assert an order of creation, in which women are to
be functionally subordinate to men, might study the precedents for

their arguments in the sixteenth-century Spanish theologians who formulated a "natural law theology for inequality" in order to enslave Indians. They declared that each person has a most appropriate social function. Some individuals' function is to work rather than to think. These biologically distinct individuals are destined by nature to be slaves, a condition beneficial to them and to society. Southerners of the last century used similar arguments to keep blacks in slavery. Most of us have changed our minds about that and it has not diminished the Bible's authority.

Those who declare that the gospel offers women spiritual equality in Christ but not in this world find themselves arguing along with a theologian of the last century who wrote in defense of slavery: "Our design in giving them the Gospel is not to civilize them—not to change their social condition—not to exalt them into citizens or freemen—it is to save them. . . . Sweeten their toil—sanctify their lives—hallow their deaths."[3] How many women have been similarly treated to saccharine sermons on the blessedness of motherhood?

Some will argue that change is rebellious, that God has assigned women a subordinate role and made the divine will for them perfectly clear in Scripture. Women have been protesting such misinterpretations of the gospel since the first century. Their efforts came to a boil more than a hundred years ago when many women became active in antislavery efforts. They traveled about giving lectures in various public places, including churches. This brought stern disapproval from ministers who, even though possibly sympathetic to humanitarian causes and reform, felt women should keep silent. When Quaker Abby Kelly spoke out against slavery, one New England clergyman preached a sermon against her, using Revelation 2:20 (KJV) as his text: "I have a few things against thee, because thou sufferest that woman Jezebel, which calleth herself a prophetess, to teach and to seduce my servants to commit fornication."

When the Grimke sisters, Sarah and Angelina (also Quakers converted in Presbyterian and Methodist revivals), tried to promote abolition, the General Association of Massachusetts Congregationalist Clergy (Orthodox) in 1837 issued a pastoral letter forbidding clergymen to allow them to speak. Woman's power lies in her dependence, the letter declared, and flows from "the consciousness of that weakness which God has given her for her protection." Women were commended for promoting piety in the home and Sabbath schools but rebuked for assuming "the place and tone of men as a public reformer." Because the Grimke sisters spoke of the sexual exploitation of their black sisters and the destruction of marriages under slavery, the divines deplored "the intimate acquaintance and promiscuous conversation of females with regard to things which ought not to be named."[4]

Sarah Grimke responded with a series of articles titled *Letters on the Condition of Women and the Equality of the Sexes,* in which she answered the pastoral letter point by point and sought to show how Scripture, particularly the example and teachings of Jesus Christ, emancipates women as well as slaves. Actually the feminist movement as such was thus born out of the persecution that women abolitionists received because of their sex. Many of these women campaigned against slavery because of their deep Christian convictions, but they found themselves fighting allegedly "scriptural" arguments for both slavery and antifeminism. In self-defense they searched the Bible and discovered many of the same interpretations we have used in this book.[5]

Little by little their cause has prevailed. Some Christians, for example, originally opposed education for women on the grounds that I Corinthians 14:35 says that if a woman wants to know anything she can ask her husband at home. Education was considered contrary to God's intention for the "weaker sex," whose minds had not been created to withstand the rigors of learning. If women studied mathematics, argued some clergymen, it might cause disintegration of family life. If women learned geography, they might leave home (where God intended them to stay) and set off to explore the world. Some said the only geography women needed to know was how to get from one room to another in the house and the only chemistry they needed was how to follow a recipe.

Christians similarly argued against the use of anesthesia in childbirth on the grounds that Genesis 3:16 taught that "God's will is that women should suffer and die in childbirth."[6] In the same vein many Christians have opposed the whole idea of birth control because "God's will for women is motherhood."

At the turn of the century when suffragists had pared down their demands to merely obtaining the franchise, men declared that women should not vote because they were to keep silent and not usurp male authority according to I Timothy 2:12.

Will the church repeat its past errors or learn from them? One of the ironies of history is that in the last century while traditionalist churches opposed all change in "women's spheres" and mainline churches were only lukewarm to the issues, evangelicals were in the forefront of social reform. They led the crusades against slavery and alcoholism, they worked for peace, and they led the way in women's rights. In many early Holiness and Pentecostal churches women ministers outnumbered men![7] But now most mainline churches have accepted the ministries of women, and the conservative churches deny women their rights.

Paul laid the groundwork for social change in Galatians 3:28: "There is neither Jew nor Greek, there is neither slave nor free, there is neither male nor female; for you are all one in Christ Jesus." As Krister Stendahl points out, "We would hardly expect to hear Paul say, 'These statements apply to the question of individual salvation, but in all other respects things are as they used to be.' "[8] Much of Paul's energy was devoted to combating the Judaizers who declared that reconciliation of Jews and Gentiles was only a spiritual concept and that meanwhile on earth Gentiles would have to conform to Jewish customs. The first church council (Acts 15) was called to decide that issue. The principles of equality among all believers and freedom from specific cultural customs were affirmed—principles that would eventually extend to slaves and women. But implementation of these principles has been slow and painful.

Paul himself had difficulty with some issues, particularly when it came to women. And yet in the end he affirms, "Nevertheless, in the Lord woman is not independent of man nor man of woman; for as woman was made from man, so man is now born of woman. And all things are from God" (I Cor. 11:11-12). Something happens in the new life in Christ that abolishes differences, that makes all persons one "in the Lord," mutually interdependent with one another and with Christ, mutually aware that "all things are from God." Assigning privileges, roles, and spheres of duty and ministry on the basis of sex would necessarily disappear if these teachings of Paul were carried to their logical end.

Today we stand at the crossroads. As Christians we can no longer dodge the "woman problem." To argue that women are equal in creation but subordinate in function is no more defensible than separate-but-equal schools for the races. The church must either be consistent with the theology it sometimes espouses and oppose all forms of women's emancipation—including education, political participation, and vocations outside the home—or it must face up to the concrete implications of a gospel that liberates women as well as men. To argue that women should have political and vocational freedom in the secular world while declaring that they should be subordinate in marriage and silent in church is to stand the gospel on its head.[9] The church must deal with its attitudes and practices in regard to women. To fail to come to grips with this issue is to fail both God and the world we profess to serve in God's name.

It is time for Christian men and women to take the women's movement seriously, rather than lightly or humorously or contemptuously dismiss it. Every movement, Christianity included, has its lunatic fringes, but feminists today inside and outside the church are raising important issues with which we all must grapple. Some areas cry out for Christian theological and ethical compassion and insight: the nature of sexuality, the meaning of marriage, questions about vocation, ordination, friendship, homosexuality, abortion. Other issues need Christian involvement on the practical level: equal pay, employment discrimination, child care, educational opportunity, care for the aged, complete and creative use of all women's talents (including their use in the church).

What are the basic issues of feminism? Do women want to become men? No, we simply want to be full human beings. In the minds of many, however, only men are human—women are their female relatives. Only men can participate in the full range of earth's activities—women have a "proper feminine sphere." Thus to ask for full humanity is, for many, to "want to be like men." Feminists, however, are not denying the basic biological differences between the sexes. We only ask that these differences no longer be used as the basis for judgments of superior/inferior, dominant/subordinate, wide choices/rigid roles, vast opportunities/limited spheres, and the like. Women are not asking to become men. We only want to be persons, free to give the world all that our individual talents, minds, and personalities have to offer. Nor are we interested in taking over things or pushing men out of the way. We only ask to be recognized as equal partners, "joint heirs of the grace of life" (I Pet. 3:7) and "fellow workers in Christ Jesus" (Rom. 16:3).

Nor is feminism simply a selfish drive to do our own thing. We ask for the right to make our own choices, to define our own lives, not out of selfish motivations but because God calls us and commands us to develop the gifts given us. Too long we have let men define our lives. Now we must listen to the inner voice. Of course, women will sometimes make mistakes, will succumb to the lure of money, success, power. Men have also made these mistakes. But each of us is responsible for our lives, not to the wishes of others but to the voice of God.

Is it possible to be a feminist and a Christian? The early American abolitionists were. The English Quakers and such women as Catherine Booth, cofounder of the Salvation Army, definitely were.

Phoebe Palmer, who gave birth to the Holiness churches and Pentecostalism, was a feminist. Many other deeply Christian women around the world have been. They have felt directly responsible to God for their gifts. And they have heard the command to use their gifts in service to the world. All Christians, men and women, must remain ever open to the reforming, renewing Word of God.

For men, it is true, women's liberation will mean a loss of power. The king has no place in a democracy. Christ cautioned his followers about seeking power and authority. At creation God set an example for humanity by sharing with all of us power and responsibility for the earth. Men have usurped that power for themselves alone. Redeemed men must again learn to share responsibility with women, including their wives. From one angle this represents a loss, but from another it offers freedom and a lighter load. We follow a person who once offered, "Take my yoke upon you, and learn from me. . . . My yoke is easy, and my burden is light" (Matt. 11:29-30). In turning over power to Christ we find the freedom to be our true selves. So men will find in helping to liberate women.

For Christian women, liberation may be a long and difficult process. Many women have not even begun to understand what the movement means to others or to themselves. As Mennonite author Lois Gunden Clemens notes, "Many of the older women in the church who have happily accepted the role assigned to them find it difficult to understand the attitude of the younger women. But these younger women regard this as a matter of Christian integrity. They are seriously concerned about the stewardship of their God-given powers, feeling that they should be using such abilities in the church as well as in the larger community."[10]

Liberation means an end to the self-hatred women have been taught, an end to the hatred we project on other women. Often women resist liberation because we have been taught that our bodies are weak, our powers of reasoning defective, our intellects light, our skills inferior, our emotions frivolous. And we have believed our teachers. We suffer from low self-esteem and no self-confidence. Feminism has been termed an "identity crisis." Women are beginning to ask, "Who am I? What it does it mean to say that *I* am created in the image of God?" Christ commanded us to love others as ourselves, but we women have been taught to despise ourselves.

And so we have mistrusted other women. We prefer a man to cut our hair, carve our meat, service our car, preach us a sermon. We say we wouldn't work for a woman executive or vote for a woman president. We really do believe that we and all other women are inferior to men. Men sometimes see other men as a part of the "team," but women have often viewed each other as the "competition." It is time we begin practicing sisterhood as well as brotherhood. Perhaps church circles, auxiliaries, or women's missionary societies could become consciousness-raising groups where we begin to share our experiences honestly and learn to appreciate one another as sisters in Christ. Those of us who have "made it" must stop pushing our sisters back with clichés such as "Any woman who works hard enough can get to where I'm at—I've never felt discriminated against." We must begin to share our struggles and help one another, particularly those unable to help themselves.

The end of male chauvinism will also mean the end of chivalry in the traditional sense of men continually smoothing the way for the "weaker sex." Women can no longer expect doors to open, seats to become vacant, packages to be carrried for them simply because they are women. Women can no longer rely on tears and manipulation rather than reason and hard work to achieve their ends. But we hope that courtesy and consideration will be extended to all persons on an equal basis. Each of us will learn to help the other, to reach out whenever aid is needed, to respond to all appeals for help.

No longer pampered and protected by men, we women must take responsibility for our own lives. We must shoulder our share of the cultural mandate God has given us for the development of our own talents and the preservation of the earth. The easy way out is closed. If we are to follow in Christ's footsteps, we must spend thirty years in the carpenter shop learning our trade; we must endure the wilderness testing; we must travel the land healing the sick, feeding the multitudes, teaching the disciples, freeing the oppressed, and preaching the gospel.

We cannot hide behind the skirts of our alleged inferiority or under our domestic bushels. *We* must speak out, not wait for men to do it for us. We must join with other women who are crusading for an end to discrimination and for freedom for all people. We must work side by side with men who are also seeking to implement God's will on earth.

Women today must provide role models for younger women, rather than urge them to simply get a man, get married, and beget children. We now must demonstrate for the next generation that we can be dedicated Christians as well as dedicated, competent achievers in the occupational realm; that Christian single women can be whole persons; that we can be supportive, loving wives without being subservient, self-denying, manipulative, and destructive; that we can successfully combine love of family, dedication to profession, and discipleship to Christ. We must offer both boys and girls a variety of choices, a full range of possibilities for serving God.

We must begin to implement Galatians 3:28, to transcend the limitations our culture has placed on us because of our sex. Jesus walked and taught in a Temple that segregated Jew from Gentile, man from woman, priest from laity. But he came to change things. At his crucifixion, the veil of the Temple was ripped from top to bottom. Through Christ we have direct access to God; Christ has abolished the distinction between priest and laity. In Ephesians 2:14 we are told that Christ is "our peace, who has made us both one, and has broken down the dividing wall of hostility," the "middle wall of partition," between Jew and Gentile. Only one barrier still remains—the "court of the women." It is time for the Christian church to tear it down once and for all.

In Isaiah 43:4-7, God says to the people: "You are precious in my eyes, and honored, and I love you. . . . Bring my sons from afar and my daughters from the end of the earth, every one who is called by my name, whom I created for my glory, whom I formed and made." Jesus said, "Whoever does the will of God is my brother, and sister, and mother" (Mark 3:35). God has daughters as well as sons; Christ has sisters as well as brothers. Now is the time for the church to recognize this—and to act upon it. That is what Christian woman's liberation, biblical feminism, is all about.

NOTES

<hr />

Introduction
1. Ronald J. Sider, ed., *The Chicago Declaration* (Carol Stream, Ill.: Creation House, 1974). Evangelicals for Social Action is now a national organization with offices at 712 G Street SE, Washington, D.C. 20003.

2. The Evangelical Women's Caucus has its national office in California. The address is P.O. Box 3192, San Francisco, 94119.

1. Biblical Feminism

1. Carl F. H. Henry, *The Uneasy Conscience of Modern Fundamentalism* (Grand Rapids: Wm. B. Eerdmans Publishing Co., 1947); Sherwood Wirt, *The Social Conscience of the Evangelical* (New York: Harper & Row, 1968); Timothy L. Smith, *Revivalism and Social Reform* (Nashville: Abingdon Press, 1957); Donald W. Dayton, *Discovering an Evangelical Heritage* (New York: Harper & Row, 1976); Nancy A. Hardesty, *Women Called to Witness* (Nashville: Abingdon Press, 1984). Charles G. Finney, *Lectures on Revivals of Religion*, ed. William G. McLoughlin (Cambridge, Mass.: The Belknap Press of Harvard University Press, 1960), p. 287. See also his Letter on Revival, No. 23, "The Pernicious Attitude of the Church on the Reforms of the Age," reprinted from the *Oberlin Evangelist* in Dayton's book, pp. 20-24.

2. Hardesty, *Women Called to Witness,* p. 78.

3. Elizabeth Cady Stanton, *The Woman's Bible*, 2 vols. (New York: European Publishing Company, 1895, 1898), 1:12. Reprint editions are available from Coalition Task Force on Women and Religion (4759 Fifteenth Avenue NE, Seattle, Wash. 98105) and Ayer Co. (Salem, N.H.).

4. Willard Swartley, *Slavery, Sabbath, War, and Women*, Scottdale, Pa.: Herald Press, 1983).

5. Elaine Pagels, *The Gnostic Gospels* (New York: Random House Vintage Books, 1979); Elisabeth Schüssler Fiorenza, *In Memory of Her: A Feminist Theological Reconstruction of Christian Origins* (New York: Crossroad, 1983), pp. 3-67.

6. Simone de Beauvoir, *The Second Sex,* trans. and ed. H. M. Parshley (New York: Bantam Books, 1953), p. xvi.

7. Karen Horney, *Feminine Psychology* (New York: W. W. Norton & Co., 1967), p. 116.

8. Mircea Eliade, *The Quest* (Chicago: University of Chicago Press, 1969), pp. 133-75.

9. Rosemary Radford Ruether, *Sexism and God-Talk: Toward a Feminist Theology* (Boston: Beacon Press, 1983), p. 165.

10. Rosemary Radford Ruether, *New Woman, New Earth* (New York: Seabury Press, 1975); Anne Wilson Schaef, *Women's Reality* (Minneapolis: Winston Press, 1981), pp. 149-52.

11. Eric Marshall and Stuart Hample, compilers, *Children's Letters to God* (New York: Pocket Books, 1966), as quoted in *Reader's Digest,* March 1967, p. 97.

12. James R. Edwards, "Toward a Neutered Bible: Making God S/He,"

239

Christianity Today, February 18, 1983, p. 21. The article Dr. Edwards submitted was titled simply "The Bible and the English Language." He raised the issue in the form of questions: "The question then remains whether the masculinity of Jesus implies that God is masculine. Whether God has gender, and if so which gender, is a difficult question to answer" (ms. p. 6). He proceeds to talk about the predominance of male imagery in Scripture and how metaphor is to be interpreted.

13. C. S. Lewis, "Priestesses in the Church?" in Walter Hooper, ed., *God in the Dock* (Grand Rapids: Wm. B. Eerdmans Publishing Co., 1970), p. 237.

14. Virginia Ramey Mollenkott, *The Divine Feminine: The Biblical Imagery of God as Female* (New York: Crossroad, 1983).

15. See Casey Miller and Kate Swift, *Words and Women* (Garden City, N.Y.: Anchor Press/Doubleday, 1977) and *The Handbook of Nonsexist Writing* (New York: Barnes & Noble, 1980); Sharon Neufer Emswiler and Thomas Neufer Emswiler, *Women and Worship,* rev. ed. (New York: Harper & Row, 1984) and *Wholeness in Worship* (San Francisco: Harper & Row, 1980); Keith Watkins, *Faithful and Fair* (Nashville: Abingdon Press, 1981). Nancy A. Hardesty is working on a book for John Knox Press, which should be available soon.

2. It All Started with Eve

1. Billy Graham, "Jesus and the Liberated Woman," *Ladies' Home Journal,* December 1970, p. 42.

2. Eva Figes, *Patriarchal Attitudes* (Greenwich, Conn.: Fawcett Publications, Fawcett Premier Book, 1970), pp. 40, 24, records the story of Lilith. According to seventeenth-century Jewish kabbalistic writings, "God then formed Lilith, the first woman, just as he had formed Adam, except that he used filth and sediment instead of pure dust. From Adam's union with this demoness, and with another like her named Naamah, Tubal Cain's sister, sprang Asmodeus and innumerable demons that still plague mankind." Actually this is surprising, for a twelfth-century midrash on Numbers declares: "Adam and Lilith never found peace together; for when he wished to lie with her, she took offence at the recumbent posture he demanded. 'Why must I lie beneath you?' she asked. 'I also was made from dust, and am therefore your equal.' Because Adam tried to compel her obedience by force, Lilith, in a rage, uttered the magic name of God, rose into the air and left him." The story of Lilith is also the subject of Lilly Rivlin, "Lilith: The First Woman," *Ms.,* December 1972, pp. 92-97; 114-15.

3. Phyllis Trible, *God and the Rhetoric of Sexuality* (Philadelphia: Fortress Press, 1978), chap. 4, "A Love Story Gone Awry," pp. 72-143; see also chap. 1, "Clues in a Text," on Gen. 1, pp. 1-30.

4. H. C. Leupold, *Exposition of Genesis* (Grand Rapids: Baker Book House, 1950), 1:94. Plato declared that male and female were the halves of an original sphere. Jewish speculation along the same lines saw a double creature joined back to back which God sawed in half while Adam slept.

5. Emile Cardinal Leger, *Search* 2 (August 1963): 136. Sidney Cornelia Callahan, *The Illusion of Eve* (New York: Sheed and Ward, 1965), p. 60. Alfred Lapple, *Key Problems in Genesis* (Glen Rock, N.J.: Paulist Press, Deus Book, 1967), p. 60.

6. Russell C. Prohl, *Woman in the Church* (Grand Rapids: Wm. B. Eerdmans Publishing Co., 1957), p. 37. James Hastings, *A Dictionary of the Bible* (Edinburgh: T. & T. Clark, 1899), s.v. "Help."

7. Helmut Thielicke, *The Ethics of Sex,* trans. John W. Doberstein (New York: Harper & Row, 1964), p. 4, quoting F. Delitzsch. Hastings, *A Dictionary of the Bible,* s.v. "Help."

8. Leupold, *Exposition of Genesis,* 1:94, 137, suggests that "male" and "female" in Gen. 1:27 come from *zakhar,* which has no root meaning other than "male" and *neqebhaha* from *neqab,* meaning "to perforate." The words used in Gen. 2:23 are *ish* and *issha. Ish* is said to have a root meaning "to exercise power." *Ishshah* is not really grammatically related but is a Hebrew word play. Its roots are possibly Assyrian. *The Interpreter's Bible Dictionary,* s.v. "Sex," suggests *issanu,* as a root meaning "strong," but author O. J. Baab dismisses this immediately as "improbable" without explanation. A second possible root is *anasu,* which can mean either "to be weak or sick" or "to be inclined to, to be friendly, social." A word with the same Hebrew spelling *(anasu)* means "soft, delicate."

9. Paul King Jewett, "The Doctrine of Man: The Divine Image—Man as Male and Female," course outline for T21 Systematic Theology, Fuller Theological Seminary, Pasadena, California, 1973, p. 114. See his *MAN as Male and Female* (Grand Rapids: Wm. B. Eerdmans Publishing Co., 1975), p. 128.

10. Augustine, "The Good of Marriage," trans. Charles T. Wilcox, in *Treatises on Marriage and Other Subjects,* The Fathers of the Church, ed. Roy Joseph Defarrari (Washington, D.C.: Catholic University of America Press, 1955), 27:9.

11. J. B. Phillips, *The Ring of Truth* (New York: Macmillan, 1967), p. 28. "Sometimes you can see the conflict between the Pharisaic spirit of the former Saul (who could say such grudging things about marriage and insist upon the perennial submission of women) and the Spirit of God, who inspired Paul to write that in Christ there is neither 'Jew nor Greek . . . male nor female.'" Jewett, "The Doctrine of Man," p. 98: "Because these two perspectives—the Jewish and the Christian—are incompatible, there is no satisfying way to harmonize the Pauline argument for female subordination with the larger Christian vision of which the great apostle to the Gentiles is the primary New Testament architect. Paul himself, judging from the evidence, was not wholly unaware of the tension in his thoughts." See his *MAN as Male and Female,* pp. 112-13. Richard N. Longenecker, "Can We Reproduce the Exegesis of the New Testament?" *Tyndale Bulletin* 21 (1970): 3-38.

12. Jewett, "The Doctrine of Man," p. 99. See *MAN as Male and Female,* p. 113.

13. Dick and Joyce Boldrey, "Women in Paul's Life," *Trinity Studies* 2 (1972):13. Morna D. Hooker, "Authority on Her Head: An Examination of I Cor. XI:10," *New Testament Studies* 10 (1963–64):410-16.

14. Thielicke, *Ethics of Sex,* p. 10.

15. Augustine, *The Trinity,* trans. Stephen McKenna, The Fathers of the Church, 45:351-55 (bk. 12, chap. 7).

16. James Moffatt, *The First Epistle of Paul to the Corinthians* (New York: Harper and Bros., Publishers, n.d.), p. 151. Margaret E. Thrall, *The First and Second Letters of Paul to the Corinthians* (London: Cambridge University Press, 1965), pp. 79-80.

17. Peter Brunner, *The Ministry and the Ministry of Women* (St. Louis: Concordia Publishing House, 1971) has developed this argument most fully. John Reumann, "What in Scripture Speaks to the Ordination of Women?" *Concordia Theological Monthly* 44 (January 1973): 25-26, offers a reply.

18. For a biblical study of head versus heart, note such references as "Wisdom resteth in the heart of him that hath understanding" (Prov. 14:33 KJV); "the good man out of the good treasure of his heart produces good, and the evil man out of his evil treasure produces evil; for out of the abundance of the heart his mouth speaks" (Luke 6:45). See also Ps. 44:21; I Chron. 28:9; Rom. 10:9-10; Mark 2:6-8.

19. Martin Luther, *Luther's Commentary on Genesis*, trans. J. Theodore Mueller (Grand Rapids: Zondervan, 1958), p. 68.

20. E. A. Speiser, *Genesis* (Garden City, N.Y.: Doubleday, 1964), p. 21.

21. Johanna Timmer, " 'Women's Lib'—A Misnomer?" *The Outlook* 23 (April 1973): 9-10. "The devil's first customer was Eve, who, horror of horrors! lent him a ready ear. . . . In a sense Eve may be said to have started the 'Women's Lib.' movement."

22. Aileen S. Kraditor, ed., *Up from the Pedestal* (Chicago: University of Chicago Press, Quadrangle Books, 1968), p. 38.

23. Dave Scaer, "What Did St. Paul Want?" *His*, May 1973, p. 13.

24. David Hubbard, "When Man Was Human," *His*, October 1971, p. 3.

25. John Peter Lange, *A Commentary on the Holy Scriptures*, trans. Philip Schaff (New York: Charles Scribner's Sons, 1905), 10:229. Augustine, *The City of God* (Garden City, N.Y.: Doubleday, Image Books, 1958), p. 256 (bk. 19, chap. 2).

26. Leupold, *Exposition of Genesis*, p. 12.

27. Dietrich Bonhoeffer, *Creation and Fall; Temptation* (New York: Macmillan, 1959), p. 75.

28. E. J. Young, *Genesis 3* (London: The Banner of Truth Trust, 1966), pp. 70, 91.

29. Boldrey and Boldrey, "Women in Paul's Life," p. 33. The first reference to women's "pain" in Gen. 3:16 is the Hebrew word *itstsabon*, which is used again in v. 17 of man's "toil" or "labor." Likewise, *etzev*, the second word of "pain" in 3:16, is translated "labor" in Gen. 5:29 (NEB) and Prov. 14:23 (KJV).

30. Young, *Genesis 3*, p. 124.

31. Leupold, *Exposition of Genesis*, p. 172.

32. Young, *Genesis 3*, p. 127. Cf. C. F. Kell and F. Delitzsch, *Biblical Commentary on the Old Testament* (Grand Rapids: Wm. B. Eerdmans Publishing Co., n.d.), 1:103.

33. S. R. Driver, *The Book of Genesis* (London: Methuen & Co., 1911), p. 49.

34. Katharine C. Bushnell, *God's Word to Women* (ca. 1919; reprint, North Collins, N.Y.: Ray B. Munson, n.d.), Lessons 16-20.

35. Helen B. Andelin, *Fascinating Womanhood* (Santa Barbara, Calif.: Pacific Press, 1963), p. 89.

36. Prohl, *Woman in the Church*, p. 39.

37. Thielicke, *Ethics of Sex*, p. 8.

38. Luther, *Commentary on Genesis*, p. 82.

39. Andre Dumas, "Biblical Anthropology and the Participation of Women in the Ministry of the Church," in *Concerning the Ordination of Women* (Geneva: World Council of Churches, Department on Faith and Order, 1964), p. 32.

3. Women in the Bible World

1. Richard Gilman, "Where Did It All Go Wrong?" *Life*, August 13, 1971, p. 48.

2. Simone de Beauvoir, *The Second Sex*, trans. and ed. H. M. Parshley (New York: Knopf, 1953; Bantam Books, 1961), pp. 75-76 in Bantam edn.

3. See, for example, Phyllis M. Kaberry, *Women of the Grassfields* (London: Her Majesty's Stationery Office, 1952); Peggy R. Sanday, "Toward a Theory of the Status of Women," *American Anthropologist* 75 (1973): 1682–1700; Letha Dawson Scanzoni and John Scanzoni, *Men, Women, and Change*, 2d ed. (New York: McGraw-Hill, 1981), chap. 3.

4. Peggy R. Sanday, "Female Status in the Public Domain," in Michelle Zimbalist Rosaldo and Louise Lamphere eds., *Woman, Culture, and Society* (Stanford, Calif.: Stanford University Press, 1974), p. 206. See also Peggy Reeves Sanday, *Female Power and Male Dominance* (New York: Cambridge University Press, 1981).

5. H. W. F. Saggs, *The Greatness That Was Babylon* (London: Sidgwick and Jackson, 1962), pp. 186-87. See also Elise Boulding, *The Underside of History: A View of Women through Time* (Boulder, Colo.: Westview Press, 1976).

6. Edward B. Pollard, *Oriental Women*, vol. 4 of *Woman in All Ages and in All Countries* (Philadelphia: The Rittenhouse Press, 1907), pp. 104-5. Elise Boulding, in her massive study of the status of women from earliest times, has found evidence that legends about Semiramis are based upon the actual life and accomplishments of an actual Assyrian queen, Sammuramat, who lived in the late ninth and early eighth centuries B.C. See Boulding, *Underside of History*, p. 225.

7. Saggs, *The Greatness That Was Babylon*, p. 214.

8. "Women's Rights Becoming Issue in Morocco," UPI report in Bloomington (Ind.) *Herald-Telephone*, September 29, 1971.

9. See Eva Matthews Sanford, *The Mediterranean World in Ancient Times* (New York: Ronald Press, 1938), pp. 45, 110; Pollard, *Oriental Women*, p. 106; Charles Seltman, *Women in Antiquity* (London: Thames and Hudson, 1956), pp. 30-32; "The Code of Hammurabi," in James B. Pritchard, ed., *The Ancient Near East* (Princeton: Princeton University Press, 1958), pp. 138-67.

10. de Beauvoir, *Second Sex*, pp. 78-79.

11. Seltman, *Women in Antiquity*, p. 42.

12. de Beauvoir, *Second Sex*, p. 79. See also Boulding, *Underside of History*, pp. 184-86, 227-35.

13. Seltman, *Women in Antiquity*, p. 43.

14. de Beauvoir, *Second Sex*, p. 80.

15. Roland de Vaux, *Ancient Israel*, trans. John McHugh (London: Darton, Longman & Todd, 1961), p. 20.

16. Ibid., p. 40.

17. Krister Stendahl, *The Bible and the Role of Women*, trans. Emilie T. Sander (Philadelphia: Fortress Press, 1966), p. 27.

18. Ze'ev W. Falk, *Hebrew Law in Biblical Times* (Jerusalem: Wahrmann Books, 1964), p. 111.

19. Ibid., p. 169.

20. de Vaux, *Ancient Israel*, pp. 54-55.

21. See David R. Mace, *Hebrew Marriage* (New York: Philosophical Library, 1953), pp. 230-31. Also William N. Stephens, *The Family in Cross-Cultural Perspective* (New York: Holt, Rinehart and Winston, 1963), pp. 225 ff.

22. Mary Douglas, *Purity and Danger* (Middlesex, England; Baltimore: Penguin, Pelican Books, 1970), p. 160.

23. de Vaux, *Ancient Israel*, p. 36.

24. Michael Grant, *The World of Rome* (New York: New American Library Mentor Book, 1960), p. 91.

25. de Beauvoir, *Second Sex*, p. 86.

26. E. M. Blaiklock, *From Prison in Rome—Letters to the Philippians and Philemon* (Grand Rapids: Zondervan Publishing House, 1964), p. 47; and "Luke" in *Zondervan Pictorial Bible Dictionary* (Zondervan Publishing House, 1963), p. 495.

27. Plato, *The Republic*, trans. Francis MacDonald Cornford (New York: Oxford University Press, paperback, 1945), pp. 149, 153.

28. Quoted in de Beauvoir, *Second Sex*, p. 81.

29. Seltman, *Women in Antiquity*, p. 115.

30. Boulding, *Underside of History*, pp. 259-63.

31. Ibid., p. 258.

32. Sarah B. Pomeroy, *Goddesses, Whores, Wives, and Slaves: Women in Classical Antiquity* (New York: Schocken Books, 1975), pp. 79-80.

33. See for example Jerome Carcopino, *Daily Life in Ancient Rome* (New Haven: Yale University Press, 1940), pp. 92-93.

34. Suetonius, *The Twelve Caesars*, trans. Robert Graves (Middlesex, England; Baltimore: Penguin Books, 1957).

35. Grant, *World of Rome*, chap. 6.

36. Stendahl, *Bible and the Role of Women*, p. 25.

4. Woman's Best Friend: Jesus

1. Seltman, *Women in Antiquity*, p. 184.

2. C. F. D. Moule, *The Phenomenon of the New Testament* (Naperville, Ill.: Alec R. Allenson, Co., 1967), p. 65.

3. Dorothy Sayers, *Are Women Human?* (Grand Rapids: Wm. B. Eerdmans Publishing Co., 1971), p. 46.

4. Charles Caldwell Ryrie, *The Place of Women in the Church* (Chicago: Moody Press, 1958), p. 23, quoting James Hastings.

5. Virginia Ramey Mollenkott, *Speech, Silence, Action!* (Nashville: Abingdon Press, 1980), p. 81.

6. Sondra Henry and Emily Taitz, *Written Out of History: Our Jewish Foremothers*, 2d rev. ed. (Fresh Meadows, N.Y.: Biblio Press, 1983), pp. 48-53. Rabbi Eliezer ben Hyrcanus is well known as being more misogynistic than most of the rabbis of the Talmud. He was married to Ima Shalom, sister of the famous Rabbi Gamaliel. She is one of the few women whose wisdom is cited in the Talmud.

7. Women are still banned from formal study among orthodox Jews. They were admitted to conservative Jewish seminaries for the first time in late 1983. Cf. "Toppling a Jewish Tradition," *Time*, November 7, 1983, p. 83.

8. Edward L. Kessel, "A Proposed Biological Interpretation of the Virgin Birth," *Journal of the American Scientific Affiliation* (September 1983): 129-36. Cf. John Money and Anke A. Ehrhardt, *Man and Woman, Boy and Girl* (New York: New American Library, 1972).

9. Graham, "Jesus and the Liberated Woman," p. 46.

10. Sayers, *Are Women Human?* pp. 46-47.

11. Interestingly, Matthew, writing to the Jewish community, includes Joseph's genealogy and all that we know about him. Luke, on the other hand,

a liberated physician writing to a Gentile, mentions many women, often placing them parallel with his mention of men:

Zechariah	Luke 1:5-22, 26-38	Mary
Simeon	2:25-38	Anna
Naaman	4:27, 25-26	widow of Zarephath
demoniac at		
Capernaum	4:31-39	Peter's mother-in-law
centurion's servant	7:1-17	widow of Nain
Simon the Pharisee	7:36-50	public sinner
The Twelve	8:1-3	women followers
Gerasene demoniac	8:26-56	woman with hemorrhage, Jairus' daughter
good Samaritan	10:29-42	Mary and Martha
men of Nineveh	11:32, 31	queen of the South
man with dropsy	14:1-6; 13:10-17	crippled woman
man with mustard seed	13:18-21	woman with yeast
man with 100 sheep	15:4-10	woman with 10 coins
two men sleeping	17:34-35	two women grinding
Pharisee and publican	18:9-14, 1-8	importunate widow
scribes	20:45-47; 21:1-4	widow who gave mite
Joseph of Arimathea	23:50-56	women from Galilee
Emmaus disciples	24:13-35, 1-11	women at the tomb
Eleven, Jesus' brothers	Acts 1:13-14	women, Mary, Jesus' mother
sons, menservants	2:17-18	daughters, maidservants
Ananias	5:1-11	Sapphira
Aeneas	9:32-42	Tabitha (Dorcas)
Philippian jailer	16:25-34, 14-15	Lydia
Dionysius	17:34	Damaris
Apollos	18:24-28	Priscilla
Agabus	21:10, 9	Philip's four daughters

Other interesting parallels could be drawn between Nicodemus and the Samaritan woman (John 3:1-21; 4:1-42); the conscientious steward and the ten bridesmaids (Matt. 24:45–25:13); Judas who sold Christ for money and Mary who anointed him with the most costly thing she owned (Matt. 26:14-16; 6-13); the disciples in the upper room and Mary Magdalene at the tomb (John 20:19-29; 20:11-18). Such parallelism has been suggested by Helmut Flender, *St. Luke, Theologian of Redemption History* (Philadelphia: Fortress Press, 1967), pp. 9-10.

12. Schussler Fiorenza, *In Memory of Her*, pp. xiii-xiv.

13. Paul ignores women in his summary of resurrection witnesses (I Cor. 15:4-8). As Josephus records, "But let not a single witness be credited; but three or two at the least, and those such whose testimony is confirmed by their good lives. But let not the testimony of women be admitted, on account of the levity and boldness of their sex." *The Works of Flavius Josephus*, "The Antiquities," trans. William Whiston (London: William W. Nimmo, n.d.), p.

97 (bk. 6, chap. 8, v. 15). This anti-feminine tradition had grown up in Jewish law despite the fact that Deut. 17:6 and 19:15 say nothing about the inadmissibility of women's testimony.

14. This point was most movingly made in a devotional talk by Virginia Mollenkott at the Conference on Contemporary Issues, "Evangelical Perspectives on Woman's Role and Status," May 30, 1973, at Conservative Baptist Theological Seminary, Denver.

15. Noted by Paul King Jewett in a speech at the Conference on Contemporary Issues, May 31, 1973.

16. Is there any connection between the murderous rage displayed by the people of Nazareth in Luke 4:28 and the fact that "Joseph's son" had compared his mission to Elijah's being sent to a Sidonian widow or to Naaman's being healed on the suggestion of his Jewish maid? Note the reactions also in Matt. 26:8; Luke 7:39, 13:14; John 4:27, 8:9-10.

5. Your Daughters Shall Prophesy

1. Lucy S. Dawidowicz, "On Being a Woman in Shul," *Commentary,* July 1968, p. 72.

2. In Romans 16 Paul mentions ten women: Phoebe (v. 1), Prisca (Priscilla, v. 3), Mary (v. 6), Junias (Junia, v.7, see KJV), Tryphaena and Tryphosa (v. 12), Persis (v. 12), Rufus' mother (v. 13), Julia, Nereus' sister (v. 15). Junia(s) is sometimes considered a masculine name. However, Junia was a common woman's name and is more likely feminine rather than a shortened form of a very obscure man's name. The case ending on the name in the Greek could be either masculine or feminine.

3. Fiorenza, *In Memory of Her,* pp. 160-204.

4. Ruth Hoppin, *Priscilla: Author of the Epistle to the Hebrews* (New York: Exposition Press, 1969). Other scholars who share this opinion which was first proposed by Adolf Harnack are James Rendel Harris (*Sidelights on New Testament Research*), Arthur S. Peak (*A Critical Introduction to the New Testament*), and James Hope Moulton. Lee Anna Starr, *The Bible Status of Women* (Zarephath, N.J.: Pillar of Fire, 1926, 1955), pp. 392-415, reprints a translation of Harnack's essay.

5. Ryrie, *Place of Women,* pp. 87-88. Prohl, *Woman in the Church,* pp. 70-71. Boldrey and Boldrey, "Women in Paul's Life," p. 1. J. Massyngberde Ford, "Biblical Material Relevant to the Ordination of Women," *Journal of Ecumenical Studies* 10 (Fall 1973): 677, notes that the masculine form *prostates* (fem. *prostatis*) is used repeatedly in the LXX of stewards (I Chron. 27:31), officers (I Chron. 29:6; II Chron. 8:10), governors (I Esdras 2:12; II Macc. 3:4).

6. Prohl, *Woman in the Church,* p. 70. Ryrie, *Place of Women,* pp. 85-86. Catherine Beaton, "Does the Church Discriminate Against Women on the Basis of Their Sex?", *Critic* 24 (June-July 1966): 25. Elsie Culver, *Women in the World of Religion* (Garden City, N.Y.: Doubleday, 1967), p. 68. Apostolic Constitutions 2:57; 3:5; *Didascalia* 2:26, 3:12. Cf. Roger Gryson, *The Ministry of Women in the Early Church* (Collegeville, Minn.: The Liturgical Press, 1976), pp. 8-10, 25-29, 35-41.

7. Ryrie, *Place of Women,* pp. 82, 84, 99-100, 128, 130.

8. Ibid., pp. 128, 131-32, 140.

9. Ford, "Biblical Material Relevant to the Ordination of Women," pp. 683, 685, 677-78. Though there is no biblical evidence that women also functioned

as bishops, there are several inscription references to *presbutera* and *episcopa,* indicating women. See Joan Morris, *The Lady Was a Bishop* (New York: Macmillan, 1973), pp. 3-8.

10. Chrysostom, *The Homilies of St. John Chrysostom,* Nicene and Post Nicene Fathers, First Series (Grand Rapids: Wm. B. Eerdmans Publishing Company, 1956), 11:555. Elsie Gibson, *When the Minister Is a Woman* (New York: Holt, Rinehart and Winston, 1970), pp. 9-10. Prohl, *Woman in the Church,* p. 72. Some suggest that Junia was not an apostle but simply one known by the apostles. This is not the best translation of the text.

11. Prohl, *Woman in the Church,* p. 55. Tertullian, *Ante-Nicene Fathers* (New York: Charles Scribner's Sons, 1885), 4:48.

12. Abel Isaksson, *Marriage and Ministry in the New Temple,* vol. 24 Acta Seminarii Neotestamentici Upsaliensis (Lund, Sweden: C. W. K. Gleerup, 1965), and James B. Hurley, "Did Paul Require Veils or the Silence of Women?" *Westminster Theological Journal* 35 (Winter 1973):190-220, argue that the issue here is not veils but loose hair as opposed to hair braided in a manner indicative of marriage. The word for "veil" appears only in v. 15 where it says a woman's hair is given her instead of a veil. These authors note that the phrases used for head covered and uncovered in I Cor. 11:4-5 are the same as those used by the LXX to translate "the hair of his head hang loose" in Lev. 13:45 and "unbind the hair of the woman's head" in Num. 5:18. They see a similar parallel in Ezek. 44:20 which explains why Paul prohibited long hair on men.

13. Johannes Weiss, *The History of Primitive Christianity,* trans. Frederick C. Grant (New York: Wilson-Erickson, 1937), p. 584. Clarence Tucker Craig, "The First Epistle to the Corinthians," in *The Interpreter's Bible* (New York: Abingdon Press, 1955), 10:126. Prohl, *Woman in the Church,* pp. 28, 51-52.

14. Eugenia Leonard, "St. Paul on the Status of Women," *The Catholic Biblical Quarterly* 12 (July 1950): 319. Moffatt, *First . . . Corinthians,* p. 149. Boldrey and Boldrey, "Women in Paul's Life," p. 28. Culver, *World of Religion,* p. 55.

15. Morna D. Hooker, "Authority on Her Head: An Examination of I Corinthians XI.10," *New Testament Studies* 10 (1963–64):410-16. J. A. Fitzmyer, "A Feature of Qumran Angelology and the Angels of I Cor. XI.10," *New Testament Studies* 4 (1957–58): 48-58.

16. John Reumann, "What in Scripture Speaks to the Ordination of Women?" *Concordia Theological Monthly* 44 (January 1973): 16; Isaksson, *Marriage and Ministry,* pp. 179-80.

17. Joseph Yoder, *The Prayer Veil Analyzed* (Huntingdon, Pa.: Yoder Publishing Co., 1954).

18. See Hooker, "Authority on Her Head," and Fitzmyer," A Feature of Qumran Angelology." H. A. Ironside, *Addresses on the First Epistle to the Corinthians* (New York: Loizeaux Brothers, 1938), pp. 337-38. Thielicke, *Ethics of Sex,* p. 10.

19. Moffatt, *First . . . Corinthians,* p. 154. Chrysostom, *Homilies,* p. 349. Isaksson, *Marriage and Ministry,* suggests that Paul is thinking of Ezek. 44:20, where the priests serving God must not wear long, unkempt hair.

20. Scaer, "What Did St. Paul Want?" p. 12.

21. Moffatt, *First . . . Corinthians,* pp. 231-32.

22. Dawidowicz, "On Being a Woman in Shul," pp. 73-74.

23. Boldrey and Boldrey, "Women in Paul's Life," p. 19.

24. Marga Buhrig, "The Question of the Ordination of Women in the Light of Some New Testament Texts," in *Concerning the Ordination of Women* (Geneva: World Council of Churches, Department of Faith and Order, 1964), pp. 51-53. Fred D. Gealy, "I Timothy," in *The Interpreter's Bible*, 11:403-6.

25. Stendahl, *Bible and the Role of Women*, p. 32.

6. He, She, or We?

1. Sigmund Freud, "Femininity," in his *New Introductory Lectures on Psychoanalysis*, trans. and ed. James Strachey (New York: W. W. Norton, 1965), p. 113.

2. Christian Reformed Church, *Study Committee Reports*, "Report 39: Women in Ecclesiastical Office," 1973, pp. 388, 382, 383.

3. Betty Friedan, *The Feminine Mystique* (New York: Dell Books, 1964), pp. 37, 69.

4. Bernard Ramm, "A Total Way of Existing," a brief, boxed response to Nancy Hardesty's article, "Women: Second Class Citizens," *Eternity*, January 1971, p. 15.

5. John Money and Patricia Tucker, *Sexual Signatures: On Being a Man or a Woman* (New York: Little, Brown and Co., 1975), chap. 2.

6. Ibid., p. 38.

7. Gary Seldon, "Frailty, Thy Name's Been Changed: What Sports Medicine Is Discovering about Women's Bodies," *Ms.* 10 (July 1981): 96.

8. Money and Tucker, *Sexual Signatures*, p. 41.

9. Seldon, "Frailty, Thy Name's Been Changed," p. 96.

10. Richard and Joyce Boldrey, *Chauvinist or Feminist? Paul's View of Women* (Grand Rapids: Baker Book House, 1976), pp. 50-51. Cf I Cor. 1:27 where "weak" is equated with "base, despised, without boast," or 4:10 where it means "undistinguished, without honor."Compare Acts 20:35; I Cor. 2:3; 11:30; 15:43 (where weakness is paralleled with dishonor); II Cor. 11:21, 29, 30; 12:5, 9, 10; 13:3, 4, 9; I Thess. 5:14.

11. Talcott Parsons, *Essays in Sociological Theory*, rev. ed. (New York: The Free Press, 1954), p. 330.

12. See, for example, Estelle Ramey, "Sex Hormones and Executive Ability," *Annals of the New York Academy of Sciences* 208 (March 15, 1973): 237-45; and Naomi Weisstein, "Tired of Arguing about Biological Inferiority?" *Ms.* 11 (November 1982): 41-46, 85. For a summary of gender-role research, see Letha Dawson Scanzoni and John Scanzoni, *Men, Women, and Change*, 3d. ed. (New York: McGraw-Hill, in press), chaps. 2 and 3.

13. Margaret Mead, *Sex and Temperament in Three Primitive Societies* (New York: William Morrow and Co., 1935, 1963), p. 280.

14. Roy G. D'Andrade, "Sex Differences and Cultural Institutions," in Eleanor E. Maccoby, ed., *The Development of Sex Differences* (Stanford, Calif.: Stanford University Press, 1966), pp. 174-204.

15. Michael Lewis, "There's No Unisex in the Nursery," *Psychology Today*, May 1972, pp. 54-57.

16. Dean Walley, *What Girls Can Be* and *What Can Boys Be* (New York: Hallmark Children's Edition, n.d.).

17. Sarah Bentley Doely, ed., *Women's Liberation and the Church* (New York: Association Press, 1970), pp. 119-24. Study by Miriam Crist and Tilda Norberg for the New York Conference Task Force on the Status of Women, United Methodist Church.

18. Patricia Cross, "The Undergraduate Woman," Research Report Number 5 from the American Association for Higher Education, March 15, 1971. Florence Howe, "Sexual Stereotypes Start Early," *Saturday Review* 16 (October 1971): 76-82, 92-94.

19. William Law, *A Serious Call to a Devout and Holy Life* (London: Printed for the Proprietors and sold by all Booksellers, 1837), pp. 202-3.

20. Marlene Pringle, "Counseling Women," *Caps Capsule* 4 (Spring 1971): 11-15. Entire issue devoted to the subject. See also Eleanor E. Maccoby, "Woman's Intellect," in Seymour Farber and Roger H. L. Wilson, *The Potential of Woman* (New York: McGraw-Hill, 1963), pp. 24-39. Also Alice S. Rossi, "Women in Science: Why So Few?" in Constantina Safilios-Rothschild, *Toward a Sociology of Women* (Lexington, Mass.: Xerox College Publishing, 1972), pp. 141-53.

21. Matina Horner, "Fail: Bright Women," *Psychology Today*, November 1969, pp. 36-38, 62. Judith M. Bardwick, *Psychology of Women* (New York: Harper & Row, 1971), pp. 167-87.

22. Kate Millett, *Sexual Politics* (Garden City, N.Y.: Doubleday, 1970), pp. 176-203.

23. Erik H. Erikson, "Inner and Outer Space: Reflections on Womanhood," in Robert Jay Lifton, ed., *The Woman in America* (Boston: Beacon Press, 1964), pp. 19, 5. For a criticism see Millett, *Sexual Politics*, pp. 214-15.

24. Donald and Inge Broverman, "Sex Role Stereotypes and Clinical Judgments of Mental Health," *Journal of Consulting and Clinical Psychology* 34 (1970):1-7. Published in summary form by Jo-Ann Gardner, *The Face across the Breakfast Table* (Pittsburgh: Know, Inc., 1970). For similar studies concerning children see Eleanor Maccoby, "Is There Any Special Way of Thinking, Feeling, or Acting that Is Characteristically Female . . . ?" *Mademoiselle*, February 1970, pp. 180-81, 277-78.

25. In Doely, *Women's Liberation*, p. 52.

26. John Money and Anke Ehrhardt, *Man and Woman, Boy and Girl* (Baltimore: Johns Hopkins University Press, 1972). Mentor Books paperback edition, p. 14.

27. See Letha Dawson Scanzoni, "Can Homosexuals Change? Understanding the Nature of the Homosexual Orientation" and "Putting a Face on Homosexuality," in *Christians and Homosexuality*, a reprint booklet published by *The Other Side* magazine (300 W. Apsley St., Philadelphia, Pa. 19144), 1984, pp. 1-7. See also Letha Dawson Scanzoni and Virginia Ramey Mollenkott, *Is the Homosexual My Neighbor?* (San Francisco: Harper & Row, 1978).

28. Sandra Bem, "Psychological Androgyny," in Alice G. Sargent, ed., *Beyond Sex Roles* (St. Paul: West Publishing Co., 1977), p. 319.

29. Sandra Lipsitz Bem, "Gender Schema Theory and Its Implications for Child Development: Raising Gender-aschematic Children in a Gender-schematic Society," *Signs* 8 (Summer 1983): 615-16.

30. Schaef, *Women's Reality*.

31. Carol Gilligan, *In a Different Voice* (Cambridge, Mass.: Harvard University Press, 1982), p. 4.

32. In Martha Saxton, "Are Women More Moral than Men? An Interview with Psychologist Carol Gilligan," *Ms.* 10 (December 1981): 63-64.

33. Ibid., p. 66.

34. Gayle Graham Yates, *What Women Want* (Cambridge, Mass.: Harvard University Press, 1975).

35. Jean Baker Miller, *Toward a New Psychology of Women* (Boston: Beacon Press, 1976), p. 1. See also Lindsay Van Gelder, "Carol Gilligan: Leader for a Different Kind of Future," *Ms.* 12 (January 1984): 37ff.

7. Love, Honor, and ———?

1. William J. Lederer and Don D. Jackson, *The Mirages of Marriage* (New York: W. W. Norton, 1968), p. 18.

2. John Stuart Mill, "The Subjection of Women," as reprinted in John Stuart Mill and Harriet Taylor Mill, *Essays on Sex Equality*, edited and with an introductory essay byyAlice S. Rossi (Chicago: University of Chicago Press, 1970), pp. 235-36.

3. John Milton, *The Doctrine and Discipline of Divorce* (London: Sherwood, Neely, and Jones, 1820), p. 126.

4. "Women's Lib: Friend or Foe?" *The Alliance Witness* 28 (October 1970): 23.

5. James Henley Thornwell, "The Rights and Duties of Masters, A Sermon Preached at the Dedication of A Church, erected in Charleston, S.C., for the Benefit and Instruction of the Coloured Population" (Charleston, 1850), as reprinted in Robert L. Ferm, ed., *Issues in American Protestantism* (Garden City, N.Y.: Doubleday Anchor Books, 1969), pp. 193, 191.

6. Sir William Blackstone's interpretation of English Common Law, as reflected in his *Commentaries* of the late eighteenth century, influenced the laws and customs of both Great Britain and America so that sex discrimination was legally sanctioned. Upon marriage, a woman lost her individual rights and became a nonperson in the eyes of the law. In his seventh edition (1775) Blackstone said, "By marriage, the husband and wife are one person in law; that is, the very being or legal existence of the woman is suspended during the marriage, or at least is incorporated and consolidated into that of the husband; under whose wing, protection, and *cover*, she performs every thing." Quoted in Mary T. Beard, *Woman as Force in History* (New York: Collier Book edition, 1962), p. 89. On the history of a woman's taking her husband's name, see Una Stannard, *Mrs Man* (San Francisco: Germainbooks, 1977).

7. Mill, "Subjection," pp. 168-69.

8. Johs. Pedersen, *Israel: Its Life and Culture, I-II* (London: Oxford University Press, Geoffrey Cumberlege, 1926), p. 343.

9. Falk, *Hebrew Law in Biblical Times*, p. 154. Also see Deut. 24:1-4, which Jesus said was given because of the hardness of men's hearts (Matt. 19:7-8). The requirement of a *written* bill of divorce was perhaps a protection of sorts for women. At least she knew where she stood—as compared with an angry spur-of-the-moment demand by a husband that she get out. The requirement of signed papers probably made divorce a bit more difficult and forestalled capriciousness somewhat. But it was far from God's intended ideal (cf. Mal. 2:16).

10. de Vaux, *Ancient Israel*, p. 39.

11. Andre S. Bustanoby, "Love, Honor, and Obey," *Christianity Today* 13 (June 6, 1969): 4. Larry Christenson uses this same quotation to buttress his own similar arguments. See Christenson, *The Christian Family* (Minneapolis: Bethany Fellowship, 1970), p. 41.

12. Winnie Christensen, "What Is Woman's Role?" *Moody Monthly* 71 (June 1971): 83. Also see Bob Mumford, *Living Happily Ever After* (Old

Tappan, N. J.: Fleming H. Revell Company, 1971), pp. 28-38.

13. Mumford makes the point that Sarah submitted to her husband even though she knew he was wrong. In obeying her husband she was obeying God, he writes. "Had she disobeyed, she would only have added her own disobedience to the disobedience of her husband." Elsewhere, Mumford uses the passage regarding vows (Num. 30) to tell Christian husbands they may nullify a woman's promises to God. As an example, he speaks of a wife who announces to her husband she has promised the Lord to serve in some capacity in the local church (such as teaching Sunday school). The husband says she may not do it because the family needs her time and energies at home, assuring her that God will not hold her to her promise because the husband is her head and refuses to give her permission! See Mumford, *Living Happily Ever After,* pp. 29-30, 45. Similar reasoning is found in the Bible study notebook for the course entitled, "A Woman More Precious than Jewels," written by Bonnie Trude and privately published with the cooperation of the Greater Minneapolis Association of Evangelicals (rev. ed., 1976). Also see Elizabeth Rice Handford, *Me? Obey Him?* (Murfreesboro, Tenn.: Sword of the Lord Publishers, 1972), a book that is required reading for engaged couples in some fundamentalist churches. In reply to the question of a wife's responsibility if she feels God is leading her in a way opposite to her husband's command, Handford writes that "the Scriptures say a woman must ignore her 'feelings' about the will of God and do what her husband says," obeying her husband "as if he were God Himself." Handford asserts that a wife "can be as certain of God's will, when her husband speaks, as if God had spoken audibly from Heaven!" (p. 34).

14. John A. Newton, *Susanna Wesley and the Puritan Tradition in Methodism* (London: Epworth Press, 1968), pp. 84-93.

15. Expressing a similar point of view, Dick and Joyce Boldrey make the clever observation that the Eph. 5 passage on marriage contains a built-in "self-destruct" with regard to authority. See Boldrey and Boldrey, "Women in Paul's Life," p. 22; reprinted as *Chauvinist or Feminist? Paul's View of Women,* p. 50.

16. James Montgomery Boice, "Marriage by Christ's Standard," *Eternity* 21 (November 1970): 21.

17. Callahan, *Illusion of Eve,* p. 201.

18. Donald Grey Barnhouse, *This Man and This Woman* (Philadelphia: The Evangelical Foundation, Inc., 1958), p. 10.

19. Donald Grey Barnhouse, "The Wife with Two Heads," *Eternity* 14 (July 1963): 3. (Reprinted from the December 1958 issue.)

20. Kathryn Kuhlman, "Healing in the Spirit" (an interview with Kathryn Kuhlman), *Christianity Today* 17 (July 20, 1973):7.

8. Living in Equal Partnership

1. Jean Stapleton and Richard Bright, *Equal Marriage* (Nashville: Abingdon, 1976), pp. 125-27.

2. Jessie Bernard, *Women and the Public Interest* (Chicago: Aldine-Atherton, 1971), pp. 88 ff. Psychotherapists of the transactional analysis school also emphasize the need for stroking in human relationships. It is a need for recognition and approval which Harris calls "the psychological version of the early physical stroking" so crucial to infants. See Thomas A. Harris, M.D., *I'm OK—You're OK* (New York: Harper & Row, 1967), chap. 3. Also see Eric

Berne, M.D., *Games People Play* (New York: Grove Press, 1964), "Introduction." On the cost to women in bearing a disproportionate responsibility for taking care of others, see Tillie Olsen, *Silences* (New York: Delacorte Press/Seymour Lawrence, 1978), esp. pp. 16-118.

3. Stephen B. Clark, *Man and Woman in Christ* (Ann Arbor: Servant Books, 1980), p. 649; see also pp. 622, 635-49. For a brief critical summary of Clark's book, see Letha Dawson Scanzoni, "Human and Mrs. Human," *The Christian Century* 98 (March 11, 1981): 268-73.

4. Elizabeth Blackwell, *The Human Element in Sex: Being a Medical Inquiry into the Relation of Sexual Physiology to Christian Morality* (London: J. A. Churchill, 1894). Material quoted is from an excerpted portion of this work appearing in Nancy Cott, ed., *The Root of Bitterness* (New York: E. P. Dutton, 1972), pp. 299-303.

5. The Masters and Johnson research shows that there is only one kind of orgasm, which we may simply call a sexual orgasm (rather than trying to make a distinction between a "clitoral" orgasm and a "vaginal" orgasm, as was the custom in the past—particularly among those of Freudian persuasion). The most sensitive organ of erotic arousal is the clitoris, with the surrounding labia and mons area also being quite sensitive. The vagina itself is supplied with very few nerve endings in contrast to the richly supplied vulva (external female genitalia). During orgasm, the reaction involves and is generalized throughout all the pelvic sex organs regardless of the mode of stimulation, with the clitoris having the role "as the center of female sensual focus." In other words, all orgasm involves clitoral-body stimulation—whether it is direct manual or mechanical stimulation applied to the clitoral shaft or glans, or indirect stimulation through mons area manipulation, breast stimulation, or actual intercourse. See William H. Masters, M.D., and Virginia E. Johnson, *Human Sexual Response* (Boston: Little, Brown, 1966). See also Shere Hite, *The Hite Report* (New York: Dell Publishing Co., 1976); Lonnie Garfield Barbach, *For Yourself: The Fulfillment of Female Sexuality* (Garden City, N.Y.: Doubleday, 1975); and Lonnie Barbach, *For Each Other* (Anchor Press/Doubleday, 1982).

6. For a detailed discussion of what the Song of Solomon has to say to Christian couples today, see Letha Dawson Scanzoni, *Sex Is a Parent Affair*, 2d ed., rev. (New York: Bantam Books, 1982), chap. 2, and *Sexuality* (Philadelphia: Westminster Press, 1984), chap. 3. See also Trible, *God and the Rhetoric of Sexuality*, chap. 5.

7. Abraham H. Maslow, *Motivation and Personality*, 2d ed. (New York: Harper & Row, 1970), chap. 12.

8. Philip Blumstein and Pepper Schwartz, *American Couples* (New York: William Morrow, 1983), p. 222. These authors found that, among the couples in their study, those who went beyond equality to *role reversal* (with the woman more active and the man more reticent) were *unhappy* with their relationship in contrast to couples who stressed equality. (Many persons who fear equality have a misconception of what it means. What they really fear is role reversal—the same old parts to play but with a switch in who plays them. This is quite different from the sharing and mutuality inherent in a truly equal relationship, one that is free from power struggles and game playing.)

9. Womb-Man

1. Augustine, *De Genesi ad Litteram*, VII, 3; and IX, 5, as quoted in Daniel Sullivan, "A History of Catholic Thinking on Contraception," in William

Birmingham, ed., *What Modern Catholics Think about Birth Control* (New York: Signet Books, 1964), pp. 32-33.

2. Sigmund Freud, "Femininity," p. 128.

3. Gerhard Lenski, *Human Societies* (New York: McGraw-Hill, 1970), p. 156. A certain amount of debate has taken place among scholars over the precise origin, meaning, and purpose of these figurines. It is possible certain figurines were designed by females as well as males and may have been used in ceremonies over which women presided. Some scholars believe they were used for puberty rites; others have suggested they were used as dolls for children as well as fertility charms for their mothers. Ruether points out their connection to goddess worship but sees their faceless appearance as suggesting that "the Goddess is not a focus of personhood, but rather an impersonalized image of the mysterious powers of fecundity." See Ruether, *Sexism and God-Talk,* p. 48. See also the drawings of the figurines and a discussion of various viewpoints in Boulding, *Underside of History,* pp. 90-107. Sarah B. Pomeroy also has a brief discussion on the topic in her book, *Goddesses, Whores, Wives, and Slaves,* pp. 13-15.

4. John Langdon-Davies, *A Short History of Women* (New York: Viking Press, 1927), pp. 149-51.

5. Mircea Eliade, *The Sacred and the Profane* (New York: Harcourt, Brace & World, Harvest Books, 1959), p. 145. also see Lenski, *Human Societies,* pp. 219-21.

6. See the section, "The Birth of Reason," in Langdon-Davies, *Short History of Women,* pp. 162-65.

7. Horney, *Feminine Psychology,* pp. 114-15.

8. Ashley Montagu, *The Natural Superiority of Women* (New York: Macmillan, 1952), p. 33.

9. Hays, p. 23.

10. Margaret Mead, *Male and Female* (New York: Dell Publishing Co., Laurel ed., 1968), pp. 119-20.

11. Max Weber, *Ancient Judaism,* trans. and ed. Hans H. Gerth and Don Martindale (New York: The Free Press, 1952), p. 190.

12. *Artharva Veda,* XIV, 2, 14, as quoted in Eliade, *Sacred and Profane,* p. 166.

13. *Koran,* II, 225, as quoted in Eliade, p. 166.

14. Sophocles, *Oedipus the King,* in David Grene and Richmond Lattimore, eds., *Greek Tragedies,* vol. 1 (Chicago: University of Chicago Press, 1942), p. 166, lines 1256-58.

15. Aeschylus, *The Eumenides,* in David Grene and Richmond Lattimore, eds., *Greek Tragedies,* vol. 3 (Chicago: University of Chicago Press, 1953), p. 28.

16. Paul Isaac Hershon, *A Rabbinical Commentary on Genesis* (London: Hodder and Stoughton, 1885), p. 33.

17. de Vaux, *Ancient Israel,* p. 271.

18. Ibid., p. 460.

19. William Graham Cole, *Sex and Love in the Bible* (New York: Association Press, 1959), pp. 281-83.

20. See Fred E. D'Amour, *Basic Physiology* (Chicago: University of Chicago Press, 1961), pp. 477-78.

21. *The Babylonian Talmud,* 'Erubin, translated under the editorship of Rabbi Dr. I. Epstein (London: The Soncino Press, 1936), pp. 697-98.

22. P. Thomas, *Indian Women Through the Ages* (Bombay: Asia Publishing House, 1964), p. 163.

23. See the chapter, "The Abominations of Leviticus," in Douglas, *Purity and Danger,* pp. 54-72.

24. Maurice Lamm, *The Jewish Way in Love and Marriage* (San Francisco: Harper & Row, 1980), pp. 22-23, 191.

25. Roland B. Gittelsohn, *Love, Sex, and Marriage: A Jewish View* (New York: Union of American Hebrew Congregations, 1980), pp. 134-35.

26. Lamm, *Jewish Way in Love and Marriage,* p. 193.

27. Douglas, *Purity and Danger,* p. 179.

28. *The Babylonian Talmud,* 'Erubin, pp. 697-98.

29. *The Babylonian Talmud,* Niddah, pp. 218-19. Also see *Midrash,* "Genesis," translated under the editorship of Rabbi Dr. H. Freedman and Maurice Simon (London: Soncino Press, 1939), 1:166.

30. S. H. Kellogg, "The Book of Leviticus," in *The Expositor's Bible,* 1:316.

31. Ibid., p. 318.

32. Cole, *Sex and Love in the Bible,* p. 283.

33. Hays, *Dangerous Sex,* p. 44.

34. de Vaux, *Ancient Israel,* p. 41.

35. *The Babylonian Talmud,* Niddah, section 31a, pp. 218-19.

36. Ibid., pp. 208 ff.

37. Ibid., p. 213.

38. Panos D. Bardis, "Family Forms and Variations Historically Considered," in Harold T. Christensen, ed., *Handbook of Marriage and the Family* (Chicago: Rand McNally & Co., 1964), p. 417.

39. *Midrash,* Thazria, "Leviticus," 4:187.

40. Gittelsohn, *Love, Sex, and Marriage,* p. 184.

41. Troeltsch makes the point that Christian teachings on virginity and the institutionalization of it in the convents gave value and position to the unmarried woman, providing a sphere of great influence that had a part in raising the position of women generally. See Ernst Troeltsch, *The Social Teaching of the Christian Churches,* trans. Olive Wyon, vol. I (London: George Allen and Unwin, 1931), p. 131.

42. On this point, see Rosemary Radford Ruether, "An Unrealized Revolution: Searching Scripture for a Model of the Family," *Christianity and Crisis* 43 (October 31, 1983):399-404.

10. Reproduction and the Modern Woman

1. U.S. Bureau of the Census, Special Demographic Analyses, CDS-80-8, *American Women: Three Decades of Change* (Washington, D.C.: U.S. Government Printing Office, 1983), p. 4.

2. Letty Cottin Pogrebin, "Motherhood!", *Ms.* 1 (May 1973): 97.

3. Of course, it depends upon the society in which one lives. At this writing, China's official policy is no more than one child per family, whereas in Romania, the government has ruled that it is a woman's patriotic duty to bear four children so that the country's population and economic output will increase. See L. J. Huang, "Planned Fertility of One-Couple/One-Child Policy in the People's Republic of China," *Journal of Marriage and the Family,* 44 (August 1982):775-84; and the news item on Romanian policy in *National NOW Times* (January/February 1985), p. 5. Currently in the United States, efforts of the far right are focusing on the promotion of traditional attitudes toward motherhood as a woman's primary purpose in life (in reaction to the opening up of more options for women in recent years).

4. The possibility of voluntary childlessness as a religious calling, permitting couples to do certain work that would be impossible with children present, is discussed in John Howard Yoder, "Singleness in Ethical and Pastoral Perspective," mimeographed paper (Elkhart, Ind.: Associated Mennonite Biblical Seminaries, 1974); and William Everett and Julie Everett, "Childless Marriages: A New Vocation?" *U.S. Catholic* 40 (May 1975): 38-39.

5. David M. Kennedy, *Birth Control in America* (New Haven: Yale University Press, 1970), pp. 42, 183.

6. Until 1969, the official manual of the American College of Obstetricians and Gynecologists recommended a number of restrictions with regard to the sterilization of women for contraceptive purposes. Most hospitals followed these guidelines or even stricter regulations, although many have eased them since 1969 when the official manual removed references to such requirements for sterilization. These requirements linked permission to perform contraceptive sterilization with a woman's age and number of children. Women of 25 years of age must have five living children, women 30 years old must have four living children, and women of 35 could not be sterilized unless they had three living children. See Harriet B. Presser and Larry L. Bumpass, "The Acceptability of Contraceptive Sterilization among U. S. Couples: 1970," *Family Planning Perspectives* 4 (October 1972): 20.

7. Charles F. Westoff, "The Modernization of U. S. Contraceptive Practice," *Family Planning Perspectives* 4 (July 1972):10.

8. From summary of government report, "More Couples Choosing Sterilization," *Greensboro News and Record,* December 6, 1984, p. A-7.

9. Richard Bube, "Frozen for the Future," *Eternity* 18 (June 1967): 36.

10. See Edward Batchelor, Jr., ed., *Abortion: The Moral Issues* (New York: Pilgrim Press, 1982).

11. R. F. R. Gardner, *Abortion: The Personal Dilemma* (Grand Rapids: Wm. B. Eerdmans Publishing Co., 1972), p. 126.

12. Sarah Ragle Weddington, "The Woman's Right to Privacy," in Batchelor, *Abortion,* p. 15.

13. James E. Kraus, "Is Abortion Absolutely Prohibited?" in Batchelor, *Abortion,* p. 106.

14. J. Robert Nelson, "What Does Theology Say About Abortion?", in Batchelor, *Abortion,* p. 60.

15. See the special issue of *The Other Side* devoted to "The Agony of Abortion," June 1980.

16. Roger L. Shinn, "Personal Decisions and Social Policies in a Pluralist Society," in Batchelor, *Abortion,* p. 174.

17. "Amniocentesis is a valuable tool," letters section, *Greensboro News and Record,* February 22, 1985.

18. Beverly Wildung Harrison, *Our Right to Choose: Toward a New Ethic of Abortion* (Boston: Beacon Press, 1983), p. 252.

19. Kraus, "Is Abortion Absolutely Prohibited?", p. 109. See also the moving account of journalist Tom Braden, "A Father's Story," in Hamilton Gregory, ed., *The Religious Case FOR Abortion: Protestant, Catholic, and Jewish Perspectives* (Asheville, N.C.: Madison & Polk, Publisher, 1983), pp. 79-81. Braden's daughter was kidnapped by five strangers who brutally beat and repeatedly gang raped her. She became pregnant as a result of the horrible ordeal. Braden asks those in the right-to-life movement, who would like to see legislation passed that would forbid abortion even in cases of rape,

what they would do if *they* had been the parents of the girl. How would they view abortion then?

20. Kristin Luker, *Abortion: The Politics of Motherhood* (Berkeley: University of California Press, 1984), p. 194. A similar point is presented in Rosemary Radford Ruether's essay on the Roman Catholic Church's demand that the nuns who signed a statement saying there was a diversity of opinion on abortion either recant or face expulsion from their orders. See "Why the nuns, on abortion, at this time?" *National Catholic Reporter,* January 11, 1985, p. 12.

21. See, for example, the special issue on "What Does It Mean to be Pro-Life?" *Sojourners,* November 1980. For another view of the approach taken by the *Sojourners* writers, see Harrison's critical commentary in *Our Right to Choose,* pp. 79-83.

22. The advertisement appeared in *The Moral Majority Report,* April 1985, p. 8.

23. Shinn, "Personal Decisions," p. 168.

24. One scientist, pointing out that fertility depends on the proportion of women to men, suggests that the quickest way to curb population growth would be to cut down on the number of women in the world! Thus, he has proposed a "boy birth pill" which would bring about selective fertilization, assuring that 90 percent of babies born would be male. Associated Press report on British scientist John Postgate of Sussex University, "Scientist Proposes 'Boy' Pill," Bloomington (Ind.) *Herald-Telephone,* July 12, 1973.

11. The Single Woman

1. Augustine, *Holy Virginity* 27.

2. Athanasius, *Letters* 48.

3. Gregory of Nyssa, *On Virginity* 4.

4. Herbert J. Miles, *Sexual Understanding Before Marriage* (Grand Rapids: Zondervan, 1971), p. 177.

5. Augustine, *The Good of Marriage* 6.6.

6. Rosemary Radford Ruether, ed., *Religion and Sexism* (New York; Simon and Schuster, 1974), pp. 176-78. See also William E. Phipps, *Was Jesus Married?* (New York: Harper & Row, 1970).

7. Cyprian, *De habitu virginum* 3.

8. Justin Martyr, *Apology* 15.

9. Samuel Laeuchli, *Power and Sexuality: The Emergence of Canon Law at the Synod of Elvira* (Philadelphia: Temple University Press, 1972).

10. U. S. Bureau of the Census, Current Population Reports, Series P–20, No. 389, *Marital Status and Living Arrangements: March 1983* (Washington, D.C.: U.S. Government Printing Office, 1984), Table 1. Marital Status of Persons 15 Years Old and Over, . . . March 1983. Table A, Median Age at First Marriage, and Table C, Divorced Persons per 1,000 Married Persons.

11. See A. Lewis and B. Berns, *Three Out of Four Wives: Widowhood in America* (New York: Macmillan, 1975).

12. Jessie Bernard, *The Future of Marriage* (New York: World Publishing Company, 1972), pp. 29-30, 34, 296-97. Hugh Carter and Paul C. Glick, *Marriage and Divorce: A Social and Economic Study* (Cambridge, Mass.: Harvard University Press, 1970), p. 347.

13. Scanzoni and Scanzoni, *Men, Women, and Change,* 2d. ed., p. 488.

14. Bernard, *Future of Marriage,* pp. 32-36.

15. Germaine Greer, *The Female Eunuch* (New York: McGraw-Hill, 1970), p. 316.

16. Scanzoni and Mollenkott, *Is the Homosexual My Neighbor?*, p. 77.

17. Other resources on the issue of homosexuality and Christianity include John Boswell, *Christianity, Social Tolerance, and Homosexuality* (Chicago: University of Chicago Press, 1980); John J. McNeill, *The Church and the Homosexual* (Kansas City: Sheed Andrews and McMeel, Inc., 1976); James B. Nelson, *Embodiment* (Minneapolis: Augsburg, 1978); *The Other Side*, "Christians and Homosexuality" (1984); The United Church of Christ, *Human Sexuality: A Preliminary Study* (New York: United Church Press, 1977); Robin Scroggs, *The New Testament and Homosexuality* (Philadelphia: Fortress Press, 1983).

18. William W. Orr, *How to Get a Husband for Christian Girls* (Wheaton, Ill.: Van Kampen Press, Inc., n.d. [ca. 1956]), p. 32.

19. Dorothy Payne, *Women Without Men* (Philadelphia: Pilgrim Press, 1969), p. 72.

20. A very helpful book on intimacy is Janet Geringer Woititz's *Struggle for Intimacy* (Pompano Beach, Fla.: Health Communications, Inc., 1985). Although Woititz writes for adult children of alcoholics, the dynamics of many fundamentalist families are remarkably similar and thus the issues many of us have with intimacy are the same.

21. Most helpful in this regard are James Nelson, *Embodiment,* and Dody H. Donnelly, *Radical Love: An Approach to Sexual Spirituality* (Minneapolis: Winston Press, 1984). See also Letha Dawson Scanzoni, *Sexuality* (Philadelphia: Westminster Press, 1984), one of the "Choices: Guides for Today's Woman" series.

22. Laura Hutton, *The Single Woman* (London: Barrie & Rockliff, 1960), pp. 46-51.

23. John Dart, "Churchgoer Study Finds Many Singles Defy Sex Taboos," *Atlanta Journal,* November 18, 1983, p. 3B, reports on a study done by psychologist Bernard Spilka and clinical social worker Jean Wulf of the University of Denver. The group was split about fifty-fifty on approval of masturbation.

24. See our chapter 8, note 5. Studies have shown that masturbation is not harmful to women and may even be beneficial. See Hutton, *Single Woman,* p. 58. Paul Gebhard, et al., *The Sexuality of Women* (London: Andre Deutsch, 1970), p. 18. Sex Information and Education Council in the U.S., *Sexuality and Man* (New York: Charles Scribner's Sons, 1970), p. 67.

25. Phil Landrum, "But What About Right Now," an interview on masturbation with Letha Scanzoni, Charlie Shedd, Jim Hefley, M. O. Vincent, Herbert J. Miles, *Campus Life,* March 1972, pp. 38-42. See also Letha Dawson Scanzoni, *Sex Is a Parent Affair,* 2nd edn., rev., pp. 155-66.

26. Charlie Shedd, *The Stork Is Dead* (Waco, Tex.: Word Books, 1968), p. 73. Miles in *Sexual Understanding,* chaps. 9-10, takes this view for men but denies masturbation as a proper outlet for women.

27. Melvin Zelnik and John F. Kantner, "Sexual Activity, Contraceptive Use and Pregnancy Among Metropolitan-Area Teenagers: 1971-1979," *Family Planning Perspectives* 12 (Sept./Oct., 1980): 230-37; Koray Tanfer and Marjorie C. Horn, "Contraceptive Use, Pregnancy and Fertility Patterns Among Single American Women in Their 20s," *Family Planning Perspectives* 17 (Jan./Feb., 198):10-19.

28. Cf. James R. Edwards, "The Strange Embraces of Jesus," *Christianity Today*, March 16, 1984, pp. 26-27.

29. Marc H. Hollender, "The Need or Wish to Be Held," *Archives of General Psychiatry* 22 (May 1970): 447-48.

30. "Finding Trouble in Paradise," *Time*, January 28, 1985, p. 76.

31. Karen Lindsey, *Friends as Family* (Boston: Beacon Press, 1982).

32. Erich Fromm, *The Art of Loving* (New York: Harper & Row, Colophon Books, 1956), p. 46.

33. Mary Bosanquet, *The Life and Death of Dietrich Bonhoeffer* (New York: Harper & Row, 1968), p. 64.

34. O. Hobart Mowrer, *The New Group Therapy* (New York: Van Nostrand Reinhold Company, Insight Book, 1964), p. 31.

12. Wasting the Church's Gifts

1. "Point of View," afternoon call-in program on WBRI, Indianapolis, March 21, 1967.

2. In the United States, the Congregational Church and Disciples of Christ have the most consistent record for ordaining women. The United Methodist Church granted local preachers' licenses to women in 1919, ordained them in 1924, and finally granted them equality with men as members of annual conferences in 1956. Women have more recently become district superintendents and bishops. The United Church of Canada (Methodist, Presbyterian, and Congregational) ordained its first woman in 1936. In 1956 the United Presbyterian Church U.S.A. began ordaining women and in 1964 the Southern Presbyterian Church (U.S.) followed suit. In 1970 both the Lutheran Church in America and the American Lutheran Church ordained women.

The Baptist Church of Great Britain and the American Baptist Convention ordain women. According to *Christianity Today*, November 10, 1972, p. 62, the Southern Baptist Convention acquired a black woman pastor previously ordained by another Baptist association. Subsequently a number of local Baptist churches have ordained women, but in 1984 the Southern Baptist Convention approved a resolution opposing the practice. Interestingly, Dr. Charles F. Stanley, Atlanta pastor and president of the Convention, in an article in the *Atlanta Journal and Constitution* (July 8, 1984, 1C, 8C) admitted that he was saved under the ministry of a woman preacher but opposed the practice on the basis of tradition, ignoring such traditional Baptist criteria for ministry as testimony to a call and evidence of effective ministry.

The Episcopal Church at the 1970 Houston Convention recognized women as deacons on a par with men, but in 1973 they refused to take the next step and admit women to full orders of priest and bishop. They finally voted to admit women in 1976 after eleven women were irregularly ordained on July 29, 1974. As of late 1984 the Episcopal Church had 474 ordained women priests. Anglican women have also been ordained in Canada, New Zealand, Hong Kong, Uganda, and Kenya. The Church of England is moving with glacial speed toward ordaining women, perhaps by 1990, according to a plan adopted in November 1984.

Conservative groups which ordain women include the Assemblies of God, Church of God, Church of the Nazarene, Churches of Christ in Christian Union, International Church of the Foursquare Gospel, United Missionary Church, and the Salvation Army. *Christianity Today*, 21 February 1973, p. 43, reported that a woman has also been licensed by the North American Mennonites. Some groups like the Christian and Missionary Alliance have a long history of ordaining women but have more recently banned the practice, as they become more deeply infected with fundamentalism and upward mobility, and abandon their Holiness roots.

Within the Roman Catholic church a very active and persistent group of women and men (many of them religious) have been pushing for the ordination of women, although Polish Pope John Paul II is staunchly opposed. Girls and women have been allowed more liberties in acting as acolytes, lectors, and ministers of communion.

Within the Jewish tradition, the Reform wing began accepting women as rabbis in 1972, followed by the small, liberal Reconstructionist movement in 1974. In 1983 women were admitted to the Conservative Jewish Theological Seminary of America, making them eligible upon graduation for membership in the Rabbinical Assembly.

3. Basic sources on the question of the ordination of women are: Peter Brunner, *The Ministry and the Ministry of Women* (St. Louis: Concordia Publishing House, 1971), Lutheran, negative. *Concerning the Ordination of Women* (Geneva: World Council of Churches, Department of Faith and Order, 1964), ecumenical. Margaret Sittler Ermarth, *Adam's Fractured Rib* (Philadelphia: Fortress Press, 1970), Lutheran Church in America, positive. Emily C. Hewitt and Suzanne R. Hiatt, *Women Priests: Yes or No?* (New York: Seabury Press, 1973), Episcopal, positive. John Reumann, "What in Scripture Speaks to the Ordination of Women?" *Concordia Theological Monthly* 44 (January 1973): 1-30, Lutheran, scholarly, positive. Stendahl, *The Bible and the Role of Women,* Swedish, hermeneutical, positive. Few of the arguments in these books are really new. Many of them were outlined in the last century in such books as Phoebe Palmer's *Promise of the Father* (1859), Catherine Booth's *Female Ministry* (1859), B. T. Roberts' *Ordaining Women* (1891) and Frances Willard's *Woman in the Pulpit* (1888). They founded, respectively, the "Holiness Movement," the Salvation Army, the Free Methodist Church and the Women's Christian Temperance Union. See Nancy A. Hardesty, *Women Called to Witness* (Nashville: Abingdon Press, 1984), chapter 7, appendix. See also Letha Dawson Scanzoni and Susan Setta, "Women in Evangelical, Holiness and Pentecostal Traditions," in Rosemary Radford Ruether and Rosemary Skinner Keller, eds., *Woman and Religion in America: Volume III, 1900-1968: A Documentary History* (San Francisco: Harper & Row, in press).

4. "The practice of excluding women from ecclesiastical office cannot conclusively be defended on biblical grounds"—Christian Reformed Church, *Study Committee Reports,* "Report 39: Women in Ecclesiastical Office," 1973, p. 453. "Although the ordination of women raises new and difficult questions, there is no decisive theological argument against the ordination of women"—American Lutheran Church seminary position paper, in Ermarth, *Adam's Fractured Rib,* p. 113. "The objections rest on a rather literal approach to the Bible and fail to take into account the degree to which the Bible is conditioned by the circumstances of its time"—The Episcopal Church, progress report to the House of Bishops, October 1966, in Hewitt and Hiatt, *Women Priests?* p. 114. See also N. J. Hommes, "Let Women Be Silent in Church," *Calvin Theological Journal* 4 (April 1969): 6.

5. Catherine Beaton, "Does the Church Discriminate Against Women on the Basis of Their Sex?" *Critic* 24 (June-July 1966): 22.

6. Mary Daly, *The Church and the Second Sex* (New York: Harper & Row, 1968), p. 121. Mossie Allman Wyker, *Church Women in the Scheme of Things* (St. Louis: Bethany Press, 1953), pp. 50-52.

7. Leonard Hodgson, "Theological Objections to the Ordination of Women," *The Expository Times* 77 (April 1966): 212-13. Hewitt and Hiatt, *Women Priests?* pp. 75-76. Gertrud Heinzelmann, "The Priesthood and Women," *Commonweal*, 15 January 1965, p. 507.

8. From a statement to the press dated 25-8 April 1967 by the Orthodox Presbyterian Church. H. Goedhard, "Women in the Pulpit?" *Journal of Ecumenical Studies* (Fall 1968): 826. From a report concerning the Lutheran Church—Missouri Synod, *Chicago Daily News*, 25 November 1970, p. 12.

9. Nicolae Chitescu, "The Ordination of Women," in *Concerning the Ordination of Women*, p. 58. He cites the second canon of Denis of Alexandria (Synt. At., 4:7) and the sixth and seventh canons of Timothy of Alexandria (Synt. At., 4:333-36).

10. See chap. 1. This position is argued by C. S. Lewis, "Priestesses in the Church?" pp. 234-39. And by C. Kilmer Myers, Episcopal Bishop of California, "Should Women Be Ordained? No," *The Episcopalian*, February 1972, pp. 8-9. See also James L. Steele, "Caligula's Horse," *Advance*, January 1973, pp. 6-7.

11. Andre Dumas, "Biblical Anthropology and the Participation of Women in the Ministry of the Church," in *Concerning the Ordination of Women*, pp. 14-15.

12. Dated 15 October 1976 and made public 27 January 1977, the declaration was approved by Paul VI and signed by Cardinal Franjo Seper, prefect of the Vatican Doctrinal Congregation, and its secretary Archbishop Jerome Hamer. Cf. "Pope Paul to Women: Keep Out," *Time*, 7 February 1977, p. 65.

13. Hodgson, "Theological Objections," p. 211.

14. Hewitt and Hiatt, *Women Priests?*, p. 121, footnote 9. Doely, ed., *Women's Liberation and the Church*, p. 41.

15. Stendahl, *Bible and the Role of Women*, pp. 19-20.

16. Heinzelmann, "The Priesthood and Women," p. 507. Eugenia Leonard, "St. Paul on the Status of Women," *The Catholic Biblical Quarterly* 12 (July 1950): 313-14.

17. Culver, *Women in the World of Religion*, p. 71. See also Morris, *The Bishop Was a Lady*. Roger Gryson, *The Ministry of Women in the Early Church* (Collegeville, Minn.: The Liturgical Press, 1976); George H. Tavard, *Woman in Christian Tradition* (Notre Dame: University of Notre Dame Press, 1973).

18. See Culver, *Women in the World of Religion;* Edith Deen, *Great Women of the Christian Faith* (New York: Harper and Bros., 1959); Roland Bainton, *Women of the Reformation in Germany and Italy* (Minneapolis: Augsburg, 1971); Roland Bainton, *Women of the Reformation in France and England* (Augsburg, 1973).

19. Gibson, *When the Minister Is a Woman*, cites many examples, as does Hewitt and Hiatt, *Women Priests?* Many women ministers are members of The International Association of Women Ministers, which publishes *The Woman's Pulpit*.

20. Prohl, *Women in the Church*, p. 77.

21. Elizabeth O'Connor, *Eighth Day of Creation: Gifts and Creativity* (Waco, Tex.: Word Books, 1971), p. 57, quoting Frances G. Wickes, *The Inner World of Choice* (New York: Harper & Row, 1963), p. 53.

22. Christensen, "What Is a Woman's Role?" p. 82.

23. Dietrich Bonhoeffer, *Life Together* (New York: Harper & Row, 1954), p. 94.

13. Working Women: At Home and Beyond

1. L. Frank Baum, *The Marvelous Land of Oz* (New York: Dover Publications, Inc., 1969 edition), pp. 170-71.

2. Matina Horner, "Fail: Bright Women," *Psychology Today,* reprint series No. P-42 (from the November 1969 issue), as told in the author's biographical information.

3. Larry Christenson, for example, claims that a woman is not equipped by nature to sustain the psychological and emotional pressure of career commitment and leadership in the world "and still fulfill her God-appointed role as wife and mother." See Christenson, *The Christian Family*, p. 45. See also Clark, *Man and Woman in Christ.* Clark believes role differences were "created into" the human race and that "these differences correlate with a governor-protector-provider role for the man and a care-service role for the woman" (pp. 440-41).

4. *National NOW Times* 18 (January-February, 1985), special section on pay equity, pp. 6-7.

5. As quoted in Mary Hartman and Lois Banner, eds., *Clio's Consciousness Raised* (New York: Harper Colophon Books, 1974), p. 167.

6. Dr. Henry Morgan, manager of the human relations division of the Polaroid Corporation, as quoted in the *Chicago Tribune,* June 28, 1971.

7. Ann Oakley, *Woman's Work: The Housewife, Past and Present* (New York: Random House, 1974), p. 1 in Vintage paperback edition. See also Oakley's *The Sociology of Housework* (New York: Random House Pantheon Books, 1974).

8. Dee Dee Ahern with Betsy Bliss, *The Economics of Being a Woman* (New York: Macmillan, 1976), p. 3.

9. For actual case studies, see Lenore J. Weitzman, "Legal Regulation of Marriage: Tradition and Change," *California Law Review* 62 (July-September, 1974): 1189. See also her book, *The Marriage Contract* (New York: The Free Press, 1981).

10. Bardwick, *Psychology of Women,* p. 166.

11. Gerald Kennedy, "John Wesley's Life and Times," introduction to *The Journal of John Wesley,* as abridged by Nehemiah Curnock (New York: Capricorn Books edition, 1963), p. viii.

12. *Journal of John Wesley,* p. 132.

13. Ibid., p. 133.

14. Betty Friedan, *The Feminine Mystique* (New York: Dell Books, 1964), chap. 1.

15. Bardwick, *Psychology of Women,* p. 171.

16. Callahan, *The Illusion of Eve,* p. 91.

17. Sidney Cornelia Callahan, "A Christian Perspective on Feminism," in Doely, *Women's Liberation,* p. 40.

18. Quoted in Lynn Jessup, "Courage the most important virtue, Angelou tells students," *Greensboro News and Record,* March 27, 1985, p. A-13.

19. Dean Eunice Roberts, Indiana University, quoted in the Bloomington (Ind.) *Herald-Telephone,* November 9, 1969.

20. Joan Scobey and Lee Parr McGrath, "The Tandem Job," *Family Circle* (October, 1969), pp. 8ff.

21. Jessie Bernard, *Academic Women* (University Park: Pennsylvania State University Press, 1964), p. 237.

22. Eli Ginzberg and Alice M. Yohalem, *Educated American Women:*

Self-Portraits (New York: Columbia University Press, 1966), p. 135.

23. Alice S. Rossi, "Deviance and Conformity in the Life Goals of Women," lecture delivered at Wellesley College, March 12, 1970.

24. Eli Ginzberg et al., *Life Styles of Educated Women* (New York: Columbia University Press, 1966), p. 13.

25. Ginzberg and Yohalem, *Self-Portraits*. The entire book is planned around these four categories. Other insightful books on combining careers and family life are Lynda Lyttle Holmstrom, *The Two-Career Family* (Cambridge, Mass.: Schenkman Publishing Co., 1972), Michael P. Fogarty, Rhona Rapoport, and Robert N. Rapoport, *Sex, Careers and Family* (London: George Allen and Unwin, 1971); and Francine S. Hall and Douglas T. Hall, *The Two-Career Couple* (Reading, Mass.: Addison-Wesley Publishing Co., 1979).

26. Bardwick, *Psychology of Women*, p. 213.

14. Where Do We Go From Here?

1. From "The Times that Try Men's Souls," a tongue-in-cheek poem written by Maria Weston Chapman in answer to the pastoral letter directed against the Grimke sisters, as quoted in Alice Felt Tyler, *Freedom's Ferment* (New York: Harper & Row Torchbook, 1962), p. 445. The poem is quoted in full in E. C. Stanton, S. B. Anthony, and M. J. Gage, *The History of Woman Suffrage*, 6 vols. (n. p., 1881–1922), 1:82-86.

2. *The New York Times*, May 17, 1970.

3. Thornwell, "The Rights and Duties of Masters," p. 197. An interesting parallel is to be found in Luther's response to the German peasants who thought that the priesthood of all believers made them equal to their landlords. In a savage tract *Against the Thievish and Murderous Hordes of Peasants*, Luther encouraged the princes to use brutal force to put down the peasant rebellion, citing New Testament passages on spiritual warfare and texts from Rom. 13 on civil order and police power. But to the peasants his appeal was to the Sermon on the Mount. They were to turn the other cheek, not resist evil, endure hardship without complaint. He even went so far as to say that the peasants' claim that Genesis 1 and 2 taught that God created the world equally for all were not texts to be taken seriously in the New Testament age when "Moses counts for nothing." See H. Richard Niebuhr, *The Social Sources of Denominationalism* (Cleveland: The World Publishing Co., Meridian Books, 1957), pp. 34-37. See also V. H. H. Green, *Luther and the Reformation* (New York: Capricorn Books, 1964), pp. 137-39.

4. Stanton et al., *History of Woman Suffrage*, 1:81, as quoted in Tyler, *Freedom's Ferment*, pp. 444-45.

5. Letha Scanzoni, "The Feminists and the Bible," *Christianity Today* February 2, 1973, pp. 10-15.

6. See A. D. White, *The History of the Warfare of Science with Theology in Christendom* (New York: Appleton-Century-Crofts, 1955), 2:63.

7. See Hardesty, *Women Called to Witness;* Dayton, *Discovering an Evangelical Heritage;* Timothy L. Smith, *Revivalism and Social Reform* (Nashville: Abingdon Press, 1957).

8. Stendahl, *Bible and the Role of Women*, p. 33.

9. Ibid., p. 39.

10. Lois Gunden Clemens, *Woman Liberated* (Scottdale, Pa.: Herald Press, 1971), p. 141.

FURTHER RESOURCES

In this revision, we were unable to include in footnotes all of the good material published or brought to our attention since our book's original edition. The following additional resources are therefore suggested for readers interested in pursuing various topics further. Some of these resource materials take a distinctly Christian approach; others take more general approaches. Some within the Christian tradition reflect an evangelical perspective, while other books and articles reflect other perspectives. And while we don't necessarily agree totally with every item listed, we feel that it is important for biblical feminists to have some acquaintance with materials from across the wide spectrum of feminist thought and to be informed from a variety of viewpoints on subjects touching the lives of women today.

Bible

"The Bible and Feminist Hermeneutics." *Semeia* 18 (1983).

Bilezikian, Gilbert. *Beyond Sex Roles*. Grand Rapids, Mich.: Baker Book House, 1985.

Bushnell, Katharine C. *God's Word to Women*. Privately published, 1912, 1923. Reprint edition available from God's Word to Women Publishers, Box 315, Mossville, Ill. 61552.

Bynum, Carolyn Walker. *Jesus as Mother*. Berkeley and Los Angeles: University of California Press, 1982.

Fiorenza, Elisabeth Schussler. *Bread Not Stone: The Challenge of Feminist Biblical Interpretation*. Boston: Beacon Press, 1984.

———. *In Memory of Her: A Feminist Theological Reconstruction of Christian Origins*. New York: Crossroad, 1983.

Mercadante, Linda. *From Hierarchy to Equality: A Comparison of Past and Present Interpretations of 1 Corinthians 11:2-16 in relation to the Changing Status of Women in Society*. Vancouver, B.C.: G-M-H Books, Regent College, 1978.

Mollenkott, Virginia Ramey, *The Divine Feminine: The Biblical Imagery of God as Female*. New York: Crossroad, 1983.

———. *Women, Men and the Bible*. Nashville: Abingdon, 1977.

Moltmann-Wendel, Elisabeth. *The Women Around Jesus*. New York: Crossroad, 1982.

Otwell, John H. *And Sarah Laughed*. Philadelphia: The Westminster Press, 1977.

Penn-Lewis, Jessie. *The Magna Charta of Women*. Bournemouth, England: The Overcomer Book Room, 1919. Reprint edition, Minneapolis: Bethany Fellowship, 1975.

Russell, Letty M. *Feminist Interpretation of the Bible*. Philadelphia: The Westminster Press, 1985.

———, ed. *The Liberating Word*. Philadelphia: The Westminster Press, 1976.

263

Bibliography

Swartley, Willard M. *Slavery, Sabbath, War, and Women.* Scottdale, Pa.: Herald Press, 1983.

Trible, Phyllis. *God and the Rhetoric of Sexuality.* Philadelphia: Fortress Press, 1978.

———. *Texts of Terror: Literary-Feminist Readings of Biblical Narratives.* Philadelphia: Fortress Press, 1984.

Wahlberg, Rachel Conrad. *Jesus According to a Woman.* New York: Paulist Press, 1975.

Church

Carroll, Jackson W., Barbara Hargrove, and Adair T. Lummis. *Women of the Cloth.* San Francisco: Harper & Row, Publishers, 1983.

Gundry, Patricia. *Woman Be Free!* Grand Rapids, Mich.: Zondervan Publishing House, 1977.

Hearn, Virginia, ed. *Our Struggle to Serve: The Stories of 15 Evangelical Women.* Waco, Texas: Word Books, 1979.

Jewett, Paul K. *The Ordination of Women.* Grand Rapids, Mich.: Wm. B. Eerdmans Publishing Company, 1980.

Weidman, Judith, ed. *Women Ministers.* San Francisco: Harper & Row, Publishers, 1981, 1985.

Feminist Movement: Past and Present

Flexner, Eleanor. *Century of Struggle: The Woman's Rights Movement in the United States.* Cambridge, Mass.: Harvard University Press, 1959.

Lerner, Gerda, ed. *Black Women in White America: A Documentary History.* New York: Random House Pantheon Books, 1972.

———. *The Grimké Sisters from South Carolina: Pioneers for Woman's Rights and Abolition.* New York: Houghton Mifflin, 1967. Schocken Books edition, 1971.

Morgan, Robin, ed. *Sisterhood Is Global: The International Women's Movement Anthology.* Garden City, NY: Doubleday Anchor Books, 1984.

Rossi, Alice S., ed. *The Feminist Papers.* New York: Columbia University Press, 1973.

Feminist Theology

Christ, Carol P. *Diving Deep and Surfacing: Women Writers on Spiritual Quest.* Boston: Beacon Press, 1980.

——— and Judith Plaskow, eds. *Womanspirit Rising: A Feminist Reader in Religion.* San Francisco: Harper and Row, 1979.

Daly, Mary. *Beyond God the Father.* Boston: Beacon Press, 1973.

Hearn, Virginia. "A Liberating Word: Feminist Theology as a Theology of Liberation." In Deane William Ferm, *Liberation Theology: North American Style.* New York: Paragon House, in press.

Heyward, Carter: *Our Passion for Justice.* New York: Pilgrim Press, 1984.

Jewett, Paul K. *MAN as Male and Female.* Grand Rapids, Mich.: Wm. B. Eerdmans Publishing Company, 1975.

Kalven, Janet, and Mary I. Buckley, eds. *Women's Spirit Bonding.* New York: Pilgrim Press, 1984.

Mollenkott, Virginia Ramey. *Speech, Silence, Action!* Nashville: Abingdon, 1980.

Moltmann, Elisabeth Wendel, and Jurgen Moltmann. *Humanity in God.* New York: Pilgrim Press, 1983.

Bibliography

Ruether, Rosemary Radford. *Disputed Questions: On Being a Christian.* Nashville: Abingdon, 1982.
———. *New Woman, New Earth: Sexist Ideologies and Human Liberation.* New York: The Seabury Press, 1975.
———. *Sexism and God-Talk: Toward a Feminist Theology.* Boston: Beacon Press, 1983.
———. *Womanguides: Readings Toward a Feminist Theology.* Boston: Beacon Press, 1985.
Russell, Letty. *The Future of Partnership.* Philadelphia: The Westminster Press, 1979.
———. *Human Liberation in a Feminist Perspetive—A Theology.* Philadelphia: The Westminster Press, 1974.
Schaef, Anne Wilson. *The Addictive System.* Minneapolis: Winston Press, 1985.
———. *Women's Reality: An Emerging Female System in a White Male Society.* Minneapolis: Winston Press, 1981, 1985.
Soelle, Dorothee. *The Strength of the Weak: Toward a Christian Feminist Identity.* Philadelphia: The Westminster Press, 1984.
Tennis, Diane. *Is God the Only Reliable Father?* Philadelphia: The Westminster Press, 1985.
Weidman, Judith L., ed. *Christian Feminism: Visions of a New Humanity.* San Francisco: Harper & Row, Publishers, 1984.
Wilson-Kastner, Patricia. *Faith, Feminism, and the Christ.* Philadelphia: Fortress Press, 1983.

Friendship

Bell, Robert R. *Worlds of Friendship.* Beverly Hills, Calif.: Sage Publications, 1981.
Brenton, Myron. *Friendship.* New York: Stein and Day, 1974.
Hinnebusch, Paul. *Friendship in the Lord.* Notre Dame, Inc.: Ave Maria Press, 1974.
Lindsey, Karen. *Friends as Family.* Boston: Beacon Press, 1981.
Marty, Martin. *Friendship.* Allen, Texas: Argus Communications, 1980.
Stringfellow, William. *A Simplicity of Faith: My Experience in Mourning.* Nashville: Abingdon, 1982.

Gender Role Issues

Follis, Anne Bowen. *"I'm Not a Woman's Libber, But . . . ": And Other Confessions of a Christian Feminist.* Nashville: Abingdon, 1981.
Gilligan, Carol. *In a Different Voice: Psychological Theory and Women's Development.* Cambridge: Harvard University Press, 1982.
Gundry, Patricia. *The Complete Woman.* Garden City, NY: Doubleday & Company, Inc., 1981.
Heilbrun, Carolyn G. *Reinventing Womanhood.* New York: Norton, 1979.
Kolbenschlag, Madonna. *Kiss Sleeping Beauty Good-Bye.* Garden City, N.Y.: Doubleday, 1979.
Maccoby, Eleanor Emmons and Carol Nagy Jacklin. *The Psychology of Sex Differences.* Stanford, Calif.: Stanford University Press, 1974.
Miller, Jean Baker. *Toward a New Psychology of Women.* Boston: Beacon Press, 1976.
Scanzoni, Letha Dawson, and John Scanzoni. *Men, Women, and Change.* New York: McGraw-Hill Book Co., 1976, 1981, 3rd. ed. in press.

265

Bibliography

Yoder, Perry, and Elizabeth Yoder. *New Men, New Roles*. Newton, Kansas: Faith and Life Press, 1977.

Inclusive Language

Crawford, Janet, and Michale Kinnamon, eds. *In God's Image: Reflections on Identity, Human Wholeness, and the Authority of Scripture*. New York: Friendship Press, 1983.

Daughters of Sarah, January/February 1985; March/April 1985.

Guidelines for Eliminating Racism, Ageism, Handicappism and Sexism from United Methodist Resource Materials. Dayton, Ohio: United Methodist Church General Council on Ministries, 1983.

Hardesty, Nancy A. Title forthcoming. Atlanta: John Knox, 1986.

Mickelson, Berkeley, and Alvera Mickelson. "Does Male Dominance Tarnish Our Translations?" *Christianity Today*, 5 October 1979, pp. 23-27.

Neufer Emswiler, Sharon, and Thomas Neufer Emswiler, *Women and Worship*. San Francisco: Harper & Row Publishers, 1974, rev. ed., 1984.

Neufer Emswiler, Thomas, and Sharon Neufer Emswiler. *Wholeness in Worship*. San Francisco: Harper & Row, Publishers, 1980.

Miller, Casey, and Kate Swift. *Words and Women*. Garden City, N.Y.: Anchor Press/Doubleday, 1977.

Presbyterian Church in the U.S. "Language about God." Atlanta: Office of the Stated Clerk of the General Assembly, 1980.

Presbyterian Church U.S.A. Task Force on Language about God. "Language about God—Opening the Door" and "The Power of Language Among the People of God." New York: Advisory Council on Discipleship and Worship, 1975, 1979.

Watkins, Keith. *Faithful and Fair*. Nashville: Abingdon, 1981.

Watley, William D. *The Word and Words: Beyond Gender in Theological and Liturgical Language*. Princeton, N.J.: Women's Task Force and Worship Commission of the Consultation on Church Union, 1983.

Withers, Barbara A., ed. *Language and the Church*. New York: Division of Education and Ministry, National Council of the Churches of Christ in the U.S.A., 1984.

Marriage (Additional books are listed under Women and Economic Issues)

Bender, Ross T. *Christians in Families*. Scottdale, Pa: Herald Press, 1982.

DeJong, Peter, and Donald R. Wilson. *Husband and Wife: The Sexes in Scripture and Society*. Grand Rapids, Mich.: Zondervan Publishing House, 1979.

Gundry, Patricia. *Heirs Together: Mutual Submission in Marriage*. Grand Rapids, Mich.: Zondervan Publishing House, 1980.

Rose, Phyllis. *Parallel Lives: Five Victorian Marriages*. New York: Random House Vintage Books, 1983.

Rubin, Lillian B. *Intimate Strangers: Men and Women Together*. New York: Harper & Row, Publishers, 1983.

Stapleton, Jean, and Richard Bright. *Equal Marriage*. Nashville: Abingdon, 1976.

Reproduction and Parenting Issues (See also single parenting books under *Singleness*)

Batchelor, Edward, Jr., ed. *Abortion: The Moral Issues*. New York: The Pilgrim Press, 1982.

Bibliography

Bengtson, Vern L. and Joan R. Robertson. *Grandparenthood: Emergent Perspectives on Traditional Roles.* Beverly Hills, California: Sage Publications, Inc., 1985.

Bloomfield, Harold H. *Making Peace with Your Parents.* New York: Ballantine Books, 1983.

Borhek, Mary V. *Coming Out to Parents: A Two-Way Survival Guide for Lesbians and Gay Men and Their Parents.* New York: Pilgrim Press, 1983.

Boston Women's Health Book Collective. *Ourselves and Our Children.* New York: Random House, 1978.

Calderone, Mary, and James Ramey. *Talking with Your Child about Sex.* New York: Random House, 1982.

Gordon, Sol,and Judith Gordon. *Raising a Child Conservatively in a Sexually Permissive World.* New York: Simon and Schuster, 1983.

Halpern, Howard. *Cutting Loose: An Adult Guide to Coming to Terms with Your Parents.* New York: Simon and Schuster, 1977.

Hanson, Shirley M. H., and Frederick W. Bozett, eds. *Dimensions of Fatherhood.* Beverly Hills, Calif.: Sage Publications, Inc., 1985.

Harrison, Beverly Wildung. *Our Right to Choose.* Boston: Beacon Press, 1983.

Lenz, Elinor. *Once My Child, Now My Friend.* New York: Warner Books, 1981.

Luker, Kristin, *Abortion and the Politics of Motherhood.* Berkeley and Los Angeles: University of California Press, 1984.

Miller, Alice. *The Drama of the Gifted Child: How Narcissistic Parents Form and Deform the Emotional Lives of Their Talented Children.* Former title, *Prisoners of Childhood.* New York: Basic Books, Inc., 1981.

Pogrebin, Letty Cottin. *Family Politics: Love and Power on an Intimate Frontier.* New York: McGraw-Hill Book Company, 1983.

————. *Growing Up Free: Raising Your Child in the 80s.* New York: McGraw-Hill Book Company, 1980.

Scanzoni, Letha Dawson. *Sex Is a Parent Affair.* Glendale, Calif.: Regal Books, 1973; rev. ed. New York: Bantam Books, 1982.

Silverstone, Barbara, and Helen Kandel Hyman. *You and Your Aging Parent.* New York: Pantheon Books, 1976, 1982.

Switzer, David K., and Shirley Switzer. *Parents of the Homosexual.* Philadelphia: The Westminster Press, 1980.

Sexuality

Barbach, Lonnie. *For Each Other: Sharing Sexual Intimacy.* Garden City, N.Y.: Doubleday & Co. Anchor Books, 1982.

————. *For Yourself: The Fulfillment of Female Sexuality.* Garden City, N.Y.: Doubleday & Co., 1975.

Batchelor, Edward, Jr., ed., *Homosexuality and Ethics.* New York: Pilgrim Press, 1980.

Boston Women's Health Book Collective. *The New Our Bodies Ourselves.* 3rd ed. New York: Simon and Schuster, 1984.

Boswell, John. *Christianity, Social Tolerance, and Homosexuality.* Chicago: University of Chicago Press, 1980.

Calderone, Mary, and Eric Johnson. *The Family Book about Sexuality.* New York: Harper & Row, Publishers, 1981.

Bibliography

Donnelly, Dody H. *Radical Love: An Approach to Sexual Spirituality.* Minneapolis: Winston Press, 1984.

Fortunato, John E. *Embracing the Exile: Healing Journeys of Gay Christians.* New York: The Seabury Press, 1983.

Goergen, Donald. *The Sexual Celibate.* New York: The Seabury Press, 1974.

Hardesty, Nancy A. "God Has No Sexual Preference." Pamphlet available from Evangelicals Concerned, Room 1403, 30 East 60th Street, New York, New York 10022.

McNeill, John J. *The Church and the Homosexual.* Kansas City: Sheed Andrews and McNeel, Inc., 1976.

Nelson, James B. *Embodiment.* Minneapolis: Augsburg Publishing House, 1978.

The Other Side Magazine. *Christians and Homosexuality* (a booklet bringing together reprints of articles from a special 1984 series. Available from Reprint Dept., *The Other Side,* 300 W. Apsley St., Philadelphia, Pa. 19144).

Penner, Clifford, and Joyce Penner. *The Gift of Sex: A Christian Guide to Sexual Fulfillment* (Waco, Texas: Word Books, 1981).

Scanzoni, Letha Dawson. *Sexuality.* Philadelphia: The Westminster Press, 1984.

Scanzoni, Letha, and Virginia Ramey Mollenkott. *Is the Homosexual My Neighbor?* San Francisco: Harper & Row, Publishers, 1978.

Shedd, Charlie, and Martha Shedd. *Celebration in the Bedroom: The Joy of Sex for Christians.* Waco, Texas: Word Books, 1979.

Small, Dwight Hervey. *Christian: Celebrate Your Sexuality.* Old Tappan, N.J.: Fleming H. Revell Co., 1974.

Smedes, Lewis. *Sex for Christians.* Grand Rapids, Michigan: Wm. B. Eerdmans Pub. Co., 1976.

United Church of Christ. *Human Sexuality: A Preliminary Study.* New York: United Church Press, 1977.

Singleness

Collins, Gary R. *It's O.K. to Be Single.* Waco, Texas: Word Books, 1976.

Edwards, Marie, and Eleanor Hoover. *The Challenge of Being Single.* Los Angeles: J. P. Tarcher, Inc., 1974. Signet paperback edition, 1975.

Evening, Margaret. *Who Walk Alone.* Downers Grove, Ill.: InterVarsity Press, 1975.

Marindin, Hope, ed. *The Handbook for Single Adoptive Parents.* 1985 edition. Published by the Committee for Single Adoptive Parents, P.O. Box 15084, Chevy Chase, Maryland 20815.

Murdock, Carol Vejvoda. *Single Parents Are People, Too.* New York: Butterick Publishing, 1980.

Payne, Dorothy. *Singleness.* Philadelphia: The Westminster Press, 1983.

Peterson, Nancy L. *The Ever-Single Woman.* Former title, *Our Lives for Ourselves.* New York: Quill, 1982.

Russianoff, Penelope. *Why Do I Think I Am Nothing Without a Man?* New York: Bantam Books, 1982.

Towns, Jim. *Solo Flight.* Wheaton, Ill.: Tyndale House, 1979.

Weiss, Robert S. *Going It Alone: The Family Life and Social Situation of the Single Parent.* New York: Basic Books, Inc., Publishers, 1979.

Violence Against Women and Children

Adams, Caren, and Jennifer Fay. *No More Secrets: Protecting Your Child from Sexual Assault.* San Luis Obispo, Calif.: Impact Publishers, 1981.

Bibliography

Fortune, Marie Marshall. *Sexual Violence: The Unmentionable Sin.* New York: Pilgrim Press, 1983.

Forward, Susan, and Craig Buck. *Betrayal of Innocence: Incest and Its Devastation.* Los Angeles: J. P. Tarcher, Inc., 1978. New York: Penguin Books, 1979.

Gordon, Sol, and Judith Gordon. *A Better Safe than Sorry Book: A Family Guide for Sexual Assault Prevention* (a picture book for young children). Fayetteville, N.Y.: Ed-U Press, Inc., 1984.

Herman, Judith Lewis. *Father-Daughter Incest.* Cambridge, Mass.: Harvard University Press, 1981.

Hofeller, Kathleen. *Battered Women, Shattered Lives.* Palo Alto, Calif.: R & E Research Associates, Inc., 1983.

NiCarthy, Ginny. *Getting Free: A Handbook for Women in Abusive Relationships.* Seattle: The Seal Press, 1982.

Russell, Diana E. H. *Rape in Marriage.* New York: Macmillan Publishing Co, 1982.

Shainess, Natalie. *Sweet Suffering: Woman as Victim.* Indianapolis: Bobbs-Merrill Co., 1984.

Walker, Lenore F. *The Battered Woman.* New York: Harper & Row, Publishers, 1979.

Women and Economic Issues

Ahern, Dee Dee, with Betsy Bliss. *The Economics of Being a Woman.* New York: McGraw-Hill Book Company, 1976.

Bird, Caroline. *The Two-Paycheck Marriage.* New York: Pocket Books, 1979.

Chapman, Jane Roberts and Margaret Gates. *Women into Wives: The Legal and Economic Impact of Marriage.* Beverly Hills, Calif.; Sage Publications, 1977.

Hall, Francine S., and Douglas T. Hall. *The Two-Career Couple.* Reading, Massachusetts: Addison-Wesley Publishing Co., 1979.

Oakley, Ann. *Subject: Women.* New York: Pantheon Books, 1981.

Pleck, Joseph H. *Working Wives, Working Husbands.* Beverly Hills, Calif.: Sage Publications, Inc., 1985.

Rapoport, Rhona, and Robert Rapaport. *Dual-Career Families Re-Examined.* New York: Harper & Row, Publishers, 1976.

Rosenthal, Lois. *Partnering: A Guide to Co-Owning Anything from Homes to Home Computers.* Cincinnati: Writer's Digest Books, 1983.

Scott, Hilda. *Working Your Way to the Bottom: The Feminization of Poverty.* Boston: Pandora Press/Routledge & Kegan Paul, 1984.

Ward, Patricia, and Martha Stout. *Christian Women at Work.* Grand Rapids, Mich.: Zondervan Publishing House, 1981.

Weitzman, Lenore J. *The Marriage Contract.* New York: The Free Press, 1981.

———. *The Divorce Revolution.* New York: The Free Press, 1985.

Women in Church History

Bainton, Roland H. *Women of the Reformation.* 3 vols. Minneapolis: Augsburg Publishing Company, 1971, 1973, 1977.

Dayton, Donald W. *Discovering an Evangelical Heritage.* New York: Harper & Row, Publishers, 1976.

Bibliography

Hardesty, Nancy A. *Great Women of Faith.* Grand Rapids, Mich.: Baker Book House, 1980; Nashville: Abingdon, 1982.

————. *Women Called to Witness: Evangelical Feminism in the Nineteenth Century.* Nashville: Abingdon, 1984.

Hassey, Janette. *No Time for Silence: Turn-of-the Century Evangelical Women in Public Ministry.* Grand Rapids, Mich.: Zondervan Publishing House, in press.

Ruether, Rosemary Radford, ed. *Religion and Sexism.* New York: Simon and Schuster, 1974.

————, and Rosemary Skinner Keller, gen. eds. *Women and Religion in America.* Vol. 1, *The Nineteenth Century.* San Francisco: Harper & Row, Publishers, 1981. Vol. 2, *The Colonial and Revolutionary Periods,* 1983. Vol. 3, 1900-1968, in press.

————, and Eleanor McLaughlin, eds. *Women of Spirit: Female Leadership in the Jewish and Christian Traditions.* New York: Simon and Schuster, 1979.

Women in Transition

Boyle, Sarah-Patton. *The Desert Blooms.* Nashville: Abingdon Press, 1983.

Bozarth-Campbell, Alla. *Life is Goodbye, Life is Hello: Grieving Well Through All Kinds of Loss.* Minneapolis: CompCare Publications, 1982.

Colgrove, Melba, Harold H. Bloomfield, and Peter McWilliams. *How to Survive the Loss of a Love.* Allen Park, Mich.: Leo Press, Inc., 1976. New York: Bantam paperback edition, 1977.

Correu, Larry M. *Beyond the Broken Marriage.* Philadelphia: The Westminster Press, 1982.

Cutler, Winifred Berg, Celso-Ramon Garcia, and David A. Edwards. *Menopause: A Guide for Women and the Men Who Love Them.* New York: Norton, 1983.

Fisher, Bruce. *Rebuilding: When Your Relationship Ends.* San Luis Obispo, Calif.: Impact Publisher, 1981.

Halpern, Howard M. *How to Break Your Addiction to a Person.* New York: Bantam Books, 1982.

Hosier, Helen. *To Love Again: Remarriage for the Christian.* Nashville: Abingdon Press, 1985.

Richards, Larry. *Remarriage: A Healing Gift from God.* Waco, Texas: Word Books, 1981.

Rubin, Lillian B. *Women of a Certain Age: The Midlife Search for Self.* New York: Harper & Row, Publishers, 1979.

Small, Dwight Hervey. *The Right to Remarry.* Old Tappan, N.J.: Fleming H. Revell Co., 1975.

Smoke, Jim. *Growing Through Divorce.* Irvin, Calif.; Harvest House Publishers, 1981.

Stearns, Ann Kaiser. *Living Through Personal Crises.* Chicago: The Thomas More Press, 1984.

Weiss, Robert S. *Marital Separation.* New York: Basic Books, 1975.

INDEX

Index

inclusive language. *See* language
inheritance, 53, 58-59
instincts, 91-92, 95, 184
Isaiah, 17, 32, 33-34, 78, 150, 238

Jesus, 17, 22, 24, 29, 31, 32, 33, 34, 39, 42-43, 44-45, 49, 51, 69-75, 76, 81, 82, 89, 107-8, 121-26, 132, 157-58, 161, 172-73, 176, 186, 188, 191, 193, 194, 197, 199-200, 205-6, 230, 233, 238, 240
Judaism, 24, 42, 57, 68, 71, 76-77, 82-86, 89, 144, 148-50, 157, 244, 259
justice, 11-12, 21, 23, 32, 35, 106, 108, 128, 148, 191

language, 19, 32-34, 42, 266
  about God, 32-34, 240, 266
  about people, 32, 34, 42, 266
Law, Old Testament, 57-63, 87
legal rights, 19, 26, 53, 55, 56, 57-62, 67-68, 164, 165, 176, 190, 215, 250
Levitical law, 25, 29, 58, 61, 62-63, 73, 76, 144-55, 157, 158
love, 10, 15, 31-32, 34, 35, 36, 44, 45, 56, 65, 72, 74, 109, 112, 117, 121-23, 126, 127-29, 132-39, 149, 178, 180, 182, 185-86, 187, 193-94, 221, 230
Luke, 17, 21, 24, 32, 43, 65, 69-70, 72-74, 77, 78, 108, 157, 200, 244-45
Luther, Martin, 22, 46, 49, 50, 203, 262

marriage, 14, 26, 29, 35, 36, 39-44, 47, 49, 51, 55-58, 65-68, 82, 83, 89, 91, 97, 99, 108, 109-26, 127-39, 159-61, 163, 171-77, 179, 180-81, 187, 190, 194, 202, 208, 211, 219, 234, 250, 252, 266
Mary, Virgin, 21, 70, 71, 76, 157
Mary Magdalene, 74-75, 77, 245
masculinity, 33, 47, 62, 70, 90-108, 130, 133, 199, 218, 240, 265-66
masturbation, 185-86
Matthew 19:4 ff., 29, 39-40, 90, 177, 250
maturity, 45, 100, 106, 108, 112, 124, 126, 134, 171, 179-80, 191, 231
Mead, Margaret, 95, 142
menstruation, 28, 71, 73, 93, 141-42, 145-52, 153, 157-58, 198
militarism, 18, 22, 23, 25, 32, 91, 108, 184
Mill, John Stuart, 110, 113, 129

ministry, 10, 28, 45, 73-75, 76-90, 101, 110, 196-208, 217-18, 229, 234, 258-59
missions, 77-78, 196-97, 201, 204, 206-7
Mollenkott, Virginia Ramey, 10, 32, 33, 34, 70
Money, John, 93-94, 103
motherhood, 33-34, 37, 65, 67, 91-92, 97, 100, 107, 118, 140-45, 151-58, 159-70, 211, 217, 229, 232, 233

Numbers
  chap. 5, 60-62, 144
  chap. 27, 58-59
  chap. 30, 62-63, 251. *See* vows

"order of creation," 40-41, 42, 44, 50, 91, 198, 231-32
ordination, 10, 19, 23, 81, 89, 97, 197-204, 208, 234, 235, 258-59
original sin, 21, 26, 30, 32, 35, 47-51, 146, 151, 152, 154

parenthood, 37, 58, 63, 93, 96, 99, 100, 130-31, 144, 159-70, 179, 191-92, 266-67
partnership, 18, 109, 110, 113, 114, 127-39
patriarchy, 17, 21, 33, 39, 52, 57, 62, 69, 70, 72, 76, 107, 109, 111, 114, 121, 146, 153, 154, 155, 199
Paul, 19, 24, 26, 37, 40-41, 42, 43-45, 77-90, 110, 115, 136, 156, 172-73, 177, 195, 200, 201, 202-3, 208, 215, 234, 241, 245
Pentecost, 70, 77
personality, 100-102, 104, 116, 126
personhood, 96, 104-8, 126, 128, 131, 231
I Peter chap. 3, 25, 88, 94-95, 98, 115-18, 235, 248
Phoebe, 78, 79, 86, 110, 212, 246
Plato, 36, 38, 65, 141, 240
poverty, 17, 18, 23, 30, 32, 49, 66-67, 157, 190-91, 210
presbyters, 80-81, 201, 247. *See* elders
Priscilla, 78, 79, 81, 86, 110, 202-3, 212, 246
procreation, 35, 36, 39, 48, 49, 140-45, 156, 165, 172, 266-67. *See also* childbirth; motherhood
property rights, 52-53, 55, 56, 58-59, 61, 65, 114
prophecy, 25, 26, 77, 79, 84, 85, 86, 199
prophets, female, 24, 64, 74, 77, 78-79, 84, 86, 196, 199, 202, 204, 232
Proverbs chap. 31, 64, 130, 132, 155, 212-13